CSS for Windows 8 web App Development

Jeremy Foster

Apress·

CSS for Windows 8 App Development

ISBN-13 (pbk): 978-1-4302-4983-2

ISBN-13 (electronic): 978-1-4302-4984-9

Trademarked names, logos, and images may appear in this book. Rather than use a trademark symbol with every occurrence of a trademarked name, logo, or image we use the names, logos, and images only in an editorial fashion and to the benefit of the trademark owner, with no intention of infringement of the trademark.

The use in this publication of trade names, trademarks, service marks, and similar terms, even if they are not identified as such, is not to be taken as an expression of opinion as to whether or not they are subject to proprietary rights.

While the advice and information in this book are believed to be true and accurate at the date of publication, neither the authors nor the editors nor the publisher can accept any legal responsibility for any errors or omissions that may be made. The publisher makes no warranty, express or implied, with respect to the material contained herein.

Distributed to the book trade worldwide by Springer Science+Business Media New York, 233 Spring Street, 6th Floor, New York, NY 10013. Phone 1-800-SPRINGER, fax (201) 348-4505, e-mail orders-ny@springer-sbm.com, or visit www.springeronline.com. Apress Media, LLC is a California LLC and the sole member (owner) is Springer Science + Business Media Finance Inc (SSBM Finance Inc). SSBM Finance Inc is a Delaware corporation.

For information on translations, please e-mail rights@apress.com, or visit www.apress.com.

Apress and friends of ED books may be purchased in bulk for academic, corporate, or promotional use. eBook versions and licenses are also available for most titles. For more information, reference our Special Bulk Sales–eBook Licensing web page at www.apress.com/bulk-sales.

Any source code or other supplementary materials referenced by the author in this text is available to readers at www.apress.com. For detailed information about how to locate your book's source code, go to www.apress.com/source-code/.

To Suzanne - you inspire me.

Contents at a Glance

Contents

About the Author

Jeremy Foster was educated in computer engineering and mathematics, and has gathered disparate industry experience in education, aerospace manufacturing, and insurance. With just enough and not nearly enough education and experience, he finally joined Microsoft with the goal of informing and inspiring other software developers to write code and write it right.

When he is not working, Jeremy is likely spending time with his wife and son, hiking and camping, sailing, scuba diving, or working on house projects. Find him online codefoster.com or on Twitter at @codefoster.

About the Technical Reviewer

Andrew Zack is the CEO of ZTMC, Inc. (`www.ztmc.com`), which specializes in search engine optimization (SEO) and Internet marketing strategies. His background includes almost 20 years of site development and project management experience and more than 15 years as an SEO and Internet marketing expert.

Andrew has been very active in the publishing industry, having co-authored Flash 5 Studio (Apress, 2001) and served as a technical reviewer on more than 10 books and industry publications.

Having started working on the Internet close to its inception, Andrew continually focuses on the cutting edge and beyond, concentrating on new platforms and technology to stay at the forefront of the industry.

Acknowledgments

Enormous thanks are in order.

Above all, my gracious wife and son have put up with more than their fair share of me hiding in my office. They were encouraging, patient, and extremely supportive. Suzanne and Wyatt, I love you and I thank you.

My team at Microsoft is second to none. They challenge, teach, stretch, and encourage me almost every day. It's a constant source of inspiration to work with such an amazing team in such an excellent company. I only hope I have passed a bit of their inspiration on through this book. To Joe, Scott, MJ, Matt, Daniel, Jerry, Bret, Alice, Doris, Michael, Bruno, Randy, Sam, Chris, and Harold, thank you.

My team at Apress has held my hand all along this journey. To Ben, Ana, Andrew, Elise, Kathleen, and the many others that worked behind the scenes, thank you.

And finally, to you my readers, you have read this far in the acknowledgements and that's admirable. Furthermore, you are a member of the development community at large that walks by my side as we trek in this exciting territory, as we strive to keep up in a constant torrent of information, and as we create awesome digital solutions to people's problems. To all of my readers, thank you.

Introduction

Note The world's population of web developers is enormous, and each one of these developers is now a Windows 8 developer—targeting the largest device market ever to exist.

Are you a web developer? I am. I started reverse engineering web pages in 1994 and have since been rather captivated by the platform. It has been wrought with constraints from the start, yet it draws in developers and consumers alike even today, roughly two decades later. My experience with the very elegant and powerful XAML, Microsoft's own user interface (UI) technology, has occasionally reminded me of the limitations of HTML, but I just keep coming back to the web stack with its open and forgiving syntax and its worldwide reach.

Perhaps you have some experience with web technologies and you're ready to write an app for the Windows 8 audience. You'll need to have skills in the three core web technologies: HTML (Hypertext Markup Language) for document structure, CSS (Cascading Style Sheets) for laying out and styling those documents, and JavaScript for implementing the application logic. This is a book about the CSS part and how CSS behaves in Windows 8 app development. Whether you have existing experience with CSS or none at all, you'll learn about using this ubiquitous styling language.

I'm guessing you're at least a little bit familiar with Windows 8. This current iteration of Microsoft's extremely popular Windows operating system is a very interesting release. It's interesting because it's dramatically different, and because developers can build apps using a few different technologies including HTML, CSS, and JavaScript—what I like to call the web stack.

With Windows 8, you can create apps using the web stack and they'll run natively on the operating system. They'll have access to the device's sensors and other native implements, and they'll even be hardware accelerated.

I want to emphasize that I don't want this to be merely a technical reference book. Of course, there are facts to relay, but what's more important than the mere transit of facts is the conveyance of a concept. If you are interested only in the definition of the CSS standard or the syntax of the APIs, you could easily look online. In my opinion, however, development is one part *education* (merely knowing the facts) and one part *experience*—that is, having run the gamut of successful and unsuccessful implementations enough times to really learn what the online documentation can never relay.

And by the way, development has a third part—*inspiration*. You really have to love what you're doing and have a vision for where you're going with it, and this must generate enough excitement in you to fuel you through the rough patches. If you don't find yourself staying up late or waking up early to write some code, then you should ask yourself if this is truly your field.

So consider this not only a book about CSS and about Windows 8, but also a book about style. Consider it a book about productivity and beauty and achieving those ends through expressive syntax.

One of the unique offerings of this book over one that is dedicated strictly to the CSS3 standard is that all along the way, I'm going to point out ways that the standard properties and templates will or will not help you with your Windows 8 app. I'll also point out the Microsoft vendor-specific properties and values that will give you added oomph. You'll also learn about the guts of the Windows 8 controls provided by the WinJS library and what class names you'll need to know so that you can properly style them.

Since you have picked up a book about CSS in Windows 8, I imagine there's a good chance you're writing an app. Perhaps the app is your brain child and you really hope to see it succeed in the marketplace. If this is the case then that's great, because the number one criterion for the success of your app is the experience that the user has with it. You've probably heard this called UX (user experience). When a user has an experience that thrills him because it saves him time, brings him information or insight, or even just thrills him because it looks like good art, he is more often than not willing to pay real money to you the author, and he's willing to review and recommend your app highly.

Microsoft made a huge step in implementing the web stack in Windows 8. I think it's a step in the right direction, and I think they've been very smart about how it was done. Microsoft now understands that we're in a world that loathes all things proprietary and for good reason. We don't want to be married to one way of solving a problem. We want general skills and lots of options. We don't want to be married to a single company either, but rather to use technologies that are based on standards resulting from the collaboration of many.

Independent standards are a good thing—a great thing in fact, and that's why the world loves the web stack. Developers will usually choose an open standard even when the best implementations are somewhat lacking compared to proprietary alternatives.

Microsoft has used the same engine that powers Internet Explorer 10 to power Windows Store apps that are made with the web stack. This means that with little or no exception, if your markup and CSS work in IE10, it will work in your Windows app and vice versa.

Note In implementing the web stack, Microsoft has *thoroughly* adhered to the standards.

When HTML, CSS, or JavaScript have a standard for a feature, it is adopted, and generally, when a feature doesn't exist, a standard is recommended to W3C. When it is unfeasible for recommended standards to be implemented in a reasonable timeline, extended functionality is added by way of the industry-standard vendor-specific tags, properties, and values. There are always going to be holes in even the most rigorous of standards, and the fact that vendors can backfill these with some of their own properties is excellent. It's even more excellent that these tags, properties, and values are all prefixed so they can be differentiated from the standards.

For example, in CSS, properties and values begin with a dash (-) followed by a vendor-specific identifier, another dash, and finally the property name. Microsoft's vendor-specific identifier is ms, so an example of a vendor-specific tag would be ms-grid.

Developers love their tools, and I suppose there's a good chance you already have your tools of choice installed and running. If you're new to development, web development, or just looking for some guidance on what to use to create and maintain your CSS, look no further than Visual Studio.

Visual Studio is one of the most powerful and popular IDE's (Integrated Development Environment) in the world and with good reason. The latest iteration is called Visual Studio 2012 and you can get a free version—Visual Studio Express 2012—for Windows 8 from Microsoft's website at http://aka.ms/win8downloads. This Express version doesn't have all of the bells and whistles of the professional version that you would pay for, but it has everything you need to create Windows 8 apps.

Visual Studio offers excellent support for CSS whether you're working with a web application or a Windows 8 app using HTML/JS. You'll get IntelliSense support which suggests property names and valid values and you'll get some other helpful features like a glyph that renders when you specify a CSS color.

And Visual Studio isn't the only tool in your tool belt. You've also got Blend. Blend comes with Visual Studio in the same install whether you have the free Express version of Visual Studio or a paid version.

Both Blend and Visual Studio are app-building machines. You can create an app from end to end in either tool, but Blend is more of a designer-friendly tool and Visual Studio is more of a developer-friendly tool. You can use both of them and you can do so side by side because they both work on the same kind of project files. So if you want some design help, open up Blend and if you want to do some debugging or write some serious code, open Visual Studio.

And now it's time to dig in to CSS and discover how fun it is to use it for styling your Windows 8 apps.

CHAPTER 1

Windows 8 Design

Note "And now for something completely different." (Monty Python)

Windows Reimagined

No doubt you've heard Windows 8 introduced as "Windows reimagined," and you simply cannot argue with how huge the paradigm shift is between Windows 8 and any previous iteration of Windows.

I remember well the first time I used Windows 8 and tried to grasp the concepts around using the edges and corners of the screen, discerning the desktop from the new UI, searching within an app from the Charms bar, and even just restarting the system!

The departure from an old paradigm is evident from the very first screen. Figure 1-1 shows what a user sees when logging in to Windows 8.

Figure 1-1. The start screen in Windows 8

Compare this to Figure 1-2, which is what we saw just after logging in to Windows 7.

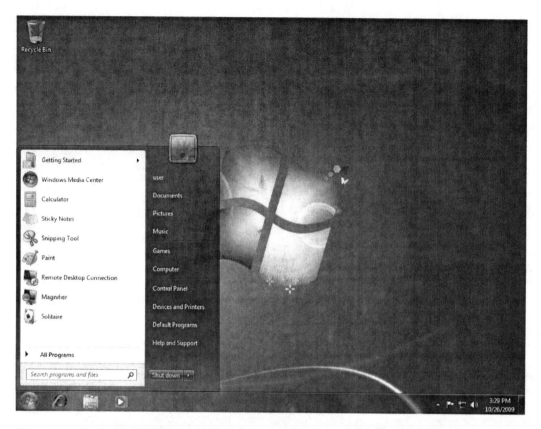

Figure 1-2. *The desktop in Windows 7 showing the start menu*

The start screen replaces the start menu. Eye tracking studies have proved that once a user has opened the start menu in Windows 7, an overwhelming majority of them did not look anywhere else on the screen. The concept of a full screen being dedicated to the start experience then makes perfect sense. Think of the start screen as an app and see how Windows has created an immersive start experience.

In fact, of all the changes introduced by Windows 8, I think the most relevant to us as app designers is this immersion of the user into their task and into their content. Windows 8 dedicates every pixel of the screen to your app, and your app stands alone on stage to be tried and judged by the user.

You don't have to go far to find a good example of an app with an immersive experience. The built-in Maps app in Figure 1-3 is an excellent one.

Figure 1-3. *The Maps app demonstrates well how immersive Windows 8 apps are. Absolutely every pixel on the screen is dedicated to the app*

With Windows 8, Microsoft delivers us not just a good design, but a good *design framework*. Microsoft is delivering not only an app development language, but a *design language* as well. This design language is very thoroughly documented and forms a foundation for your app's design.

The design language for Windows 8 is documented at `http://design.windows.com`. This subsection of MSDN's robust developer site focuses on the entire design process that a great app demands. This includes advice on things like:

- Scoping your app and helping you decide what your app will be great at

- The monetization strategy for your app

- The recommended size of the left margin

- The placement of commands in the app bar

Designing your app precludes your choice of UI language. You can implement good design using Microsoft's XAML language just as well, but we're going to be using HTML and CSS. We're going to design first and then implement that good design. Some of the design principles might seem a bit esoteric at first, but it's important to see what they offer for guidance. Don't worry because we'll get much more concrete near the end of the chapter when we learn how to implement our good design.

We'll explore good Windows 8 app design by looking at some traits of a well-designed app.

Traits of Great Windows 8 App Design

Some characteristics of a well-designed Windows 8 app are enumerated in the `design.windows.com` site at `http://msdn.microsoft.com/en-us/library/windows/apps/hh464920.aspx`. In this chapter, I will step through each of these traits exactly as they are presented on Microsoft's site and unpack them each with my own perspective and experience.

Use Microsoft Design Style

If there is one concept you take away from a chapter on Windows 8 design, may it be this: *Windows 8 design is all about immersing the user in their content.*

What is content? An app's content is the reason a user launched the app. For a financial app, the content is the stock price or a financial article. For a social app, the content is the friend or the conversation. For a photo app, the content is the photos.

Instead of wrapping content with ancillary information *about* the content, Windows 8 pretty much just shows the content. When you're looking at a photo, you'll usually just see a photo stretched from one edge of the screen to another, and when you're looking at a friend's profile on a social network, you'll see a view dedicated to the essence of information about that friend.

This is not the next step in the evolution of user interface. This is a departure from the current trend, which has been to cram everything into one screen so that everything is a single click away. It's not uncommon to find 25% or even less of a view's design surface dedicated to the content itself. The trend's flaw, however, is that when too much is added to a view, then none of it serves its purpose of making life easier for the user because the individual parts lose their significance and the whole of the parts loses the user.

Everything on the screen that is not content is *chrome*. Chrome is a term from the automobile industry where polished metal parts are added to attract buyers even though they play no role in the vehicles function. There's nothing wrong with a mere aesthetic, but the problem with chrome in an app is that it detracts from the app by distracting the user from their content.

The Windows 8 design principles attempt to put *content before chrome*. It's not that chrome will never exist, but an app designer should be careful to introduce it. Your app should always prioritize content and eliminate distractions. Notice in Figure 1-4 how the Xbox Music app in Windows 8 shows only content from edge to edge.

Figure 1-4. Windows 8 apps dedicate 100% of the space to content

There are three classic reasons that chrome is added to a view: navigation, interactions, and layout. These play a significant role in an app's usability, however, so we must replace them—not remove them. Let's take a look at how the function of each of these types of chrome is facilitated without distracting from the content.

Navigation

Static navigation is guilty of creating a lot of chrome. We're all familiar with the standard website model containing a header at the top of the page with navigation links just below or along the left side of the page.

In an effort to avert the click, many go so far as to fill in the navigation menu with multiple levels of hover-activated popout menus or even include a tree view of the entire site's structure. Tabs are another popular, modern form of static navigation.

The problem with static navigation is that it doesn't fall in line with our app's primary purpose which is to deliver the user's content. Static navigation is information about where a user might want to go next, but it tells the user nothing about where they are, therefore it's not a recommended practice in a Windows 8 app. How do we facilitate navigation then? We do so by designing our app with a clear information hierarchy that naturally directs the user to subordinate or subsequent content.

There are two primary recommended navigation models for Windows 8 apps. I'll cover each briefly, but read more at http://msdn.microsoft.com/en-us/library/windows/apps/hh761500.aspx#hierarchical_system.

Three-tier navigation

The first model is the three-tier, hierarchical navigation model. In this model, all site content exists in three tiers—the *hub*, the *section*, and the *detail*. This navigation model is just the right number of levels for a content-driven app. Any fewer and an app would not be able to categorize, and thus facilitate, navigation for all of its content. Any more and users tend to get disoriented and lose their place.

Hub

The hub is the entry point to an app and serves as an overview of the entire app. A hub can't show all content in the app, of course, but it can show just enough of each section to interest the user. A shopping app, for instance, wouldn't show all products from a category, but might instead show the first few featured products and invite the user in to see more.

Section

If the user chooses the header of one of the hub's sections, they will be taken to the section page. The section page is responsible for relaying any general information about the section as well as giving the user access to all of the individual items or entities that fall under that section. To use the cliché products and categories example again, the *tools* section would be responsible for getting the user to all available tools. That doesn't necessarily mean that all tools show up immediately on the section page. Often times filter and sort functionality makes the user's life easier.

Detail

After the user has reached an individual entity in the app, such as a specific product, they are brought to the detail page. The detail page is responsible for presenting all of the information about that specific entity. A detail page might contain a photo, a description, some related entities, a list of categories, or who knows what else. The bottom line is that the detail page is the dedicated place for informing the user about an entity.

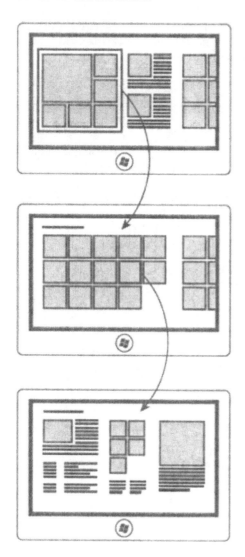

Figure 1-5. *A diagram of the three-tier navigation model showing the hub, section, and detail tiers*

Flat navigation

Content-driven apps work well in a three-tier navigation structure, but some apps don't really have a content structure. Some apps are just a collection of similar views—all peers to one another. Internet Explorer is a great example and it follows the flat navigation pattern, because the browser instances in a session don't relate hierarchically to each other.

In an app that implements flat navigation, the upper app bar (which is conventionally used for navigation) provides access to these peer pages as seen in Figure 1-6.

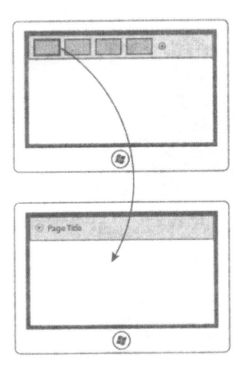

Figure 1-6. *A diagram of the flat navigation model*

Interactions

The second common reason that chrome is added to a page is for interactions. Interactions are things like buttons that give the user a chance to *interact* with the app.

Giving your user an opportunity to interact with your app is certainly a good idea, but traditional controls on the design surface are not necessarily the best way to provide that interaction. Crowding the design surface with controls that the user may or may not even need is secondary to immersing the user while still giving them an opportunity to call up some interactions when and if they need to.

On-screen content can often speak for itself and a user will know or learn quickly how to interact with it. A user (even a young child) will often be able to intuit that touching some bit of content will bring you more information about it. Likewise, you don't need to repeat other commands to affect the content on screen, but can instead allow the user to select one or more items and then select a command from the app bar. Putting commands in the app bar puts the user in control because the app bar doesn't take any space at all until the user elects for it to.

We want to design our Windows 8 apps so that the *content commands for itself*. Usually, that simply means that content is clickable. You can see an example of content commanding for itself in Figure 1-7.

Figure 1-7. *Extra command buttons for seeing more information about content items is often unnecessary. It's better to let users interact directly with content*

Sometimes commands can't be represented directly by the content, and in that case we are advised to *leverage the edge.* This means that some of the commands which would otherwise be cluttering our design surface can be relegated to the system-wide Charms bar or to the lower or upper app bar. It's called leveraging the edge because these bars are "hiding" off the edge of the screen precisely until the user calls upon them. Here we are putting the user in control again.

Figure 1-8 shows an app with its app bar visible. This app bar is called up by the user by a swipe gesture from off screen, by right clicking the mouse, or by pressing WIN + Z on the keyboard. This bar is the home for commands that belong to the app. More specifically, it is where you put the commands that affect the view the user currently has in context.

Figure 1-8. *The app bar is always ready to bring app-level commands to the user, but it's not there until the user actually requests it*

Figure 1-9 shows an app with the Charms bar visible. This bar is called in by the user by a swipe gesture from off screen right, by hitting the top-right or lower-right corner of the screen with the mouse, or by pressing WIN + C on the keyboard. The Charms bar is not something that we as developers actually change. It is baked in by Windows. We are able to implement certain code contracts in our apps however, so that our app will respond to the user activating the charms. For instance, our app can be enabled to share, search, share to a device, and provide application settings.

Figure 1-9. *The Charms bar brings system-level commands to every app in a predictable way*

Commands on the app bar are specific to a given app and it's nice that they're in a consistent location, because users that have spent any time at all with Windows 8 will know exactly where to find them. Users will quickly get used to the workflow of searching and sharing and will be glad to have the same workflow in every app.

Keep in mind that if a command is a part of an essential workflow, then it should not be hidden from the user, but should instead be placed on the design surface. The start and stop buttons for a stopwatch app are a good example of this. Hiding those buttons would make no sense at all and in fact an argument could be made that these commands are actually themselves the app's content.

Layout

Finally, apps get cluttered by chrome that serves merely to separate content. We're talking about lines and boxes and dividers. Actually, in most cases layout chrome tends to disappear when navigation and interaction chrome does, because layout chrome is often separating content from navigation or content from interactions more than content from content.

Because we're starting with the entire screen as the canvas for our app, instead of drawing lines and boxes, we can spend the space on just space—empty space as shown in Figure 1-10. In Windows 8, we're not afraid to put breathing room between things.

Figure 1-10. *Windows 8 is not afraid to use significant amounts of space as breathing room for your content*

We also create good layout with good typography. The typography in Windows 8 has meaning and purpose. The standard font and standard font sizes give us a *type ramp* for representing hierarchical relationships between elements on the screen and naturally separating them by their role or significance as shown in Figure 1-11.

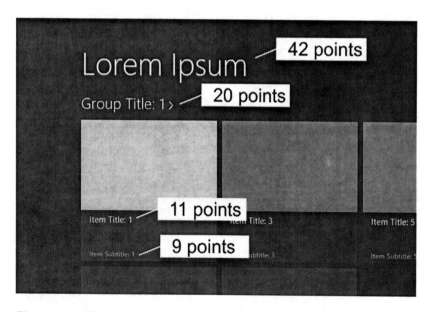

Figure 1-11. *The type ramp conveys the significance and hierarchy of type*

Your app should also implement what's called the *Windows 8 design silhouette*. The design silhouette is the standard margins, header placement, content padding, type faces, and type sizes that give users a strong familiarity, as shown in Figure 1-12. This consistency should be coupled with unique design style that gives your app not only familiarity but also its own personality.

Figure 1-12. *Standard margins and header placement give Windows 8 users some consistency*

Be Fast and Fluid

Windows 8 apps should always operate in a fast and fluid way. A fast and fluid app responds immediately, flows nicely, and uses purposeful animations and sharp, clean graphics.

Part of a great user experience is a user feeling like they are directly interacting with information instead of with a system that is relaying that information. Touching content and dragging it around in real time is a great user experience, but only if the content precisely follows the user's finger instead of jittering, lagging, or falling behind.

For the most part, Windows 8 apps that you create will be fast and fluid even if you don't think about it. This is because a lot of the built-in controls and functions are designed with this in mind, and it's also because the Windows API—the Windows Runtime or WinRT—provides asynchronous calls only for any method that might take too long (and too long in this case is defined as 50 ms).

Sometimes, however, you as the developer will be in direct charge of the performance of elements moving around on the screen and interacting with the user. Whenever this is the case, you should make certain that the performance would be considered *fast and fluid*.

Animations also do a great deal toward making a user feel like he's interacting with an organic system. We'll talk in much more depth about animations in Chapter 6.

Snap and Scale Beautifully

Windows 8 is not bound to fixed hardware. There are hundreds of PC models and many form factors that will be happy to run Windows 8 and your app. Consequently, your app should be adaptable and you should intentionally consider the appearance of every page in every possible view state.

The typical Windows 8 view states that you'll be dealing with are:

- Fullscreen landscape: the entire screen, which is more wide than tall

- Fullscreen portrait: the entire screen, which is more tall than wide

- Snapped: just the left (or right), and is 320 pixels of landscape

- Fill: remaining space when another app is snapped

You don't have to support portrait view, but you must support snapped and fill views. Your user will be able to snap your app or snap an app next to yours whether you like it or not. Even if your app makes it through certification without intentionally handling these states, it will be embarrassing when your users discover it.

Use the Right Contracts

One of the main reasons we put operating systems on our computers is to abstract away all of the menial tasks that we want to work in a consistent way without our having to recreate them for each app. Printer drivers didn't used to exist, so instead each app had to be programmed to talk to any printer that might possibly be in use. Arduous is a suitable word for this task.

One modern-day norm that is a candidate for abstraction is social networking, or to be even more general—*sharing*. Windows 8 abstracts the concept of sharing away from our apps and wraps it in what's called a *contract* that you as a developer can implement. A contract, in case you're not familiar, is simply a pattern that is followed in your code that fulfills what Windows is expecting to find when it attempts to ask your app to share or search or whatever. Implementing a contract in your code is not a difficult endeavor. The tremendous advantage of this is that as long as your app is capable of sharing and correctly implements the contract and then it is suddenly capable of sharing with every app that participates in the same contract. It's even capable of sharing with apps that didn't exist until after you put yours into the Store!

Searching is another popular and often used contract. With the right contract implementation (again a rather simple task), your app can be searched by a user even before they've launched your app, and you get to determine what happens when your app is searched and how to bring about search results.

There are plenty for Windows 8 contracts and I recommend adding any to your app that can add real value.

Invest in a Great Tile

Live tiles are Start screen tiles that are updated with new information or imagery. Live tiles are effective because they're informational. I find myself getting all the information I need sometimes with only a quick glance at my start screen. I can see the weather for the day, my next appointment, and the headline news without launching any apps at all.

Keep in mind that the tile for your app not only informs the user, but it also invites them into your app. You want your user to use your app and use it often, and you can promote that usage by investing in the quality and functionality of your live tile.

There's little reason not to put in the miniscule time required to create rich tile support. Making a wide version of your tile is excellent and allows a user to make your app more prominent on their start screen. If you make a wide tile, it's recommended that you give it live tile functionality. A double wide that does nothing at all is a bit disappointing.

Feel Connected and Alive

One of the design goals of a Windows 8 app should be to help users feel less like they're interacting with a device and more like they're interacting directly with their information.

Many of the principles we've talked about so far help to achieve this, but one especially critical way to keep users connected and give their information a sense of vitality is to actually interrupt whatever they're doing with an onscreen notification and audio prompt. After all, live tiles are informative, but more of a user's time will be spent working in an app than staring at their start screen. For notifications that the user deems significant, they'll expect to be interrupted from whatever they happen to be doing at the time.

Make a user feel like their device is alive by notifying them when they receive a call or instant message, when they are outbid in an online auction, and certainly when their lottery ticket is drawn.

Roam to the Cloud

Roaming to the cloud is a catchy, modern phrase that simply means that we save certain information to an internet-hosted location instead of to the device. That way when the user reloads the operating system on his device or logs in to another one, the settings and preferences they've elected in the past are seamlessly available.

The great thing about roaming in Windows 8 is that it's extremely easy for the developer. All that's required is that you save settings through the roaming storage API that Windows provides. The setting is actually stored locally, but Windows is responsible for synchronizing all of those settings with the user's Microsoft account (not to their SkyDrive). Listing 1-1 shows an example setting saved to roaming storage just to show you how easy it really is.

Listing 1-1. The user's favorite color being saved to a roaming setting so it will be available on any device

```
//JavaScript snippet
var appData = Windows.Storage.ApplicationData.current;
appData.roamingSettings.values["favoriteColor"] = "blue";
```

Consider roaming not only your user's data, but also their tasks. If a user is in the middle of something, help them to pick it back up when they continue on a different computer. If you've used the Netflix app that's already in the Windows Store, you may have noticed that it saves the timestamp that represents where you are in the movie you're watching and restores it when you return even if you return to a different device. Users love that and you should look for applications of the principle in your own app.

Follow the Design Principles

We've looked at a number of traits of well-designed Windows 8 apps, and we have one more. The final trait is that an app should follow the Windows design principles. I'll enumerate and explain the design principles next. These principles are a bit less pragmatic and seemingly more esoteric than the traits we've been looking at, but I would caution you not to overlook them. Understanding and following these general principles will guide you in designing your app even when you're not starting with a project template.

Microsoft Design Principles

The Windows 8 design principles are fully documented and more extensively explained on MSDN at http://msdn.microsoft.com/en-us/library/windows/apps/hh464920.aspx#traits_8_embrace_metro. They are simple, high-level, guiding principles. They are values that Windows 8 apps should respect for the purpose of making apps that do their job and delight the user.

According to Microsoft, the principles are:

- Show pride in craftsmanship

- Do more with less

- Be fast and fluid

- Be authentically digital

- Win as one

Show Pride in Craftsmanship

The principle that an app designer/developer should show pride in craftsmanship certainly illustrates how general these principles are. It means that you should never avoid spending the extra time it takes to get the details right. You should worry about just how the animation behaves and just how the colors match. You should concern yourself with the exact size of the left margin and the user's experience in the edge cases.

Let me put some teeth to this principle with an illustration that I run into unfortunately often. Tell me if you can see anything wrong with the view in Figure 1-13.

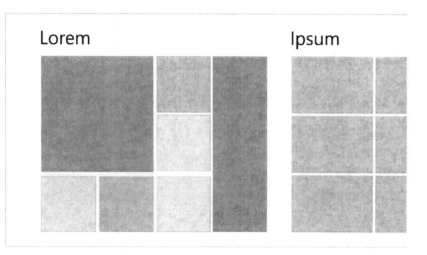

Figure 1-13. *A typical grid layout but with one subtle design flaw*

I hope you noticed that the list items in the left most group of tiles are almost but not quite in alignment. Even if your user doesn't consciously notice something so apparently trivial, they will notice it subconsciously and it will be a detractor.

Do More with Less

To do more with less means that you break the modern trajectory of adding so much stuff to the screen that none of it even serves its purpose.

The word to keep in mind when you're designing the usage flow that your user will follow is *essence*. Ask yourself if you're presenting the *essence* of the information and giving the user the *essential* commands. Information and commanding that is not essential will be not only superfluous but worse yet it will be distracting.

Remember, just like Windows itself, you're not trying to be ultimately discoverable. It's far better to be ultimately immersive.

Be Fast and Fluid

This principle will sound familiar because it's a repeat from the design traits, which speaks to the significance of the concept. The feeling a user gets when he uses an app that he would describe as "fast and fluid" is one of those things that's hard to describe, but you know it when you see it.

Don't be afraid to spend some money on professional design help that has experience not just with static graphics, but with dynamic screens and user experience.

Be Authentically Digital

I believe that more philosophy than science goes into app building. If you zoom out of the last 30 years and look at the mass adoption of computing, it's quite clear that developers are still trying to figure out good architecture and usability.

We held on to the paradigms that we knew and dragged them into our digital systems all the while grimacing at their ill fit. Perhaps only now we're learning that digital systems have their own rules, and that often those rules are more liberating than those of our analog world, and that users can come to learn and even love the digital world.

As we build our apps, we take advantage of the full extent of the digital systems we have and we avoid app design that accepts constraints of the analog world that are irrelevant in the digital world. We are, after all, working with pixels on a screen—an essential truth to be embraced.

Win as One

Users don't *use apps;* they *complete tasks.* Sometimes those tasks involve a single app, but very often they involve an orchestration of apps. Imagine for a minute the following scenario.

Your app helps users make reservations at restaurants. Your user may use your app on its own, but more likely your user will:

- Step onto an escalator at the airport

- Check their trip management app to find their hotel's location

- Check for restaurants in the hotel's vicinity

- Pick a restaurant based on user reviews

- Make a reservation at the restaurant (using your app!)

- Send the reservation confirmation to a colleague and then step off the escalator

That user is a delighted user. He has not just used an app; he has accomplished something significant in very little time. All during the escalator ride, the complimentary and informative animations were important, all of the thought that went into the UX of each app was very important, and the app-to-app sharing was crucial.

To make a successful Windows 8 app, you have to think about the user. Part of that is making sure your app will work well with other apps and devices to complete entire usage scenarios.

Another aspect of this design principle is taking advantage of established conventions, standards, and recommendations. By doing so, you'll be taking advantage of what users have already learned about Windows 8 apps. They'll feel secure and familiar in your app.

We've looked at a number of design traits and principles that will hopefully help you when you're going through the process of designing an app. Let's walk through a fictional app design right now.

Design Scenario

In my opinion, there's just one measure of what makes a successful app. It's not the number of installs. It's not the number of launches. It's not the great ratings or the great reviews, and it's not even the dollars that end up in your bank account.

The measure of a successful app is the amount of value it brings to the lives of the users.

Never lose sight of that. If you build an app that brings value, you've built an app that will bring dollars. Unfortunately, we cannot directly quantify value added, so I'm sure we'll continue to measure our app on the many other factors and I'm sure you'll continue to appreciate the positive cash flow.

Scope

One of the best ways to win at app development is to do a good job at defining your app's scope. Your app should do one thing and do it well. We call this your app's "best at" statement.

Likely you notice the trend in today's software world and especially in the mobile space away from a few apps that do everything and more toward many apps that each do one thing well. You're not going to break anybody's heart if your app does also do their taxes and make their coffee. If it does the one thing it's intended to do and does it well, your users are going to love it, and rate it well, and send you cash.

Doing one thing well means scoping your app well. This means that before you write any code, you determine what it is your app *will* and *will not* do. You may already know that it's often more difficult to determine what it will not do—to say *no* to features—than it is to add new ones.

To be clear, the enormous, robust and full-featured apps have their place, and if you have the means to take that on, then let that be your scope. If you're an individual developer, however, then you'll need to practice cutting features. Just because you *can* implement something and just because it would be really cool doesn't mean you should. As developers, we tend to be idealists, and we tend to want very much to add in features to prove to ourselves that we can.

To keep features in reign, I recommend using a *best at statement*. Your best at statement is a single, concise sentence formed by filling in the blank in the following sentence:

This app is the best in its category at _____.

Be sure your answer is specific, concise, and clear. Here's an example:

This app is the best in its category at helping users find local volunteer opportunities for helping the elderly or disabled with house work, yard work, or other chores.

Notice how specific the statement is about who is involved—volunteers plus elderly and disabled people. The statement is also short and concise. The app is not going to organize volunteer events or help with fund raising or accept donations for non-profits. It's only going to help a user find a volunteer opportunity.

This statement does a great deal toward defining the scope of your app by stating clearly what it does and by exclusion what it will not do. Helping people find volunteer opportunities may, however, involve more than one usage scenario.

Usage Scenarios

The vision for our app is shaping up, but it's still abstract, so to solidify it, we will determine what the usage scenarios are. For this app, how about the following:

- Allow a user to browse **potential volunteer opportunities** in the vicinity of their current location and in the near future (next two weeks perhaps) and filter the opportunities by location and date.

- Allow a user to see all of their **current volunteer opportunities**.

- Allow a user to **communicate** with other volunteers and with those receiving assistance.

You might generate a lot of scenarios while you're brainstorming, but the list should be trimmed to include only those which directly support the best at statement.

These usage scenarios each imply a number of supporting features or functions. For instance, providing potential volunteer opportunities implies that we provide the user with full details of each opportunity to include things like its location and duration, what tools might be required, and more. Generally these usage scenarios tend to form the sections that we'll see on the hub page.

At this point, it's quite helpful to have some graph paper or even some specialized app design paper to get ideas on paper without the encumbrance of actual implementation. I have created a Windows 8 app design sheet and made it available as a PDF at http://codefoster.com/designsheet. The first page includes frames for designing the standard three-tier navigation model for your app, and the second page is simply a full-page 1366 x 768 design surface with a light grid and guidelines for the recommended margins, for snapped view, and for the app bar. Hopefully this resource will help you when designing your app.

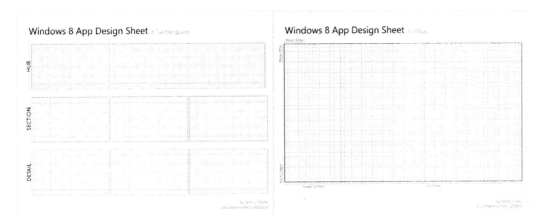

Figure 1-14. *The Windows 8 app design sheet from* codefoster.com/designsheet

Let's use this design sheet to sketch out a hub page. We'll call our app *Good Help*, and we'll have three sections: *my gigs, connect,* and *nearby gigs*. These sections map directly to our three usage scenarios.

Notice that the app does follow the basic Windows 8 design guidelines, but we've gotten a little bit creative (perhaps not enough so) with the layout to give our app some of its own personality. The opportunities in both the *my gigs* section as well as in the *nearby gigs* section are using relatively large rectangles to allow us to bring some images and a good amount of information to the hub page if necessary. The connect section provides a single column of smaller rectangles to resemble a chat session since this section facilitates communication between app members.

Remember that the hub page should serve as a glimpse of the entire scope of the application, so we should find a place for each of our usage scenarios. Users like to feel oriented in an app, and a well-designed hub can provide this by constantly offering the user an overview and making it easy to dive into more information about a given section or entity.

There's obviously not room on the hub page for everything available in the app. The *nearby gigs* section for instance may have 400 opportunities within, but the hub is only going to show some subset of those. In this case it makes sense to bring the *closest* opportunities to the user's hub as those might be the most likely for him to sign up for.

The hub is giving us access not only to the sections available in our app, but direct access as well even to some of the items. In the concept drawing in Figure 1-15, there are three items populating the *my gigs* section indicating the user has signed up for these three volunteer opportunities. Touching one of those items will navigate the user directly to the details of that opportunity.

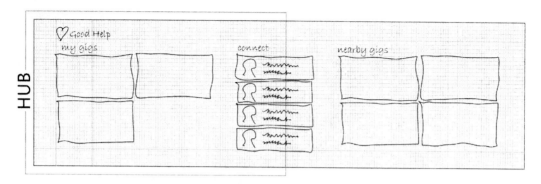

Figure 1-15. *A first sketch of the Good Help app's hub page*

Let's continue our app's design and draw the concept for one more page. We'll design the *gig* page, which will relay the complete details of any one gig. This is the page a user would navigate to by touching one of the opportunities on the hub. Figure 1-16 shows the concept.

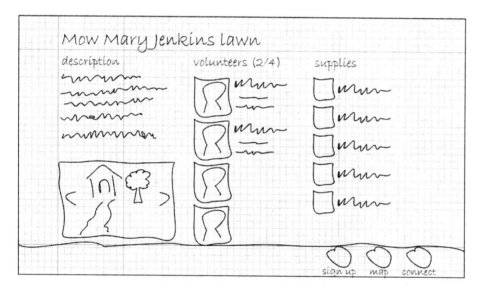

Figure 1-16. *A sketch of a detail page*

And that does it for this design scenario. I hope this obviously fictional application is close enough in concept to the app you're working on that you'll be able to apply the design principles here quickly.

Summary

In this chapter, we looked at a number of traits of a well-designed Windows 8 app as well as some design principles to keep at the front of your mind to help guide you through the process of designing and implementing your app.

The most significant design trait we visited encourages us to use Microsoft's design style which includes immersing the user in their content and doing all we can to eliminate distractions. Windows 8 apps are less about discoverability and more about content immersion and consistency.

App developers have to break the habit of using the design surface for *chrome* which might be static navigation, user interactions, or explicit layout. Instead, we learn techniques for replacing this functionality without taking the user's eye off their content. For instance, we learn how to navigate by letting content do its own commanding. We learned how to allow the user to interact by leveraging the screen's edge—using the app bar and the Charms bar. Finally, we learned how to lay out our content without explicit layout artifacts by using space and typography intentionally.

We concluded by running through part of a design scenario where we worked on the scope of our app and then roughly defined its hub page and one detail page. This exercise is roughly the same process (though on a smaller scale) as the process you'll go through on every app you create.

The design process is great and certainly critical and prerequisite, but it's time to get our hands dirty, jump into code, and learn the basics of creating an actual Windows 8 app.

■ ■ ■

CHAPTER 2

Introduction to Windows 8 Development

■ **Note**   It's an exciting time to be a software developer.

The goal of this book is to help you dive deep into CSS, particularly the way that it applies when you develop apps for Windows 8. If you don't have any experience developing Windows 8 apps, however, you're going to have a hard time practicing anything you learn. So just in case this is a whole new world for you, we're going to use this chapter to look at Windows 8 architecture, the tools that will be valuable to you when developing apps, and then how to distribute your app locally and to the Windows app store.

Windows 8 Architecture

Before Windows 8 blew into our lives, Windows applications could be written using C++ with native access to the Windows core Win32 libraries. They might rather sit a little higher (logically) and be written in C# or Visual Basic and run on the .NET framework. Or if you stretched your mind a bit and imagined a web app to be a Windows application, then an app could be written using the languages of the web, hosted in a web server (either locally or remotely), and then sit even higher still on the web browser.

Windows 8 does not do away with any of the existing paradigm for creating applications, but it does introduce a brand new and exciting one.

Windows 8 introduces WinRT. WinRT is a brand new, modern API that is designed and built from the ground up for modern apps. It's not a mere extension of either the Win32 libraries or of the .NET framework.

One of the reasons Window's new architecture is exciting is the fact that it can be targeted by a few different technology stacks. It can be targeted by C++ and XAML, by C++ and DirectX, by C#/VB and XAML, and by JavaScript and HTML. The different languages are *projected* into the WinRT domain so they don't constitute an additional layer of hierarchy, and the model leaves open the possibility of projecting other languages into WinRT down the road. Figure 2-1 shows the different language stacks that sit on WinRT today.

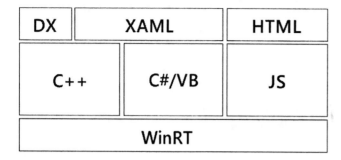

Figure 2-1. *A macro view of the languages that can target WinRT*

Each of these stacks brings along its own unique environments and advantages. If you author in C++ you can use some of your existing C and C++ components. If you author in C#/VB and XAML, you get the incredible power and familiarity of the .NET framework. It's not the entire framework, but it's a subset that's tailored for these modern apps.

If you author in JavaScript and HTML, you get the broad, standards-based web stack used by a massive number of developers around the world. You get the browser's document object model and you get the dynamic and persistent language we love a lot and hate just a little—JavaScript. Perhaps the most exciting thing you get is an incredible amount of JavaScript code that's already been written to do many of the things you might want to do.

However, when you develop an app for Windows 8 using the web stack, the app is not running in a browser against a web server; it's running natively on the platform. The app is hardware accelerated and trusted by the system to access the system itself and all attached hardware. This is a whole new space for developers.

Besides direct access to the underlying WinRT, a Windows 8 developer also gets the added assistance of the Windows Library for JavaScript (WinJS). WinJS is a standard JavaScript library like any other, but its aim is to help you make great apps that look right at home in Windows 8.

WinJS provides some JavaScript and some CSS styles. We'll be looking far more extensively at the CSS styles that WinJS provides a bit later on.

When we start to write apps, we'll want some good tooling in place and luckily the tooling that Microsoft provides is second to none. We'll take a look at that next.

Tools

Microsoft's flagship developer tool is Visual Studio. It's been around long enough to undergo some serious evolutions in design and function. Besides Visual Studio, developers also have access to Blend.

Visual Studio 2012

Visual Studio 2012 (VS2012) is the latest iteration and there's no missing the evolution in the design of this one! VS2012 barely resembles its predecessors in many ways, but it doesn't lose any of the capabilities. You can still author many different project types and can now author Windows 8 apps as well.

One of the VS2012 products—Express—targets Windows 8 apps alone and is completely free. It doesn't have all of the functionality of the higher, pay products of course, but it will still manage your app from start to finish. This is especially exciting for student developers that don't have a big developer gig or the cash lying around for development tools.

If you want to develop a Windows 8 app, you must have Windows 8 and you must have Visual Studio 2012. Earlier versions of Windows will run VS2012, but will not work to create Windows 8 apps.

Project Templates

VS2012 project templates for Windows 8 projects will get you going in a hurry. Any of these basic templates will get you to a point where you can begin playing with the CSS that we'll learn in this book, so don't feel like you've got so far to go.

Let's start with the simpler templates and work up. Create new projects from each of the following templates and then follow along as I point out the construction of the various pages that make up the project.

The Blank Template

The blank template shouldn't surprise you with its sparse contents. It is, after all, supposed to be blank. If you're the type, however, that wonders about even the small amount of apparent magic that happens with a blank template, you can visit my blog post http://codefoster.com/Windows-8-Building-Up-to-Blank and read more about what goes into this simple template.

To create a new blank project:

1. Launch Visual Studio 2012 on a machine running Windows 8

2. Click File | New Project

▓ **Note**   If you are using a professional version of Visual Studio, you'll see a screen like the one in Figure 2-2. If you're instead using Visual Studio Express then your choices will be fewer but the concept remains.

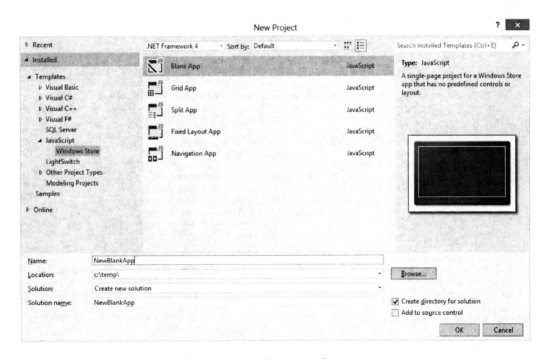

Figure 2-2. *The New Project Window gives you a few options for project types*

3. Choose JavaScript | Windows Store from the left pane, and then choose Blank App from the list of templates. Assure that you're okay with your project's location and name and then click OK.

After a few seconds, you'll have a full-fledged Windows 8 app ready to run. You can run the app locally by clicking on the green arrow on the toolbar, but the results are not so exciting quite yet. Figure 2-3 shows what a project created from the blank template looks like when you run it.

Figure 2-3. *A first run of a project created from the blank template. The white text that you can hardly read says "Content goes here" and acts as a placeholder for you to add your content*

Let's look through the project that was created for us and make sure we have a solid understanding of the files involved.

If you have any experience with websites, you might notice that the files in the Solution Explorer resemble a web project in many ways. Like a web project, there are folders like js, images, and css, and like a web project there is a default.html file at the root level. You can drill into all the levels and see for yourself that we're not dealing with too terribly many files. It's nice to have a simple start when you're trying to get the core concepts.

Before we look at the HTML, CSS, and JavaScript files involved, let's have a look at one that might not look familiar to you—package.appxmanifest. This file holds all of the meta-information about your Windows 8 app. It's important information for describing your app when it's submitted to the Windows Store, among other things.

The package.appxmanifest file (a.k.a. the manifest) is just a simple XML file, but you rarely have to stare at the XML directly, because the GUI designer that Visual Studio launches when you double-click the manifest is quite good.

Let's look at the HTML file now. Double click the default.html to open it, or just look at Listing 2-1 if you don't have your project in front of you.

Listing 2-1. The default.html file that accompanies a new blank project

```
1 <!DOCTYPE html>
2 <html>
3 <head>
4     <meta charset="utf-8" />
5     <title>NewBlankApp</title>
6
```

```
 7      <!-- WinJS references -->
 8      <link href="//Microsoft.WinJS.1.0/css/ui-dark.css" rel="stylesheet" />
 9      <script src="//Microsoft.WinJS.1.0/js/base.js"></script>
10      <script src="//Microsoft.WinJS.1.0/js/ui.js"></script>
11
12      <!-- NewBlankApp references -->
13      <link href="/css/default.css" rel="stylesheet" />
14      <script src="/js/default.js"></script>
15 </head>
16 <body>
17      <p>Content goes here</p>
18 </body>
18 </html>
```

I want to highlight the total lack of anything proprietary in this file. If you've seen HTML5, you'll recognize the terse DOCTYPE directive, the basic head section with script and style sheet links, and the world's simplest body of content stating that "Content goes here".

The script and style sheet files that are referenced on lines 13 and 14 begin with a forward slash (/) and thus start at the project's root and continue to reference the default.css file from the css folder and default.js from the js folder. You'll grow accustomed to this convention because all of the built-in template files are broken into .html, .css, and .js files that share a name.

Lines 8–10 of Listing 2-1 may appear odd at first glance, but I'll explain why even those are composed of entirely standard, HTML5 markup. A uniform resource identifier (URI) such as the ones that the link and script elements on lines 8–10 contain, begins with a scheme (such as http) and then a colon (:). Everything after the colon is defined by the scheme.

For the popular http scheme, the remainder of the URI is defined as http://{hostname}/{path} where the hostname is usually the name or IP address of a server and the path is the full path to the file being requested.

The URI's in Listing 2-1, however, have the scheme omitted, and the rule is that if a segment of the URI is omitted then it defaults to the value of the same segment for the current request. For websites, the default request is often times http, but the scheme for a Windows 8 app is ms-appx. So lines 8–10 could have been written like Listing 2-2.

Listing 2-2. The ms-appx scheme is the default for Windows 8 apps

```
 8      <link href="ms-appx://Microsoft.WinJS.1.0/css/ui-dark.css" rel="stylesheet" />
 9      <script src="ms-appx://Microsoft.WinJS.1.0/js/base.js"></script>
10      <script src="ms-appx://Microsoft.WinJS.1.0/js/ui.js"></script>
```

In the ms-appx scheme, the segment of the URI just after the double slash is the package that the code is located in. As you can see in Figure 2-4, the ui-dark.css file (from line 8 of Listing 2-2) exists in the Windows Library for JavaScript 1.0 under the project's references and the package name of that referenced package is Microsoft.WinJS.1.0.

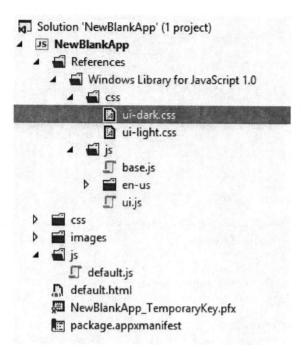

Figure 2-4. *The ui-dark.css file is inside a referenced package*

As long as requests are using the ms-appx scheme, the system knows that they are safe requests, and these requests are said to be in the *local context*. Requests made to the http scheme, on the other hand, are not assumed to be safe and Windows 8 runs them in what's called the *web context*. You can find a lot more information by visiting http://aka.ms/win8contexts.

Alright, so there's nothing magic happening in the HTML file, so I'm going to move on to assure you that there's none happening in the CSS or the JavaScript files either.

The CSS file for the blank template is found in the css folder and it's called default.css. There's no functioning code in the file, but a little bit of framework has been included to get you started. Listing 2-3 shows you what you'll find in the default instance of default.css.

Listing 2-3. The default.css file that's included with the blank project template

```
body {
}

@media screen and (-ms-view-state: fullscreen-landscape) {
}

@media screen and (-ms-view-state: filled) {
}

@media screen and (-ms-view-state: snapped) {
}

@media screen and (-ms-view-state: fullscreen-portrait) {
}
```

These are all just empty shells of style rules and media queries that are not having any effect at all. This is your blank canvas, however. When Chapter 3 starts showing you how to define style rules, this is where they'll go.

The last page we'll look at is the JavaScript. The default.js file is in Listing 2-4, and as you can see, it's longer than the HTML and CSS files.

Listing 2-4. The default.js file that's included with the blank project template

```
// For an introduction to the Blank template, see the following documentation:
// http://go.microsoft.com/fwlink/?LinkId=232509
(function () {
    "use strict";

    WinJS.Binding.optimizeBindingReferences = true;

    var app = WinJS.Application;
    var activation = Windows.ApplicationModel.Activation;

    app.onactivated = function (args) {
        if (args.detail.kind === activation.ActivationKind.launch) {
            if (args.detail.previousExecutionState !==
                activation.ApplicationExecutionState.terminated) {
                // TODO: This application has been newly launched. Initialize
                // your application here.
            } else {
                // TODO: This application has been reactivated from suspension.
                // Restore application state here.
            }
            args.setPromise(WinJS.UI.processAll());
        }
    };

    app.oncheckpoint = function (args) {
        // TODO: This application is about to be suspended. Save any state
        // that needs to persist across suspensions here. You might use the
        // WinJS.Application.sessionState object, which is automatically
        // saved and restored across suspension. If you need to complete an
        // asynchronous operation before your application is suspended, call
        // args.setPromise().
    };

    app.start();
})();
```

I won't take the time to explain everything that's happening in this file, but I would like to point out a couple of things.

First, you should know that this entire file is standard JavaScript—ECMAScript 5 technically.

Second, the Process Lifecycle Management (PLM) is handled here. PLM is the code you write to be sure that your app behaves well when it's launched, suspended, reactivated, and terminated. If you write your code right, your user's experience with your app will be fast and seamless.

Finally, notice that all of the code in the JavaScript file is wrapped in what's called an *immediate function*, as shown in Listing 2-5.

Listing 2-5. An immediate function wraps code acting like a namespace and keeping it isolated from other modules and the global namespace

```
(function () {

    ...

})();
```

This immediate function defines a function and then runs it immediately. At first, this seems an awfully strange thing to do. Why would you need to define a function and call it right away? Couldn't you just write the code and let it execute? Yes, you could. The immediate function is a common trick in JavaScript that takes advantage of JavaScript's function scoping. Functions are like Las Vegas. What happens in a function stays in a function. So you can get as crazy as you want with variable and function definitions inside that immediate function and it's not going to add a bunch of junk that the rest of the app can see that is sure to confuse and conflict.

We're just touching on JavaScript, remember, because this is after all a book about CSS. There's one more thing I want you to be able to at least recognize, though, and that is an *event*.

Events are popular in many modern programming languages. An event is a method that fires when a certain thing happens. If a user clicks a button, an event should fire. If a user scrolls something on the screen, an event should fire (even if they only scrolled a single pixel).

The JavaScript that we write should respond to events and to do that we need to define methods and tie them to the right events. I'll give a very basic example.

Let's show a dialog box when the user clicks a button. To do that, we could use the code in Listing 2-6.

Listing 2-6. A simple event handler for causing a button click to initiate a message box

```
document.getElementById("myButton").onclick = function(e) {
    Windows.UI.Popups.MessageDialog("Hello").showAsync();
};
```

Now, let's tear this code apart to understand exactly what is going on and the basics of how event handlers work.

The first part that says `document.getElementById("myButton")` is just referencing a `button` that has been defined in HTML with an id of `myButton`.

The `.onclick` is the click event for that button. Its value is `null` at first, but it wants us to provide a function to call when the button gets clicked.

The rest of the listing is the function, and it simply displays a dialog box that says "Hello" each time the user clicks the button.

Why Choose a Blank Project?

The blank project is an excellent place to start if your app does not need more than a single page. If you're working on a game where all the action happens inside a `canvas` element, then there may be no reason to navigate users to another page.

You also might choose to use the blank template if you just hate having code written for you. If you want to start from nothing (or almost nothing), then there's another good reason to start here.

There's plenty more to learn even just about the blank project template, but this is just an overview and we're going to move on to the other project templates before we get in over our heads. Next, we'll learn about the navigation project template.

The Navigation Template

Figure 2-5 illustrates an app created with the navigation template. It looks almost as sparse as the blank template in Figure 2-3, but it does have a page header. The page header isn't the only difference though.

Figure 2-5. A first run of a project created from the navigation template. We still have the small, white text that reads "Content goes here", but now we have a page header as well

The navigation project template adds a few things above and beyond the blank template that are mostly aimed at providing you with a navigation framework for getting from one page to another. This improved navigation is actually provided by the WinJS library. I'm going to show you all of the differences and tell you why this navigation framework given to us is a good thing.

If you were to use a file differencing utility to look at a blank project template and a navigation template you would see the following differences between the two. In the navigation template:

- There are some basic style changes in default.css that provide a page header that conforms to the Windows 8 design principles.

- The default.html file no longer contains the primary content ("Content goes here"), but instead has something called a *contenthost*.

- The js folder in the project contains a navigator.js file that defines how the contenthost behaves. The default.html page references navigator.js.

- The project has a *pages* folder with a *home* folder in that, and the home folder contains its own HTML, CSS, and JavaScript files. Conventionally, every page will be in its own folder in the pages folder.

Those are pretty much all of the differences. It's not a lot. Now why is this helpful?

You likely know that in HTML, you can create hyperlinks and easily navigate from one file to another, but there are at least a couple of reasons why hyperlinks are not sufficient for a Windows 8 app.

The first is that hyperlinks create a new HTTP GET request and rely on the query string parameters available in a GET request as the sole means of passing data. With the navigation framework, on the other hand, we have a means to pass robust JavaScript objects in the process of navigating from one page to the next.

The second is that hyperlinking takes the user from one page to another and lets all of the scope and context of the former page drop entirely. Each request is a completely new context. This puts a real pain on the developer, and although web developers will find this a familiar problem, it's just not necessary in a modern, client-side app. The navigation framework keeps the user on the default.html page for the entire lifecycle of the app and only appears to navigate the user to another page by replacing content in the DOM of default.html. This general pattern is called single page architecture (SPA) and it's gaining popularity, even on public web pages.

Figure 2-6 illustrates hyperlink navigation and Figure 2-7 illustrates improved navigation using a single-page architecture.

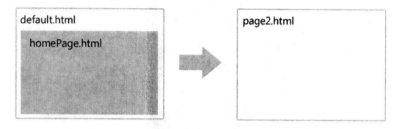

Figure 2-6. *Hyperlinking to page2.html breaks the user's context a create a new context*

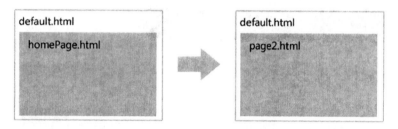

Figure 2-7. *Navigating via the WinJS library keeps context intact, making life easier for the developer*

Why Choose a Navigation Project?

The navigation project is a great place to start for any app that might implement multiple views. If your app is going to show users a list of products and then allow them to choose a product to see more info, then you likely need navigation.

I begin almost every project from the navigation template even if I know I'm going to be implementing a grid. The navigation functionality that the navigation template gives you is very helpful and tedious to write, but I like starting my grids from scratch.

The Grid Template

Next up is the grid project template, as shown in Figure 2-8. This beast of a template contains a lot of code and you'll get intimidated if you're not careful. The grid project template contains almost 500 lines of JavaScript alone. The reason for the size is that in addition to implementing the navigation framework (that we talked about in the previous section) it also defines a bunch of sample data and contains three separate, complete pages that implement good 3-tier navigation.

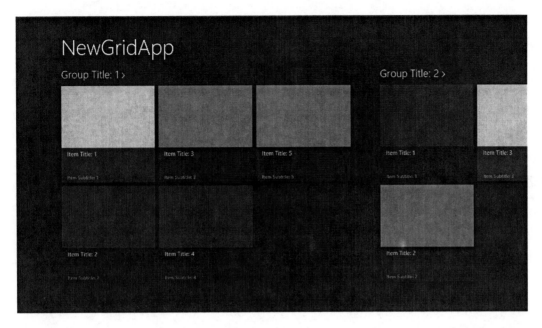

Figure 2-8. *A first run of a project created from the grid template. We're looking at the hub of a 3-tier navigation model that's been created for us*

The grid template implements an app navigation model called *3-tier navigation*. This 3-tier navigation model is very highly recommended for Windows 8 apps. Following it will give your users consistency and devising your own model risks confusing or losing them. There are two strong reasons to use this navigation model. First, is has a lot of user research behind it, and second, it's a convention that users will already be familiar with.

The heart of the grid template is the ListView. We'll look at ListViews in some depth in this book. For now, just know that the ListView is the control that gives you that familiar grid of entities. It's rather popular for these entities to appear as *tiles*, but that's certainly optional.

Why Choose a Grid Project?

A grid project takes you from 0 to 60 quickly when your app resembles the basic 3-tier navigation model. It's a great learning tool, and I recommend you create an app using this template and then just browse and attempt to reverse engineer the code. One of the biggest advantages of the grid template is that the design principles of Windows 8 are already implemented. The margins are the right width, the fonts are the right size, and the ListView groups have the right gaps between them.

When you get more proficient with creating your own ListViews and implementing the design principles using CSS, I recommend you ditch this template for the navigation template. I feel like the grid template introduces more complexity than it's worth, but that's just me.

I've introduced you to the three project templates that I think are the most significant. There are more that I'm not covering. The Split Project Template has its place but it applies to a relatively narrow set of apps. The Fixed-Width Project Template adds so little actual code that I tend to just write it myself if I need its functionality.

DOM Explorer

If you've used the developer tools for any of the major browsers, you're familiar with the concept of getting a live version of your HTML document. This live document in object form is referred to as the *Document Object Model (DOM)*.

When you run an HTML/JavaScript app for Windows 8 in debug mode using Visual Studio 2012, you get another pane in Visual Studio called the DOM Explorer. If you don't see the DOM Explorer then look in the Debug menu under Windows | DOM Explorer.

The DOM Explorer gives you a hierarchical representation of the DOM for the currently running app. It effectively shows you what the HTML looks like, but includes any dynamic additions or modifications that your script (or the WinJS script) may have made while the app was running. If you dynamically add a button to an HTML page using JavaScript, you won't see that button in your HTML file, but it will show up in the DOM Explorer.

The DOM Explorer is very helpful in developing and debugging. Figure 2-9 shows a typical view of the DOM Explorer.

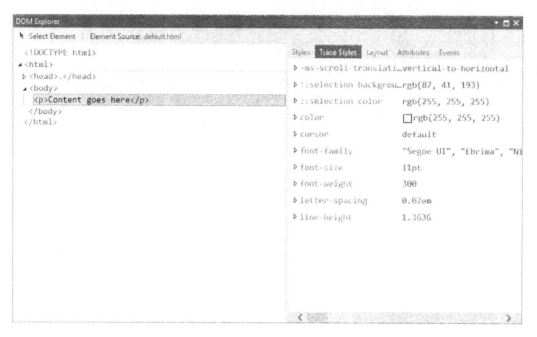

Figure 2-9. *The DOM Explorer in Visual Studio shows a live view of your Document Object Model (DOM) when your app is running in debug mode*

On the left side of the DOM Explorer (highlighted in Figure 2-10), you see the entire DOM. If you don't have any fancy JavaScript in your app then this DOM will look exactly like your default.html file.

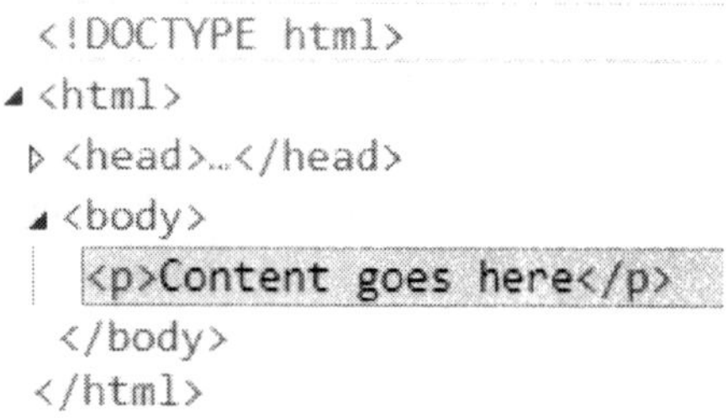

```
<!DOCTYPE html>
◢ <html>
  ▷ <head>...</head>
  ◢ <body>
      <p>Content goes here</p>
    </body>
  </html>
```

Figure 2-10. *The DOM includes the HTML that you wrote along with anything dynamically injected at runtime*

Above the DOM in Figure 2-9, notice the Select Element button. When you click that button, your app comes to focus (in front of Visual Studio) and you get an opportunity to choose an element you might be interested in. A thin, blue line assists you in this venture.

The right pane of the DOM Explorer (highlighted in Figure 2-11) provides five panels that each give us a different bit of insight into whatever element is highlighted on the left.

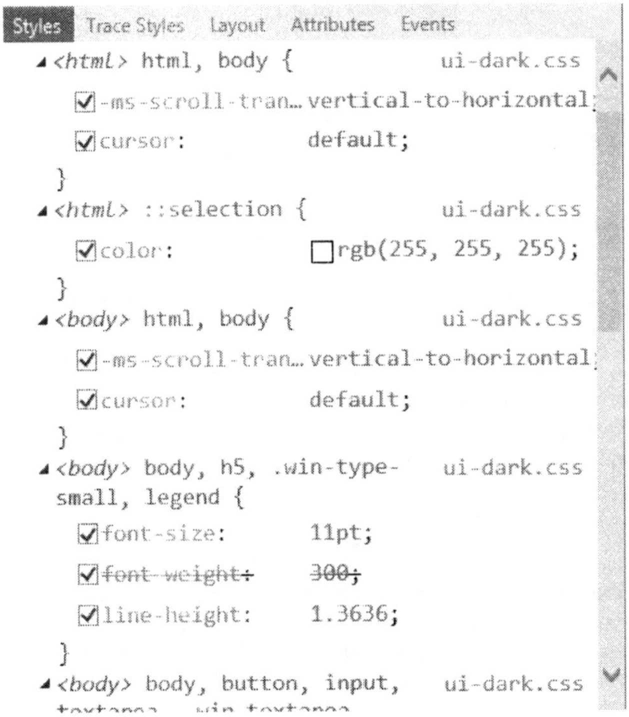

```
Styles   Trace Styles   Layout   Attributes   Events
 ◢<html> html, body {                ui-dark.css
    ☑-ms-scroll-tran… vertical-to-horizontal;
    ☑cursor:          default;
 }
 ◢<html> ::selection {               ui-dark.css
    ☑color:          ☐rgb(255, 255, 255);
 }
 ◢<body> html, body {                ui-dark.css
    ☑-ms-scroll-tran… vertical-to-horizontal;
    ☑cursor:          default;
 }
 ◢<body> body, h5,  .win-type-    ui-dark.css
   small, legend {
    ☑font-size:      11pt;
    ☑font-weight:    300;
    ☑line-height:    1.3636;
 }
 ◢<body> body, button, input,    ui-dark.css
   textarea,  win-textarea
```

Figure 2-11. *An app developer working with CSS will benefit greatly from the five tabs in the DOM Explorer*

These extra tabs are very important when you're styling your app. As you follow this book and create CSS styles that apply to the elements in your UI, those styles will appear in these tabs.

The first two tabs are very similar. The *Styles* tab shows a list of all of the styles that currently apply to the selected element arranged by the style sheet they came from. The *Trace Styles* tab also shows all of the styles that currently apply, but now they are arranged by CSS property. I find the Trace Styles tab far more helpful. The *Layout* tab shows something called the box model, which we'll talk about in Chapter 5. The *Attributes* tab allows you to add HTML attributes to the selected element, and finally the *Events* tab shows any JavaScript events that are tied to the selected element.

Debugging

Debugging is one of the strongest features of Visual Studio. The entire execution cycle can be stepped through line by line and values can be observed and even modified while your app is running. In-depth debugging is certainly out of our scope, but I hope a short introduction will help convince or encourage you in your choice of tools.

When it comes time to run your app and see how it behaves, you have a few options. The Debug Target select box on the Standard toolbar as shown in Figure 2-12, allows you to run your app locally (natively on your machine), on a remote machine, or in the Simulator.

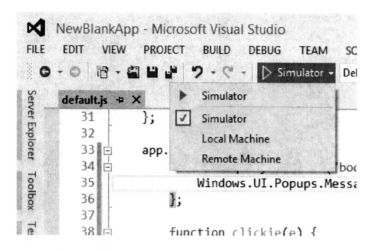

Figure 2-12. *Visual Studio allows you to debug your app to your local machine, to a remote machine, or in the Simulator*

You'll likely usually debug apps to the Local Machine. Running locally is the fastest and simplest route. When you want to target another machine, you can choose Remote Machine, and when you need to simulator features or environment conditions that you don't happen to have on your development machine you can choose Simulator.

The Simulator allows you to simulate things like touch, geo-location, screen size, and screen resolution.

Blend

Everything we've discussed so far involves Visual Studio to compose and edit the raw code that drives your app. This is the typical development approach for sure, but history has shown many attempts by many companies to implement visual tools that write the code for us. I for one have never been impressed. Every attempt I've seen falls short in some way that ends up dissuading me from using it and driving me back to editing raw code in Visual Studio. That is, until Blend.

Blend is a free product that comes with Visual Studio 2012. It even comes with Visual Studio Express 2012 which is also free, so you can use Blend without paying a dime. Blend is different from Expression Blend. Expression Blend is a tool for designing XAML components, but Blend is a tool for designing Windows 8 apps in either XAML or HTML/CSS.

Blend is an incredible tool. Most visual designers force the user to distinguish between design mode and execution mode; views are designed in one mode and then the program is executed to see the results. In Blend, you're always in design *and* execution mode. Your app, composed of HTML, CSS, and JavaScript, is running in Blend as if it's running on the machine. Consequently, Blend can give you a live DOM (like Visual Studio's DOM Explorer except it's always live!) and it can bring in all of your real data. In Figure 2-13, you can see Blend in action. Although you won't likely notice it at first, the grid item tiles in Figure 2-13 are dynamically loaded from JavaScript data.

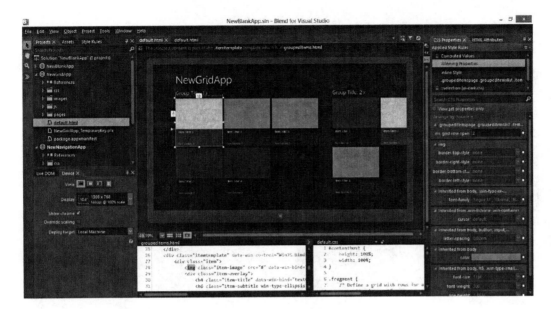

Figure 2-13. *The grid app from Figure 2-8, but now open in Blend*

When you click on a visual element such as one of the gray tiles (highlighted in Figure 2-14), Blend assumes that you want to alter its design, so it renders the typical selection rectangle and handles for resizing it. If we were to drag a handle and resize the object, the CSS that was determining the size of that tile would be modified, and you would see all other tiles change in size as well.

Figure 2-14. *Blend runs your app and yet an element can be designed*

As I said, when you click a tile, Blend assumes you're interested in highlighting the tile so you can design it, but you might want to act as a user of the app and actually navigate when you click. That's what interactive mode is for. On the top-right corner of the document area, you'll find the Interactive Mode icon that looks like Figure 2-15. Activating Interactive Mode informs Blend that you want to act like a user and actually *use* the app.

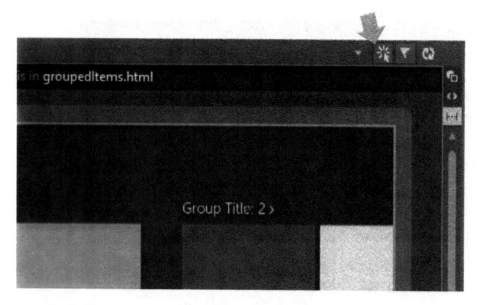

Figure 2-15. *The Interactive Mode icon in Blend*

The great thing is that when you click the Interactive Mode button again to return to design mode, Blend maintains your application state and allows you to continue designing from there.

Perhaps the most significant offering of Blend over Visual Studio is the way it lets you work visually while it manipulates the underlying style HTML and CSS code. You may have enough experience with CSS already to know that its declaration can be rather complex. The styles that apply to any given element may be cascaded down from any number of style rules each overriding each the next. Although this structure is rather complex, when you change a property in Blend, it's able to change the right style.

Also, the Applied Style Rules pane shown in Figure 2-16 (usually located in the upper-right corner of Blend's workspace) gives you a list of all of the CSS style rules that apply from various style sheets.

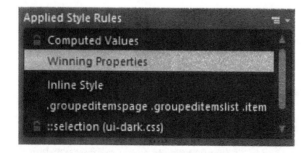

Figure 2-16. *The Applied Style Rules pane shows the entire hierarchy of styles that apply to the selected element*

When you need to create your own brand new style rule, the Style Rules tab (Figure 2-17) lists all of the style sheets that are referenced from the current page, indicates clearly which style sheet a new style will land in, and gives you a chance to change it.

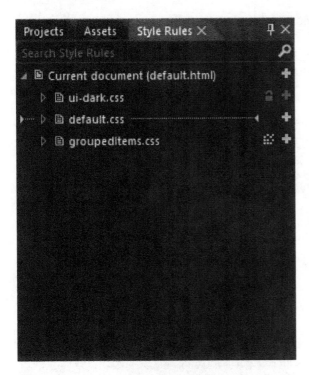

Figure 2-17. *The Style Rules tab indicates which style sheet a new rule will be created in*

One last thing I love about Blend is the 3-pane view, which works perfectly for editing an HTML file and its associated CSS and JS files all at the same time.

One thing to note, however is that Blend is not excellent at JavaScript. If you are working on programming tasks, use Visual Studio. Fortunately, the two tools both share a common project format so switching between them is seamless. In fact, Visual Studio provides an "Open in Blend" option (Figure 2-18) available by right-clicking on a project.

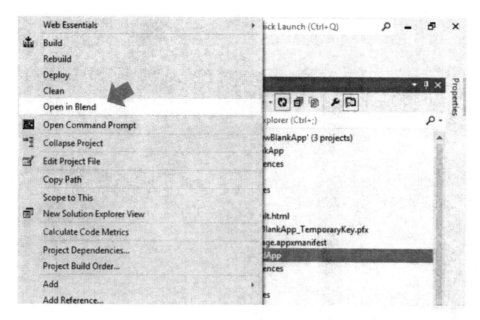

Figure 2-18. *A project shortcut makes switching from Visual Studio to Blend fast and easy*

Distributing Your App

What a great day when you finish your first app. No doubt you'll have a good deal of pride and visions of dollar signs. As of this writing, I have two apps in the Windows Store and I hope to write a lot more.

Submitting your app to the Windows Store is not a difficult venture. The process is very straightforward, the certification requirements are clear, and the feedback along the way is helpful. I won't take the time to detail the Store submission process, because the Store pretty much holds your hand the whole way anyway. I will introduce it and lead you in, however.

Also, when your app is in development and before you distribute it, you may need to install it on another device for testing, so I'm going to show you how to do that as well.

Sideloading

The act of installing a Windows 8 Store app on a device without using the Windows Store is often called *sideloading*. It's definitely a supported scenario, and I'll let you know how to do it.

You could obviously just copy your source code to another system that has Visual Studio, open the project, and run it. That would effectively install your app onto the second device. Not every device has Visual Studio on it, though, and Windows RT devices *can't* have Visual Studio. There's another way though. You can start with one of the default project templates if you'd like to practice before your app is complete. Here are the steps to sideload your app onto another device:

1. Open your app in Visual Studio on your development machine.

2. Choose Create App Packages from the Store menu (the Store menu is under the Project menu in professional versions of Visual Studio) as shown in Figure 2-19.

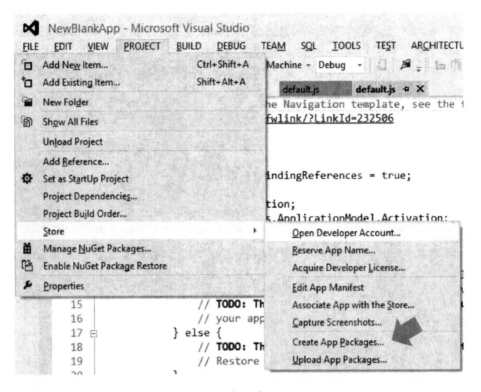

Figure 2-19. *The Create App Packages option in the Store menu*

3. Choose No when you are asked Do you want to build packages to upload to the Windows Store? as shown in Figure 2-20. Click Next.

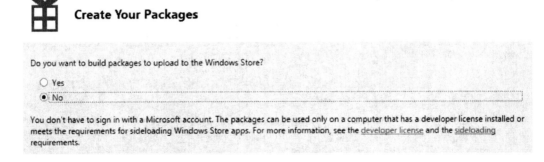

Figure 2-20. *Choose No if you know you are only going to sideload this version of your app*

■ **Note** Take a minute to read the note on the page shown in Figure 2-20 because it lets you know that the device that you install an app package on must either a) have a developer license or b) meet the requirements for sideloading Windows Store apps. You can get more information about developer licenses at `http://aka.ms/devlicenseinfo` and more information about sideloading at `http://aka.ms/sideloading`.

---

4. The defaults should be good for the Select and Configure Packages step. If you need to target different processor architectures you can, and if you don't know what that means then just leave it alone and you should be fine. Click Create.

5. The package creation should complete and indicate the location. Press OK.

6. The package that gets created consists of a folder and an .appxupload file. The .appxupload file is for uploading to the Windows Store when you're ready to submit it, but the folder is what you want for installing on another device. Use whatever means necessary to get the entire contents of that folder (Figure 2-21) copied to another device.

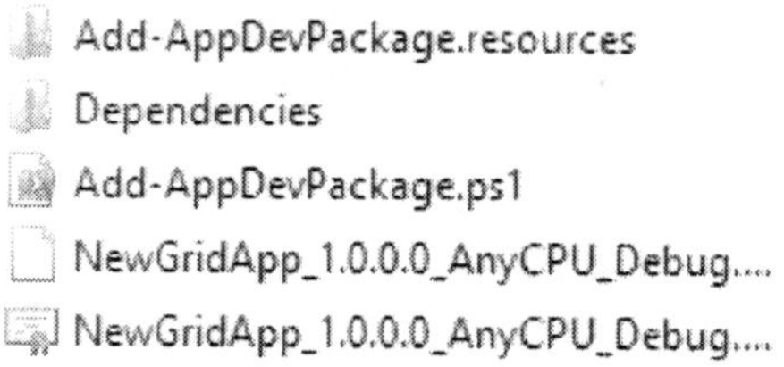

    Add-AppDevPackage.resources

    Dependencies

    Add-AppDevPackage.ps1

    NewGridApp_1.0.0.0_AnyCPU_Debug....

    NewGridApp_1.0.0.0_AnyCPU_Debug....

Figure 2-21. A sample app package after being created. The .ps1 file is responsible for installing the packaged app

7. On the new device, you only need to right-click on the Add-AppDevPackage.ps1 file and choose Run with PowerShell. PowerShell will launch and ask you a few questions to which you can accept the defaults.

And that does it for the relatively simple process of sideloading.

Of course, to increase your reach and avoid requiring a developer license on target machines, you need to submit your app to the Windows Store.

Publishing to the Windows Store

The Windows Store will get your app in front of the eyes of tens (and soon hundreds) of millions of consumers. If you provide an app that adds value to their lives, they'll happily install it and use it and if you decide to charge then they may even part with some pocket change.

To complete the process of submitting your app, start by going to `http://dev.windows.com` and following the instructions to get your developer account. After you have that set up, follow these general steps:

1. Build your app package following the same steps as you did to create a package for sideloading until you get to the first screen in the creation wizard where it asks if you want to build packages to upload to the Windows Store. You would obviously answer Yes to that question this time through.

2. Back at `dev.windows.com`, locate and click Windows Store Apps, Dashboard, and then Submit an app.

3. Fill out a lot of information about your app and in the appropriate step upload the `.appxupload` file that you generated in step 1.

For more information on the complete process of submitting your app, reference `http://aka.ms/appsubmit`.

Summary

Welcome to the extremely exciting world of Windows 8 development.

In this chapter, you've been introduced to the architecture of Windows 8 that supports a wide range of computer architectures, and a valuable set of tools and development languages. All of this is brought together, in part at least, by a new programming model and a modern API called WinRT.

You were then introduced to the world-class tooling that will be your best friend every day as you build apps. The latest iteration of the ever-popular Visual Studio invites Windows 8 Store apps into its repertoire of target projects, and it starts you off with some good project templates that get you from zero to complete product in literally a matter of seconds.

Visual Studio also welcomes Blend as a free companion to assist in the visual design of apps. The two tools sharing a common project format make collaboration between design and development a fluid experience for everyone.

Finally, you were introduced to your options for running your app locally, installing it on another device, and submitting it to the Windows Store.

I hope after reading the first two chapters, you feel like you have the basic skills at least to get started in designing and developing your first app. There's plenty more to learn and plenty of sources from which to learn. For the CSS department, just hold on, because we're about to dive deep.

CHAPTER 3

Selectors and Style Rules

Note CSS is no more than a collection of style rules, and each style rule is made up of a selector and a definition. Don't let it get more complicated than that.

A style rule's selector determines what it affects, and the definition determines how it is affected.

So, just as it is the entire job of HTML to define the document's structure, it is the entire job of CSS to lay out and style that structure to appear as it should and where it should.

With the combination of the document object model (DOM) of HTML and the element selection capability of CSS, we have a very effective and relatively unique way of expressing a potentially complex structure and then separately styling unique sets of elements in that structure without being overly obscure or repetitious.

I call it relatively unique because the styling of many other UI languages tends to get mixed in with the document structure. With HTML and CSS, however, the two can remain separate. The advantage (beyond being clearer for the developer) is the ability to easily interchange style sheets and, in doing so, completely alter an app's layout and style.

So the awesome power of CSS comes from its ability to define style rules and then determine to exactly which elements in the UI that rule should apply.

In Figure 3-1, you can find the app that precedes all others: the Windows Store app.

Figure 3-1. *The Windows Store app*

This app has content, but it has a lot of style as well. The app's title is a larger font and positioned just so; the apps have images and captions and background colors, and everything on the page has a very intentional layout. Overall, the app has good content and good presentation of that content. That's really what we're shooting for.

Style Format and Location

CSS applies to or describes HTML. Actually it describes XML in general, but as far as we're concerned in creating Windows 8 apps, HTML is our only consideration. That means that any time you create an HTML file and would like to affect the elements in that document with styles, you need to write and apply some CSS.

These styles can exist in three places:

- inline
- in an embedded style sheet
- in an external style sheet

Inline Styles

Inline styles are defined in a style attribute added directly to the elements they should affect.

Inline styles are generally considered poor form since they mingle the structure and style in your project and can quickly become unwieldy. I generally never use inline styles, and I strongly feel that there are very few, if any, cases where they should be put into production. They may be helpful for some developers for things like rapid prototyping or troubleshooting design, but they should not be used in the final product. Listing 3-1 shows what inline styling looks like.

Listing 3-1. *A simple HTML5 document with an inline style attribute on a div tag*

```
<!-- default.html -->
<!DOCTYPE html>
```

```
<html lang="en" xmlns="http://www.w3.org/1999/xhtml">
<head>
    <meta charset="utf-8" />
    <title></title>
</head>
<body>
    <div style="font-weight: bold;"></div>
</body>
</html>
```

Embedded Style Sheets

Embedded style sheets are defined on the page they affect. A style element is added to the head element of the page and contains style rules to determine how style properties are applied to various elements. An embedded style sheet is generally less common than the third option and should likely be scarce in a Windows 8 app. Listing 3-2 is an example of an embedded CSS style sheet.

Listing 3-2. A simple HTML5 document with an embedded style tag

```
<!-- default.html -->
<!DOCTYPE html>

<html lang="en" xmlns="http://www.w3.org/1999/xhtml">
<head>
    <meta charset="utf-8" />
    <title></title>
    <style>
        #myDiv { font-weight: bold; }
    </style>
</head>
<body>
    <div id="myDiv"></div>
</body>
</html>
```

External Style Sheets

Finally, external style sheets are the best method for defining and applying styles. With external style sheets, the affected HTML file is left untainted. The only trace, in fact, is the reference to the style sheet, which takes just a single line inside the head element, leaving the rest of the HTML to do its job, which is to provide the structure of the document. Another major advantage of using external style sheets is the ease of dynamically exchanging them for support of multiple themes, multiple languages, or even multiple platforms potentially.

Listing 3-3 shows a good example of an HTML file with a reference to an external style sheet.

Listing 3-3. A simple HTML5 document with a reference to an external CSS style sheet

```
<!-- default.html -->
<!DOCTYPE html>
```

```html
<html lang="en" xmlns="http://www.w3.org/1999/xhtml">
<head>
    <meta charset="utf-8" />
    <title></title>
    <link href="default.css" rel="stylesheet" />
</head>
<body>
    <div id="myDiv"></div>
</body>
</html>
```

```css
/* default.css */
#myDiv {
    font-weight: bold;
}
```

These style sheet files (.css) can be kept anywhere as long as they are accessible by way of an HTTP request from the HTML page. You could link to a style sheet that's stored on an entirely different server on the internet, or it could be in a central folder in your web project (perhaps called css or styles), or it could be right next to your HTML file, and you can use either an absolute reference or a relative reference in the link's href attribute.

It is a rather strong convention to put all style sheets in a central location in a web project, but it's also quite common, especially when creating single page web applications, to create a style sheet for each and every HTML page in the project, and this is the convention in Windows 8 apps. When you're architecting your Windows 8 app, you have the option of putting the CSS files anywhere you choose, but following the convention is a good practice. One of the built-in, Windows-8 project templates is the Navigation App template, and it follows this convention putting a CSS file, an HTML file, and a JavaScript file for each page in their own folder inside the pages folder.

Basic Style Rule Syntax

The contents of the external style sheet (and the embedded style sheet too, for that matter) are simple—composed of nothing more than a large list of one style rule after another. Occasionally, style rules may be wrapped with a media query block, but we'll save that subject for later.

Listing 3-4 shows how a style sheet (whether it's an external style sheet or an embedded one) populated with some rules would look.

Listing 3-4. Typical format for style rules

```css
selector {
    property: value;
    property: value;
    property: value;
}

selector {
    property: value;
    property: value;
    property: value;
}
```

```
selector {
    property: value;
    property: value;
    property: value;
}
```

For some of your shorter style rules, you might, like me, rather forego the line feeds between rules and format your rule on a single line, more like listing 3-5.

Listing 3-5. A more compact format for saving vertical space when style rules are simple

```
selector { property: value; property: value; }
selector { property: value; property: value; }
selector { property: value; property: value; }
```

You'll save some vertical space this way and perhaps extend the life of your mouse wheel, but like its sister technology HTML, CSS ignores extra whitespace, so you can feel free to format it however you like and know that it's going to be interpreted the same.

Another typical and very helpful convention is the indentation of style rules that affect only elements that are below the preceding style rule. Indentation is used extensively in imperative coding languages to communicate the code structure to the developer and make it easier to read. In CSS, indented code indicates the hierarchical relationship between style rules. Remember that whitespace is ignored, so this indentation has no effect on the functionality. Notice in Listing 3-6 how the second style rule contains the same selector ("selectorA") as the preceding rule, in addition to some more specifics. This means that it is in the context of its preceding rule, and this is what the indentation signifies. You'll see this convention used in the sample code in this book.

Listing 3-6. Indentation strictly as a visual aide for indicating hierarchy

```
selectorA {
    property: value;
    property: value;
    property: value;
}

    selectorA selector1 {
        property: value;
        property: value;
        property: value;
    }

selectorB {
    property: value;
    property: value;
    property: value;
}
```

You know what style rules are now, so it's time to learn how to compose them. We'll begin with a discussion on selectors.

Selectors

Imagine you are working with a typical word processor. When you are finished composing and perhaps editing your document, your job becomes one of formatting. To determine formatting for various parts of the document, you take two steps: you select the area you wish to format by dragging over it with the mouse, and then you apply various styling rules, usually by clicking command buttons or keyboard shortcuts. You might select the entire first paragraph, for example, and then determine that you want the font size to be increased to 16pt. Or you may choose only a single word and set it to be underlined.

These are exactly the steps you will take with CSS, only you select using a selector, and you apply styles using style properties. Your selector designates which HTML elements you want to select, and the associated style properties determine what should happen to that selection.

So writing selectors that select exactly what you intend is obviously a very important step, and I beg you not to skip over this section. I actually find far more developers that are weak and lacking in their CSS selection skills than I do those lacking in their formatting skills. What this amounts to is wasted time, space, and complexity, either over-defining their HTML with class and ID decorators that are not necessary or with redundant or wordy style rules in their CSS. Either misstep adds to the complexity of the project, which has obvious penalties even if the site or app works perfectly fine.

A selector is an expression that is evaluated and results in a list of zero to many DOM elements (or pseudo-elements, but we'll get to that later).

The evaluation of a selector may, for instance, result in the selection of every div element on the page, the first p in the body, or the page footer element. Selectors can get quite specific, however, and result in things like every third list item (li) in the ordered list (ol) or the first letter of the third paragraph of the div called myDiv.

The goal in defining your selector is to select what you want, and that's all. It is quite common to define a selector and style rule only to find that your rule is affecting more elements than you had intended.

There are a few different ways of referring to the same element. You can refer to it by its type (which is its tag name or element name, i.e., div, p, video, body, etc.). You can refer to it by its unique id attribute if it has one. You can refer to it by any of the values in its class attribute. Or, finally, you can refer to it using one of many other creative methods which we'll get to in due time.

Before we dig into the different selection techniques, let's define a few terms:

- **style rule.** A style rule is an entire statement that will determine which elements will be affected by a style and also define the style that will be applied. It consists of a selector and a declaration block.

- **selector.** A selector is a pattern for locating one or more elements in the DOM. A selector may be composed of multiple simple selectors combined with combinators.

- **combinator.** A combinator is a symbol that defines the contextual relationship between the element(s) targeted by the simple selector on its left and the element(s) targeted by the simple selector on its right.

- **declaration block.** A style rule's declaration block defines the style properties and their values that will be applied to the results of the style rule's selector.

Figure 3-2 illustrates these terms.

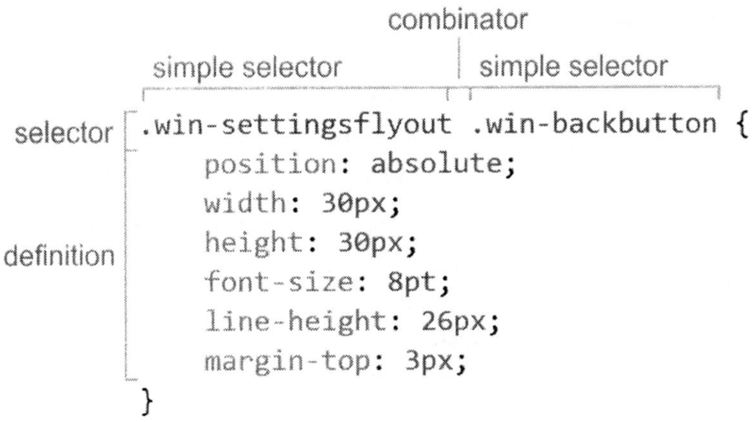

```
                           combinator
          simple selector  │  simple selector
          ┌─────────────────┴──┐┌───────────────┐
selector  ┌ .win-settingsflyout .win-backbutton {
          │     position: absolute;
          │     width: 30px;
definition│     height: 30px;
          │     font-size: 8pt;
          │     line-height: 26px;
          │     margin-top: 3px;
          └ }
```

Figure 3-2. *The anatomy of a CSS style rule*

Now, let's learn the various methods for selecting your elements.

Type Selectors

The first selector that you should know is the *type selector*. A type selector is simply the name of an HTML element; using one results in the selection of every element of that type. The selector in Listing 3-7 will locate all div elements on the page and make the text bold.

Listing 3-7. A type selector targeting every div in the document

```
/* CSS snippet */
div {
    font-weight: bold;
}
```

Listing 3-8 will bold all of the text in the entire body. Technically, this will attempt to locate all of the body elements, but let's hope you only have one!

Listing 3-8. A type selector targeting the document body

```
/* CSS snippet */
body {
    font-weight: bold;
}
```

If instead of specifying a type, you use an asterisk (*), you are using what's called the *universal type selector*, which matches all types. The CSS in Listing 3-9 will match every element on the entire page and set its font to bold!

Listing 3-9. An explicit use of the universal type selector

```
/* CSS snippet */
* {
    font-weight: bold;
}
```

This universal selector is not used on its own too often, but it's important to understand it for reasons that we'll get to very soon.

Don't forget that these type selectors, used on their own, will match any and all matching elements of the type. In order to select only one of your div elements, you'll have to be more specific (and we'll have more on that to come).

This is important. It is an absolute requirement that a type selector precede any other selectors in your expression. If you've done any CSS development already, that may come as a surprise. You may have used selectors such as the one in Listing 3-10.

Listing 3-10. Some selectors which include implicit use of the universal type selector

```
/* CSS snippet */
.first {
    font-size: 18pt;
}

#firstName {
    border: 1px solid black;
}

:hover {
    color: green;
}
```

Those examples don't seem to have a type selector preceding, in this case, a class selector, an ID selector, and a pseudo-class selector respectively. Note, though, that if you don't specify a type selector explicitly, then the universal type selector (*) is assigned for you implicitly. Therefore, the selectors in Listing 3-11 are identical to the preceding examples.

Listing 3-11. The same three rules with an exlicit universal type selector

```
/* CSS snippet */
*.first {
    font-size: 18pt;
}

*#firstName {
    border: 1px solid black;
}

*:hover {
    color: green;
}
```

And this makes sense, since what you mean to indicate with something like #firstName is any element with an id of firstName.

Class Selectors

Unlike type selectors, *class selectors* are going to rely on your doing a little bit of work in your HTML file beyond simply declaring the element. Specifically, you're going to need to decorate your element with a class. Listing 3-12 shows what it would look like to give a div element a class of important.

Listing 3-12. A div element with a class specified

```
<!-- HTML snippet -->
<div class="important"></div>
```

It's important to understand what the intended use of class selectors are. Many developers use them where they should, instead, use ID selectors (coming up).

The class names that you add to your HTML elements should generally be adjectives of the element they're associated with. Classes describe some permanent or transient characteristic of their element. A div may have a class of featured when it contains content that should be highlighted on the front page. A list item may have a class of selected when the user has chosen it. Or a video may have a class of hidden when it should wait for user action to show it.

Notice that I said that the classes may be a *transient* characteristic. In your HTML apps, you'll likely use JavaScript to add or remove classes from certain elements according to the logic of the app. When a user selects an element, a JavaScript event may fire and add the selected class to that element. In doing so, the element would suddenly take on the style rules that apply to selected elements. In Listing 3-13, for example, the div with the id of mydiv does not have a class on it to start, but when the code in the JavaScript snippet fires (which may fire in reaction to something the user does), the bigAndBold class is added to the element, and all of the style properties that are defined by that style rule suddenly take effect.

Listing 3-13. Adding a class programmatically

```
<!-- HTML snippet -->
<div id="mydiv">Lorem ipsum</div>

/* CSS snippet */
.bigAndBold {
    font-size: large;
    font-weight: bold;
}

// JavaScript snippet
document.querySelector("mydiv").className = "bigAndBold";
```

Decorating your element with a class value does not alone do anything at all to your element unless that class has a style rule defined for it. Setting a video element's class to hidden does not hide it unless you also write a style rule for the hidden class, something like display:none or visibility:hidden.

To target all of your elements with a certain class you simply prefix the class name with a period (.) in your selector, as in Listing 3-13.

Listing 3-13. A class selector referencing elements with a class of "important"

```
/* CSS snippet */
.important {
    color: red;
}
```

Elements are not limited to a single class. The HTML markup in Listing 3-14, for instance, is perfectly valid with three distinct classes defined.

Listing 3-14. An element with three defined classes

```
<!-- HTML snippet -->
<div class="important featured hidden"></div>
```

In this case, we are describing a div that is important, featured, and hidden. There's nothing wrong with that.

Similarly and perhaps obviously, the same class name may decorate as many elements as necessary. The important thing is that you never use a class to uniquely identify an element. Uniquely identifying elements is the job of the id attribute and the ID selector and we'll get to that very soon. Classes should be used when you are attempting to designate a set of entities that has something in common. Classes inherently relate to sets of elements.

Class selectors should be used in place of type selectors if the structure of your content may change. When you indicate a type in your selector, such as div, you make your style dependent on the document structure and make it more difficult to change that structure in the future. For instance, you may start with a list of div tags defining menu items, as in Listing 3-15.

Listing 3-15. A menu defined using a div

```
<!-- HTML snippet -->
<div class="menu">
    <div>Home</div>
    <div>About</div>
    <div>Products</div>
    <div>Services</div>
    <div>Contact</div>
</div>
```

You should be able to foresee, however, the possibility of this changing into something else like the unordered list in Listing 3-16.

Listing 3-16. The same menu now defined as an unordered list of list items

```
<!-- HTML snippet -->
<ul class="menu">
    <li>Home</li>
    <li>About</li>
    <li>Products</li>
    <li>Services</li>
    <li>Contact</li>
</ul>
```

In this case, you can keep your CSS styling abstract by referring to the menu by its class (menu) without indicating a type. Then the actual element type used can be changed without affecting the style.

So instead of the style rule in Listing 3-17, you should choose the one from Listing 3-18.

Listing 3-17. A type specific way of referring to the menu element

```
/* CSS snippet */
div.menu {
    /* menu styles */
}
```

Listing 3-18. A better, more abstract way of referring to the menu element

```
/* CSS snippet */
.menu {
    /* menu styles */
}
```

The first requires that you have a div of class menu. The second and preferred example simply requires that you have any element of class menu. The first would only work for the first example (the one using div elements), but the second would work for both.

Class selectors can also be chained on to one another to match only elements that have *all* of the specified classes.

ID Selectors

I mentioned that elements' class values should be thought of as adjectives of the element – things like hidden, bigger, emphasized, header. An element's id value should be its name and it must be unique. An img tag may have the id of mainLogo, which gives us a solid definition of what it is for future reference, and there will be no other mainLogo on the entire page.

You must be sure of that, too, because some strange behavior can arise if you get multiple elements with the same id value.

When you refer to elements by their class, you can expect to find anywhere from zero to many, but when you refer to an element by its ID, you should expect only one, since as we've mentioned the ID should always be unique.

To select an element by its ID, you use the hash sign (#) before it. For example, Listing 3-19 shows a selector which will select the element with an id value of mainLogo and set its width to 80px.

Listing 3-19. An ID selector which should only match a single element

```
/* CSS snippet */
#mainLogo {
    width:80px;
}
```

It is not necessary to indicate a type explicitly because ID selectors are always referencing a single, specific element. There's really nothing more to ID selection than that. It's very simple.

Attribute Selectors

So far we've seen how to select an element by its type, by its class, and by its ID. Elements often have attributes, however, and it's possible to select them based on the values of those properties.

As you can imagine, this opens up a lot of possibilities. There are a limited number of HTML elements, but there are a huge number of possible attributes and even more possible values for each of these attributes.

Look at the selector in Listing 3-20, which will set 120 pixels of left margin for all of the ListView controls on the page.

Listing 3-20. An attribute selector that matches ListView controls

```
/* CSS snippet */
 [data-win-control='WinJS.UI.ListView'] {
     margin-left: 120px;
}
```

The massive advantage here is that our HTML elements don't have to get any more descriptive than they already are. The div is already announcing that it's a ListView via an attribute, so we can use that instead of wasting bytes adding ID or class attributes.

That last example used the equality selector ([=]) to check that the value of the data-win-control attribute is WinJS.UI.ListView. There are other attribute selectors that can be used too, though.

If you specify a value in the square braces alone, it will check that that attribute exists regardless of what its value is (or even if it has a value at all!). Listing 3-21 will change the text to red for all input elements that have a required property.

Listing 3-21. An attribute selector that simply checks for the existence of a certain attribute

```
/* CSS snippet */
input[required] {
     color: red;
}
```

Remember that the required property in HTML5 does not require a value as it did in previous iterations of HTML. So, this existence comparison is helpful for these "valueless" attributes and likely for many other reasons as well.

Using the [|=] hyphen selector will match when the specified attribute's value is exactly equal to the specified value, but it will also match if the attribute's value has the specified value in it followed by a hyphen. So the attribute selector in Listing 3-22 will match paragraphs with a lang value of en, en-us, and en-au, but not es.

Listing 3-22. All lang attributes with a derivations of the English language

```
/* CSS snippet */
p[lang|='en'] {
     direction:ltr;
}
```

The [^=] selector is called the prefix selector, but I remember it as the "starts with". Use this one to see if an attribute has a value that starts with some value. Listing 3-23 will add some left margin to all div elements whose ID starts with item.

Listing 3-23. The "starts with" selector

```
/* CSS snippet */
div[id^='item'] {
    margin-left:10px;
}
```

This would match item, item1, item02, item-3, and so on, but would not match selecteditem.

The [$=] selector is similar. It's called the suffix selector (which I call "ends with") and will match when the attribute ends with the value you specify. Listing 3-24 will match selecteditem, firstitem, and item, but not itemOne.

Listing 3-24. The "ends with" selector

```
/* CSS snippet */
div[id$='item'] {
    margin-left:10px;
}
```

The substring selector [*=] is easier to remember as "contains," and it matches when any part of the attribute value matches. Listing 3-25 will match all div elements that have an ID containing the string 'sidebar.'

Listing 3-25. The "contains" selector

```
/* CSS snippet */
div[id*='sidebar'] {
    margin-left:10px;
}
```

Finally, there is a whitespace selector [~=] that will match your value in a space-delimited list of values. This one can come in very handy at times. Look at the span in Listing 3-26, which has a custom attribute called data-food-types, which will contains things like meat, vegetable, or dairy in a space-delimited attribute value. In that case, the whitespace selector would suit perfectly for determining whether meat was one of the values in the list. Values must match exactly; they cannot be partial matches.

Listing 3-26. One example use case for the whitespace selector

```
<!-- HTML snippet -->
<span data-food-types="dairy meat">meal</span>

/* CSS snippet */
span[data-food-type~='meat'] {
    font-style:italic;
}
```

Like class and ID selectors, attribute selectors default to the universal type selector, so the following two lines are identical:

```
[data-win-control='WinJS.UI.ListView']
*[data-win-control='WinJS.UI.ListView']
```

By the way, leaving the explicit type selector (div) off in this case makes perfect sense since the data-win-control is only ever found on a div element anyway.

You can create an attribute selector for any attribute that can possibly describe an HTML element. For HTML, only recognized attributes are considered valid, but for HTML5, any recognized attribute or any attribute that begins with data- is considered valid, so developers are free to add custom attributes that begin with data-. The number of possible attribute selectors is unlimited.

Listing 3-27 shows some practical examples of where you might use attribute selectors in a Windows 8 app using HTML5.

Listing 3-27. Example attribute selectors in a Windows 8 app

```
/* CSS snippet */
section[role=main] {
    /* styles to affect the main section */
}

[data-win-control] {
    /* styles to affect all Windows 8 control in the document */
}

[data-win-control^='WinJS.UI'] {
    /* styles to affect just the UI controls */
}
```

Attribute Selectors		
Symbol	**Name**	**Description**
[=]	Equality	Matches elements with an attribute that has the specified name and value
[]	Existence	Matches elements with an attribute that has the specified name
|=	Hyphen	Matches elements with an attribute that has the specified value or that has the specified value followed by a hyphen
[^=]	Prefix	Matches elements with an attribute that begins with the specified value
[$=]	Suffix	Matches elements with an attribute that ends with the specified value
[*=]	Substring	Matches elements with an attribute that contains the specified value
[~=]	Whitespace	Matches elements with an attribute that has the specified value or that has the specified value surrounded by whitespace

It may interest you to note that you could actually select an element by its ID using an attribute selector, but that would be poor form, considering there's an ID selector made just exactly for that.

Pseudo-class and Pseudo-element Selectors

I'm hoping you have the concept of a class by now. Remember, a class is an adjective. It describes the element that it decorates, and it is explicitly added by you – the developer. Pseudo-classes, on the other hand, are inherent. They are adjectives just like classes, but you don't have to specify anything in the HTML.

When the user is hovering over a table row, for instance, the word hover could be used to describe that row, right? One of the pseudo-classes is :hover (as you can see, pseudo-classes are preceded by a colon), and it could be used to select that element as long as the user is hovering his mouse over it. It's easier and cleaner to add a pseudo-class to your selector than it is to programmatically add classes to your elements.

Like the other selectors, it is possible to specify a pseudo-class on its own and invoke the default type selector. So :hover is the same as *:hover and will match any element at all that is hovered over.

The concept of a pseudo-element is very similar to that of a pseudo-class. Just like a pseudo-class acts like a class but is inherent and does not have to be designated by the developer, a pseudo-element acts like an element but is inherent and, again, does not have to be designated by the developer.

The first list item in a list is just that, whether you designate that explicitly or not, correct? One of the pseudo-classes is :first-child and it would select that first list item. Here again, we're selecting elements without being forced to write extraneous markup.

You'll likely run into some confusion over the difference between a pseudo-class and a pseudo-element, and that is because there was no difference in syntax in standards previous to CSS3. CSS3 introduced the double colon (::) syntax to refer to a pseudo-element and left the single colon (:) for the pseudo-class. The pseudo-elements that were formerly using a single colon remain in the spec for backwards compatibility, so you'll see them twice in the following complete list of standard pseudo-classes and pseudo-elements: ::after, ::before, ::first-letter, ::first-line, ::selection, :active, :after, :before, :checked, :default, :disabled, :empty, :enabled, :first-child, :first-letter, :first-line, :first-of-type, :focus, :hover, :in-range, :indeterminate, :invalid, :lang(), :last-child, :last-of-type, :link, :not(), :nth-child(), :nth-last-child(), :nth-last-of-type(), :nth-of-type(), :only-child, :only-of-type, :optional, :out-of-range, :read-only, :read-write, :required, :root, :target, :valid, :visited.

In addition to the standard pseudo-classes and pseudo-elements, there are a few that are Microsoft vendor specific, and you should be familiar with them when working in a Windows 8 app. They are :-ms-input-placeholder, :-ms-keyboard-active, ::-ms-browse, ::-ms-check, ::-ms-clear, ::-ms-expand, ::-ms-fill, ::-ms-fill-lower, ::-ms-fill-upper, ::-ms-reveal, ::-ms-thumb, ::-ms-ticks-after, ::-ms-ticks-before, ::-ms-tooltip, ::-ms-track, and ::-ms-value. The vendor specific pseudo selectors are generally used to access the sub-elements of various controls.

I won't take you through the entire list of pseudo selectors, but I want to highlight a few of the ones I find the most helpful.

:root

The :root pseudo-class has one simple function, and that is to locate the root element of the document in context. For example, when CSS is describing an HTML document, the root is always the HTML element. You never know when this is going to come in handy, so keep it in your back pocket.

::first-letter

::first-letter is excellent for creating a drop cap in your paragraph. I can't imagine what other use there might be for it, but as its name indicates, it represents the first letter in the text of the element it applies to. Remember that sometimes a pseudo-class or pseudo-element is explicitly attached to an element in the selector as in p::first-letter. Other times it's implied as in div ::first-letter. Don't miss the subtle difference there. The former means "the first letter of the paragraph tag. The latter has a space after the div and thus means "the first letter in every element that is a descendent of a div".

Listing 3-28 defines what is likely the most popular use of the ::first-letter pseudo-element—for creating a drop cap. Figure 3-3 illustrates the resulting drop cap.

Listing 3-28. Using the ::first-letter pseudo-element to target the first letter in a paragraph

```
/* CSS snippet */
.dropCap::first-letter {
    font-size: 500%;
    float: left;
    line-height: 0.8em;
    padding: 0 4px 0 0;
    font-family: Serif;
    font-weight: bold;
    position: relative;
    left: -3px;
}
```

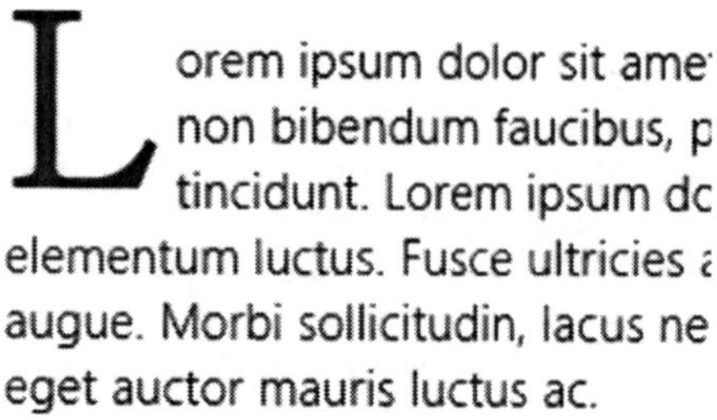

L orem ipsum dolor sit ame
non bibendum faucibus, p
tincidunt. Lorem ipsum dc
elementum luctus. Fusce ultricies ¿
augue. Morbi sollicitudin, lacus ne
eget auctor mauris luctus ac.

Figure 3-3. *The style definition creates a drop cap effect*

:checked

:checked is a pseudo-class (you can tell by the single, preceding colon) and will limit the checkboxes (or radio buttons) that are selected to only those which have been checked. Listing 3-29 and Figure 3-4 show the :checked pseudo-class in action.

Listing 3-29. The :checked pseudo-class selector in action

```
<!-- HTML snippet -->
    <div id="checkboxes">
        <input type="checkbox" />
        <input type="checkbox" checked />
        <input type="checkbox" />
        <input type="checkbox" checked />
        <input type="checkbox" />
    </div>

/* CSS snippet */
#checkboxes :checked {
    border: 1px solid red;
}
```

Figure 3-4. *Checkboxes that are marked as checked have received the border style*

::before, ::after, and content

The ::before and ::after pseudo-elements, used in conjunction with the content style property, are used to inject some content before or after the element targeted with your selector. At first, you may wonder what this functionality is even doing in CSS. It does, after all, seem like a content issue that should be handled by HTML and/or JavaScript.

There are cases, however, when the injection of content is really more of a styling concern. Imagine you want to render a small, complimentary glyph next to the hovered paragraph to indicate to the user which one is in focus. Or perhaps you want to show a check mark next to links that the user has already visited. Either of these would be impossible without the ::before and ::after pseudo-elements and the content property.

There's at least one more thing that's interesting about the content property. It allows for the use of an attr() function to refer to the value of one of the attributes of the element in context. For example, look at Listing 3-30, which will render a popup tooltip next to each link, when you hover over it, that includes the title of the link.

Listing 3-30. The ::after pseudo-element used to render a tooltip for hovered links

```
/* CSS snippet */
a:hover::after {
    content: attr(title);
    background-color: lightyellow;
    border: 1px solid black;
    color: black;
    position: relative;
    left: 10px;
    white-space: nowrap;
    padding: 5px;
}
```

:required

This :required pseudo-class is used a whole lot to add a style to fields that are marked as required. Listing 3-31 shows an example. Typically, web developers will decorate required fields with a red border or an alternate background color or a complimentary symbol. A symbol could be added to required fields without any additional markup if used in combination with the ::before and ::after pseudo-elements and the content property we just learned.

Listing 3-31. An HTML element with a required attribute and a CSS rule to style it

```
<!-- HTML snippet -->
<input type="text" required />

/* CSS snippet */
input:required {
    border: 1px solid red;
    color: red;
}
```

::-ms-expand

The ::-ms-expand pseudo-element represents the tiny drop-down arrow that renders on select controls.

::-ms-browse

You can target the browse button that is rendered when you use a file input control by using the ::-ms-browse property. Being able to target sub-elements like this gives very granular control over the details of app design.

Positional pseudo-classes

Many of the pseudo-classes relate to an element's position in the DOM. They are :first-child, :first-of-type, :last-child, :last-of-type, :nth-child(), :nth-last-child(), :nth-last-of-type(), :nth-of-type(), :only-child, and :only-of-type.

These positional pseudo-classes are extremely useful in selecting just the right elements without being forced to decorate your HTML elements with an id or a class attribute. You can use them to refer to things like

- the first div on the page

- every other table row

- the last paragraph in a section

- the odd menu items

- every third list item

- and more

You'll notice that about half of these pseudo-classes are suffixed with -child and half with -of-type. The -child do not restrict by element type, whereas the -of-type do. Consider the subtle difference between Listing 3-32 and Listing 3-33.

Listing 3-32. One of the positional pseudo-classes with the -child suffix

```
/* CSS snippet */
div p:first-child {
    font-weight: bold;
}
```

Listing 3-33. One of the positional pseudo-classes with the -of-type suffix

```
/* CSS snippet */
div p:first-of-type {
    font-weight: bold;
}
```

Listing 3-32 will select "every paragraph that is the first child among its siblings," whereas Listing 3-33 will select "every paragraph that is the first *paragraph* among its siblings". Of course, both of those matched paragraphs must also be a descendent of a div element, since the selector begins with div.

You've seen, then, what the first-child and first-of-type pseudo-classes do, and you can likely guess what last-child and last-of-type do. Look now at :nth-child(), :nth-of-type(), :nth-last-child(), and :nth-last-of-type(). These pseudo-classes are functional, and that's why they have the parentheses.

To illustrate all of these positional pseudo-classes, consider the table in Listing 3-34.

Listing 3-34. A table with five rows

```
<!-- HTML snippet -->
<table id="myTable">
    <tr><td>Beans</td><td>2.7</td><td>67%</td></tr>
    <tr><td>Corn</td><td>1.7</td><td>40%</td></tr>
    <tr><td>Beets</td><td>2.9</td><td>77%</td></tr>
    <tr><td>Carrots</td><td>7.0</td><td>62%</td></tr>
    <tr><td>Celery</td><td>12.3</td><td>50%</td></tr>
</table>
```

If our goal was to select all of the table rows and color their background to gray, we could do so using . . .

```
/* CSS snippet */
#myTable tr {
    background-color: gray;
}
```

If, on the other hand, our goal was to select only certain rows, we would use one of either first-, last-, or nth-. To select the first table row, we would use Listing 3-35.

Listing 3-35. The :first-child pseudo-class used to color the first row in a table

```
/* CSS snippet */
#myTable tr:first-child {
    background-color: gray;
}
```

To select the last table, row we would use Listing 3-36.

Listing 3-36. The :last-child pseudo-class used to color the last row in a table

```
/* CSS snippet */
#myTable tr:last-child {
    background-color: gray;
}
```

To select every other table row, we could use Listing 3-37.

Listing 3-37. The :nth-child pseudo-class used to color every other row in a table

```
/* CSS snippet */
#myTable tr:nth-child(2n) {
    background-color: gray;
}
```

Now, this one takes some explaining. The :nth-child pseudo-class acts like a function where you pass in a formula of the form an + b. The CSS engine will then plug a set of positive integers starting with 0 into the formula for n. The result will be a set of integers. CSS will omit the negative and zero values and use the resulting positive integers to determine which items should be matches.

In Listing 3-37, I just provided 2n, and that's equivalent to 2n + 0 and evaluates to $[0,2,4,6,8,...]$. The 0 is omitted, and we are left with essentially highlighting every even row. This is a common scenario, so CSS also defines the even keyword and allows us to simply use #myTable tr:nth-child(even) to create the same effect.

Consider the formula 2n-1 then, which would evaluate to an integer set that looked like $[-1,1,3,5,7,9,...]$. CSS would then ignore the –1 (since it's less than zero) and apply this style to elements 1, 3, and 5. Just like even, CSS defines the odd keyword to simplify matters.

The formula that you pass in to an nth- pseudo-class can get pretty fancy. Here are some examples . . .

Listing 3-38. Example formulas for the nth- pseudo-classes

```
2n /* every other (starting with the second) */
2n - 1 /* every other (starting with the first) */
3n /* every third */
3n + 3 /* every third starting with 3 */
-n + 3 /* only the first three */
n + 3 /* all, starting with the third */
```

Finally, let's look at the :only-child and :only-of-type pseudo-classes. Listing 3-39 uses each of them.

Listing 3-39. Example use of :only-child and :only-of-type pseudo-classes

```
/* CSS snippet */
div p:only-child {
    font-size: larger;
}

div p:only-of-type {
    font-size: larger;
}
```

The first rule would select "the paragraph in a div as long as it's the only element under that div", and the second would select "the paragraph in a div as long as it's the only paragraph element under that div".

:target

You can use the :target pseudo-class to add some fairly interesting interaction to your app without introducing any JavaScript.

Here's how it works. If you have an element in your document with an id value that matches a fragment identifier in the current URL, then that element will match the :target pseudo-class.

If your URL, for instance, is http://www.mysite.com/#image01, then the element with an id of image01 will match the :target pseudo-class.

The fragment identifier is used to navigate a user around a single document, so by using this pseudo-class, you can add styling that gives the user a sense of where his focus is or what he's doing.

:not()

The last one I want to show you is the :not pseudo-class. This one is helpful because it reverses whatever is inside the parenthesis. In an earlier example I showed you how to style all checked checkboxes using . . .

```
#checkboxes :checked {
    border: 1px solid red;
}
```

We can reverse that logic and select all unselected checkboxes using . . .

```
#checkboxes :not(:checked) {
    border: 1px solid red;
}
```

Combinators

We know now how to select an element or set of elements using:

- the element's type
- one or more of the element's classes
- the element's unique ID
- an expression to match the existence or value of an attribute of the element
- one or more pseudo-classes
- one or more pseudo-elements

That covers a lot of cases, but that's not all we can do with selectors. Selectors can work in teams. They can be combined together using combinators to specify a hierarchical and possibly complex logical relationship between elements to get to the target element or elements.

We can easily select all of the div elements on the page and add some space above them by using:

```
div {
    margin-top: 6px;
}
```

If, however, we actually wanted to only add space before the div elements that are in a section, then we would have to use a combinator. We would have to use the descendent combinator actually, and it would look like Listing 3-40.

Listing 3-40. Two simple style selectors separated by a descendant combinator (a space)

```
/* CSS snippet */
section div {
    margin-top: 6px;
}
```

The selector in Listing 3-40 has a space in it. It separates section from div, and this sets up a hierarchical relationship between the two. It indicates that only a div that is a child of a section should match. This space is called the *descendent combinator*, and we're going to look more extensively at it and three others.

Descendent

Use a space (⌴) to indicate a descendent combinator.

Using this single space between two selectors means: "select all elements that match the second selector where that element is a descendent of an element that matches the first selector". That sounds like a mouth full, but it's not difficult when you look at it. An example will clear this one up.

```
div p {
    padding: 2px;
}
```

The preceding code will add some padding around all paragraph tags that are inside of a div. This means they can be nested any number of levels deep and they can be inside of any div whatsoever. This is a very liberal selector.

Child

The *child combinator* is a greater-than sign (>).

The child combinator is similar to the descendent combinator except that it's more specific. The child combinator only matches if the element matched by the selector on the right is a direct descendent of the element matched by the selector on the left.

You might run into trouble when you forget the child combinator and lazily leave a space between your selectors. A selector of div p, for instance, will match any paragraph that is a child of a div and when you only have one level of children under your div, that works just fine. It will also match p elements that are distant descendants of your div, however, and that may or may not be what you intended.

This is where the child combinator comes in. It requires that the element on the right be a *direct* child of the element on the left.

General sibling

Descendent and child combinators indicate a vertical parent–child relationship between elements, but the *sibling combinator* (~) indicates a horizontal relationship between children of the same parent.

The general sibling implies the order of the siblings but says nothing of how close or far apart the siblings are. Given A ~ B, both A and B must have the same parent and B must come after A, but there may be many elements in between.

Adjacent sibling

The *adjacent sibling combinator* (+) is like the general sibling combinator except more specific. The adjacent sibling indicates that the elements matching the selectors on either side are not only siblings but that they are immediately next to one another and in the indicated order.

You likely won't use the adjacent sibling combinator as often as some of the others, but it's one of those assets that's great to have when you need it. Listing 3-41 shows one such case in which the intent is to remove the space above an H1 element if it comes immediately subsequent to another H1 element.

Listing 3-41. An excellent use for the adjacent sibling combinator

```
/* CSS snippet */
H1 + H1 {
    margin-top: -10px;
}
```

Selector Groups

We've looked at simple selectors that match in type, class, ID, attribute, and more. We've looked at stringing simple selectors together using combinators to form hierarchies. There's one more feature of selectors that's quite important, and that is our ability to group them. It is quite common to wish for the same style properties to describe multiple target element sets. For instance, perhaps we want to be sure there are 10 pixels of space above each heading tag whether it's an h1, an h2, or so on.

This could be described with individual style rules, but that would be quite redundant, so grouping syntax should be used. Grouping is doing by simply adding a comma between selectors. Listing 3-42 illustrates how we could add space to all of the heading tags.

Listing 3-42. A style rule that uses selector chaining to apply to five levels of header tags

```
/* CSS snippet */
h1, h2, h3, h4, h5 {
    margin-top: 10px;
}
```

It's important to note, when using more complex selectors, that the comma signifies a complete reset of the selection chain. You may be tempted to try something like the code in Listing 3-43, for instance, to apply the same style to all of the heading tags under a certain div, but the results would not be what you intended. Because the comma breaks the selection chain, the h1 is going to work correctly, but the h2, h3, and h4 selectors are actually going to match every h2, h3, and h4 in the document.

Listing 3-43. An example of a selector chain that may not act as you expect

```
/* CSS snippet */
#topDiv #childDiv h1, h2, h3, h4 {
    margin-top: 10px;
}
```

The solution to the dilemma is to include the fully qualified style selector on each term in the chain. Listing 3-44 shows this rather lengthy but accurate solution.

Listing 3-44. The selector chain corrected to add the full hierarchy to each term

```
/* CSS snippet */
#topDiv #childDiv h1, #topDiv #childDiv h2, #topDiv #childDiv h3, #topDiv #childDiv h4 {
    Margin-top: 10px;
}
```

Style Definition

Remember that a style rule is made up of its selector and its definition (aka the declaration block). Remember also the simple concept that you have to select something before you can define what it is you want to modify about it. We have looked at length at how to select what you want, and now it is time to actually do something to it!

The definition of a style rule is very easy to understand because it is simply a collection of style properties in the form of a key value pair. The key and value are always delimited with a colon (:), and pairs are delimited from each other with a semi-colon (;).

The key is one of many CSS style properties that you will soon learn and the value is one of the valid values for that property.

For instance, color is a CSS style property, and red is one of its many valid values. Defining the text color of an element would involve targeting that element with a selector and then providing the color property key with a value of red.

The rule in Listing 3-45 will make all paragraph text red.

Listing 3-45. Set all paragraph text to red

```
/* CSS snippet */
p {
    color: red;
}
```

You should recognize the selector by now. The p is the selector. It is a type selector and it will match every paragraph tag in the document. The definition consists of a single key value pair. The key is color and the value is red.

That's about as simple as a style rule gets, but they don't get much more complicated either. The selector may be longer and more specific, and multiple style property pairs replace the single pair here.

Learning CSS mostly involves two things:

1. learning how to use selectors and

2. learning what all of the possible style properties there are for you to use

The easiest way to see what style properties are available is to just use IntelliSense in Visual Studio. When you invoke IntelliSense in the style definition, you'll see a complete list of all style definitions possible (Figure 3-5). IntelliSense does not filter the list based on which properties apply to the element type you've selected.

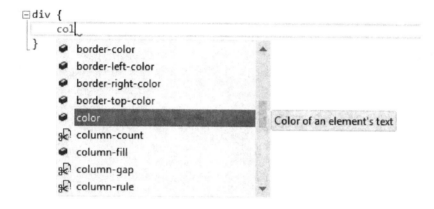

Figure 3-5. *Visual Studio's IntelliSense as it applies to CSS style properties*

There are hundreds of properties, and I'll introduce a good number of them in subsequent chapters. For now, I just want to make sure you understand a couple of fundamentals in their use.

As I said, defining a style property is pretty much as easy as typing it, typing a colon (:), typing the value, and then finishing it off with a semicolon (;).

Listing 3-46 shows a couple of style properties defined in a style rule that will apply to all p elements and will direct the text inside it to be blue and bold.

Listing 3-46. A style rule with two properties

```
/* CSS snippet */
p {
    color: blue;
    font-weight: bold;
}
```

Shorthand Properties

Your style rule may be fairly short with only a handful of properties, or it may be very long with a whole lot of properties. It all depends on how much styling needs to be applied to the target element.

Now consider the following, sizeable style rule, which will apply to all div elements and will direct it to have a border that is 2px wide, dashed, and red all the way around.

```
div {
    color: blue;
    border-left-color: red;
    border-left-style: dashed;
    border-left-width: 2px;
    border-top-color: red;
    border-top-style: dashed;
    border-top-width: 2px;
    border-right-color: red;
    border-right-style: dashed;
    border-right-width: 2px;
    border-bottom-color: red;
    border-bottom-style: dashed;
    border-bottom-width: 2px;
}
```

Formidable, isn't it? This is obviously not an elegant way to do something as simple as adding a red dashed border around an element, and that's why shorthand properties exist. Shorthand properties allow you to define multiple style properties all at once. Let's rewrite the last example taking advantage of the space and time that shorthand properties can save us.

```
div {
    color: blue;
    border: 2px dashed red;
}
```

That's much better. A single property has replaced 12! The border property is a shorthand property. It takes a list of property values in a certain order delimited by spaces, and it applies them to the longer list of actual properties.

Here again, Visual Studio is your friend. When you enter a shorthand property, you get a tool tip that shows you the list of space-delimited properties that it's expecting (Figure 3-6).

Figure 3-6. *Visual Studio's tool tip suggesting values for a shorthand property*

Take a look at these common shorthand properties . . .

```
border:3px groove black;
font:bold 12px arial;
margin:4px 7px 2px 4px; /* sets the top, right, bottom, and left margins */
padding:10px 2px 7px 1px; /* sets the top, right, bottom, and left padding values */
background:url(image.png) no-repeat gray;
```

The margin and padding properties (which we'll talk about in great length in chapter 3) have some alternate forms, even.

```
margin:4px 7px; /* sets the top/bottom margins to 4px, left/right margins to 7px */
padding:10px; /* sets padding to 10px on all sides */
```

Property Values

Valid property values (the value after the colon and before the semi-colon) differ by style property, but they all follow some basic rules. All of the properties share one common, valid value – that is inherit. A value of inherit will indicate that the property should get its value from its parent element.

Length values are required to be a numeric followed immediately by one of the standard CSS units of measure from the table below.

Unit	Description
em	the computed font size
Ex	the height of a lowercase 'x'
Px	pixels, relative to the viewing device
rem	the font size of the root element
vw	the viewport width
vh	the viewport height

(continued)

Unit	Description
vm	the smaller value of viewport width or height
ch	zero-width (width of the zero character in the rendered font)
in	inches
cm	centimeters
mm	millimeters
pt	points (1 point = 1/72 inches)
pc	picas (1 pica = 12 points)

Besides these units of measure, you can specify a value followed by a percent sign (%) to calculate your length relative to its container. A table cell with a width of 50%, for instance, will (at least attempt to) take up half of the width of the table.

CSS3 introduced some functions that can be used to add some additional oomph to the units as well. The calc() function will do some math for you even if it involves disparate units. The following code set the width of a div to be 20 pixels less than the full width of its parent container and might be very helpful when placing an object on the page.

```
div {
    width:calc(100% - 20px);
}
```

And min() and max() will take an arbitrary number of parameters and return the smaller or largest respectively. To set the left padding to the smaller of 10% and 20 pixels, you could use the following:

```
div {
    padding-left:min(10%,20px);
}
```

Cascading Order, Specificity, and Scope

The end goal in working with CSS is to get properties to apply to document elements. It's important, therefore, to consider some particulars that will affect what gets applied and what doesn't.

Cascading

The *C* in CSS stands for cascading, so you might surmise that it is one of the flagship features of this technology, and you would be right.

Cascading refers to the way style rules get applied to their target elements. One style rule may apply to an element only to be overridden by another style rule of greater importance.

The way that your browser (following the CSS standard) determines which of these rules is of greater importance is a rather complicated matter. I'm going to try to keep it simple, but you should understand what's going on here so you don't find yourself scratching your head and wondering why your text is green when you meant for it to be black.

Style rules do get applied in order. But what is that order? Remember the three ways to apply style properties to elements in your page? Inline styles, embedded style sheets, and external style sheet. The style rules in the embedded styles override those from the external style sheets, and the inline properties override them both.

Looking at the HTML page and external style sheet in Listing 3-47, can you determine whether the Hello, World! text in the div is going to be bold or not?

Listing 3-47. The cascading nature of CSS style rules

```
<!-- default.html -->
<!DOCTYPE html>
<html>
    <head>
        <title></title>
        <link href="default.css" rel="stylesheet" />
    </head>
    <body>
        <div id="myDiv" style="font-weight:normal;">
            Hello, World!
        </div>
    </body>
</html>

/* default.css */
#myDiv {
    font-weight: bold;
}
```

The answer is that it will not be bold. The external style sheet indicated that it should be, but the inline style has overridden it with the font-weight: normal property.

If you're not sure which of your rules are getting applied and which are getting overridden, use a style tracing tool. Most modern browsers contain such a feature in the developer tools, and the same thing is provided in Visual Studio when working with Windows 8 apps.

Specificity

Specificity also plays a role in the matter. Specificity is a fancy word to describe the computer's best guess at how specific your selector is and thus how much weight it should be given when competing with other rules. If two style rules end up targeting the same element, but one does so in a more specific way, then it is determined to have higher specificity, it wins, and that style rule's properties are applied instead of the other.

ID selectors, for example, are very specific. If a certain div element is targeted by two style rules, each trying to give it a different color border, but one is referencing it by its id and the other by its type, then the former will win. The div in the following example, then, would have a red border even though we've given it a class of blue.

Listing 3-48. A div with an ID and a class and style rules targeting both

```
<!-- HTML snippet -->
        <div id="myDiv" class="blue">
            Hello, World!
        </div>

/* CSS snippet */
#myDiv {
    border: 1px solid red;
}
```

```
.blue {
    border: 1px solid blue;
}
```

For a more in-depth look at CSS specificity, I recommend David Powers' book *Beginning CSS3*.

Scope

When you study JavaScript, you'll learn a pattern called the modular pattern, which is intended to give scope to certain blocks of JavaScript that are otherwise fully exposed to the global namespace and thus to all other code in the application.

CSS doesn't have anything like this. CSS doesn't have any scope! This means that if 100 style sheets were referenced on any given HTML page, then all of the CSS styles are available to all of the page.

Windows 8 apps, though, tend to follow a navigation pattern that keeps the user on a single page (default.html) and loads the HTML, CSS, and JavaScript of the page that the user navigates to instead of actually changing scope. This is a very good practice both for the developer and the user. It's actually a very popular trend in modern website applications as well, but if you define a style rule in CSS on one page of a single page application, you can accidentally let that rule bleed over to other pages. For this reason, it's recommended that you prefix your CSS style rule selectors with the class that Windows 8 gives to all page fragments, which is simply the name of the page.

If you create new item in a Windows 8 project in Visual studio called `orders.html`, then by default your page's HTML will contain a `div` of class `orders`. If you precede all of your selectors with `.orders` and then a space (remember, that's the descendant combinator), then your style rules will only match elements that exist inside your page. This is a very good practice to implement.

Media Queries

CSS2, the predecessor to CSS3, had media types. Media types allowed for the application of different style sheets, depending on the designated media value. Two common media values are `screen` or `print`. This meant that the developer could specify one style sheet that would be applied to the document when the user agent (the browser usually) was rendering it to the screen, and a different style sheet for rendering it to a printer.

CSS3 evolved nicely with the introduction of media queries, which greatly increase the functionality.

With media queries, instead of referencing an entirely different style sheet, we're able to more granularly designate blocks of CSS style rules that apply to various media-related characteristics.

Instead of merely determining that a style sheet should apply in a given case (though this is still possible), a media query can determine that a single style rule (more granular than the whole sheet) should apply.

With media queries, it's possible to distinguish not only between the various media types (things like `screen` and `print` and also `handheld`, `projection`, and `tv`), but also between orientations (portrait and landscape) and between various sizes, resolutions, and aspect ratios.

The ability to apply different styles to different media configurations is absolutely critical for Windows 8 development. Windows 8 can be installed on a huge number of systems; most of those systems have different size and resolution screens—some can be rotated—and to top it off, Windows 8 offers the ability to snap an app, setting it to just 320 pixels wide and placing it next to another app on the screen. This introduces even more possible rendering configurations.

Thankfully, media queries make our job as developers a lot easier.

Media queries start with the `@media` keyword, continue with a media type and some number of features, and end up resulting in a true or false value. A media query is true only if the type and all of the features match.

So valid media query syntax would look something like the following:

```
@media type and feature1 and feature2 and featureN {
    styleRule1;
    styleRule2;
    styleRuleN;
}
```

The valid values for the type are: screen, print, braille, handheld, print, projection, tty, tv, embossed, speech, and all, and the valid values for feature are width, height, device-width, device-height, orientation, aspect-ratio, device-aspect-ratio, color, color-index, monochrome, resolution, scan, grid, and Microsoft has extended this list with two additional, vendor-specific values: -ms-high-contrast and -ms-view-state. When working on a Windows 8 app, the -ms-view-state is going to be your best friend. This is how you determine which view state your app is in. It could be fullscreen landscape, fullscreen portrait, snapped, or filled (when an app is snapped next to yours).

A subset of the feature values enumerated above can be prefixed with min- and max-. A value of min-device-width: 800px, for instance, would be valid and helpful in specifying a media query that only matched if the device in use was at least 800 pixels wide. Additionally, a value of max-color-index: 256 would be valid and would match if the device supported 256 colors or less.

A media query list can be built up from multiple media queries by separating them with commas. All this does is apply the same set of style rules in multiple cases. In Listing 3-49, the color style property will apply to all paragraphs when the output medium is either on a screen or on a color printer.

Listing 3-49. A media query targeting the screen and color printers

```
/* CSS snippet */
@media screen, print and (color) {
    p {
        color: red;
    }
}
```

Besides specifying the media type that your media query should apply to, you can also specify the media type that your media query should exclude. You could make a media query that would apply to everything except for the printer by using . . .

```
@media not print {
    p {
        color: red;
    }
}
```

This would apply a color in every case except for print, where perhaps the desire is to save color ink.

If you're creating a Windows 8 app, you'll most certainly want to handle at least a couple of view states— full screen landscape and snapped view, if nothing else, and media queries are the way to go.

Summary

We've learned that the purpose of CSS is to affect your HTML with styles, and that affecting your HTML with styles is a two-fold process of, first, making a selection of one or more HTML elements and, second, defining the styles that should apply to that selection.

We looked in detail at the selection process—at the use of multiple selector types and the use of multiple combinator types for putting them together so our selections can be more specific.

We looked in detail at style definitions and how to define multiple properties in a style definition. We also saw shorthand properties in action, making our style properties easier to write.

We saw how style rules cascade, take effect, and possibly override each other, and we saw how we're given the ability to use media queries to make our style rules take effect only in certain cases regarding the device, device size, and view state.

Next, we'll look at real, live style properties, and we'll start with properties that pertain to styling text.

CHAPTER 4

Text Properties

Note There's something extremely compelling about great typography that will make users love your app.

If you have already read the first chapter then you know how to select elements and you know how to define style rules for those elements, and now, you are ready to turn mere structure into something beautiful as well as functional.

We're going to take a detailed look at some of the many style properties. In this chapter we'll cover typography-related properties—the properties that pertain to the text in your app. We'll look at text color and font properties for determining things like what font face your text is rendered in and what size and weight it is. We'll explore multi-column layouts that are much more popular in Windows 8 apps than in traditional web design, and we'll learn how to control the hyphenation in our text columns.

Let me take the time to convince you of the importance of high-quality typography in your Windows 8 app. Typography is more than just making text look fancy—at least it is in a Windows 8 app. In Windows 8, typography is used to convey style, but also to convey structure and hierarchy. It helps a user's eye and brain quickly determine the significance of the content on the screen. It's used to help them differentiate between the title of your app, the category of a section, and the body of text that makes up the app's content.

So, spend the time to learn how to get great control over the display of text inside your app, and then consider the very first of the Microsoft design style principles—*show pride in craftsmanship*. This means you should take the time to make sure your app is polished, and being intentional and beautiful with your typography is one massive way to polish your app.

Text

Text on a page has a basic function of relaying information, but being careful about your choice of typography and your text layout can spell the difference between an app that looks like a dictionary and one that really draws users in.

In this section, we're going to look at some basic text properties that will give us control over things like the color, opacity, weight, size, and font face of our text. Let's start with color and opacity.

Color and opacity

The color property determines the foreground color of the selected element. It primarily affects the text that an element contains.

There are three common places to define color: the color property, the background-color property (see Chapter 3), and the border-color property (again, see Chapter 3), and colors are always defined the same way—*ways* actually—there are four common ways to define a color:

- by color name
- by hex value
- by the rgb() or rgba() functions
- by the hsl() or hsla() functions

Named Colors

Defining colors using their name is likely the most intuitive for most people, so if a named color exists that fits your requirement then by all means use it. You define color by name by simply providing the color name as the value to the color property. There are 147 named colors in the HTML/CSS standards, and you can see a list of all of them at http://www.w3.org/TR/css3-color/#svg-color. Some of them are basic like: Red, Green, and Blue. Some of them are derivations of the basics like DarkRed, LightGreen, and DarkSlateBlue. And some of them are altogether esoteric like DarkGoldenRod, LemonChiffon, and PapayaWhip. The named colors are not case sensitive, so papayawhip works just as well as PapayaWhip.

Hex Colors

Defining colors using their hex value opens you up to far more than 147 colors—actually it's more like 16.8 million colors. Perhaps you recall the advice from earlier days in web development that you should stick to a narrow band of "web safe colors," but that advice is hardly relevant in this modern age where browsers that are limited to a narrow color palette are extremely few and far between. If you're creating a Windows 8 app, then you know you're working with the very latest in web standards with the Internet Explorer browser engine and you certainly don't need to worry about legacy compatibility issues like this.

A hex color value is a six-digit hexadecimal value preceded by a hash (#). For example, #FFEFD5 would give you the equivalent of PapayaWhip, and the hex values are not case sensitive either, so #ffefd5 would work fine as well. The first pair of hexadecimal digits represents the level of red, the second the level of green, and the third the level of blue.

Table 4-1. *A few hex values and their color equivalents*

Hex Value	Color
#000000	black
#ffffff	white
#ff0000	red
#00ff00	green
#0000ff	blue
#ffff00	yellow
#00ffff	cyan
#ff00ff	magenta

Even the more avid number jockeys among us take some time to convert decimal and hexadecimal, so it's convenient that any modern graphics software package should provide the hex equivalent of any color you choose. Designating colors using a hex value makes no provision for opacity, so if you need some degree of transparency in your color then just read on.

A shorthand method for designating hex values exists for hex values with repeating pairs like #000000, #ffffff, or even #aa33dd. If you designate a hex value with only three characters, then it will repeat each of the three values into pairs. Use this shorthand technique to use #000 for #000000 (black), #fff for #ffffff (white), or #ff0 for #ffff00 (yellow).

RGB Colors

Defining colors with the rgb() and rgba() functions is quite simple. The rgb() function works just like the hex value except the three color components are passed in as decimal arguments to the function instead of being three hexadecimal pairs. A color value of rgb(0,0,0) will result in black just like a hex value of #000000. The rgba() function goes an extra step in accepting an alpha value. The alpha value defines the opacity of the color; that is, it determines to what degree the color appears versus letting its background come through. It's the opposite of transparency. The color blue at full opacity (zero transparency) is the color blue and completely covers its background, whereas, the color blue at half opacity (half transparency) let's some of the background through as if it were blue tinted glass. As an example, rgb(0,0,255) would be entirely blue and rgba(0,0,255,0.5) would result in something like the blue tinted glass.

The values for red, green, and blue can either be an integer value from 0 to 255 or a percentage value (succeeded by a % symbol). The alpha value should always be a decimal value from 0.0 (fully transparent) to 1.0 (fully opaque).

HSL Colors

Similar to rgb() and rgba(), you can use the hsl() and hsla() functions to specify a color based on its hue, saturation, and lightness values. HSL is an alternate method for representing unique colors. The hue represents the color's position in the rainbow, the saturation roughly corresponds to how rich the color is, and the lightness is how light or dark the color appears. The nice thing about using HSL values instead of RGB is their relative intuitiveness. Once you have the right hue, you can adjust its saturation and lightness values to make sensible adjustments to the color, which can't be said for RGB. Small changes to any of the RGB values results in colors of an entirely different hue. This is especially useful when creating color ramps where a hue is chosen as a theme color and varying saturation or lightness value are used to create the application's visual assets.

The functions take their first argument (hue) as an integer from 0 to 255, their second and third arguments (saturation and lightness) as a percentages, and hsla() takes the fourth argument (alpha) as a decimal from 0.0 (fully transparent) to 1.0 (fully opaque).

Opacity

The opacity property is related. The opacity of text determines how much of the background is allowed to show through the text. Setting the opacity of text explicitly is the same as (and can be used in conjunction with) using the alpha value in the rgba() or hsla() function. Opacity is actually the inverse of transparency, so a maximum value of 1.0 will result in text that does not allow any of the background through (100% opacity or entirely opaque) and a minimum value of 0.0 will let the background through fully (0% opacity or entirely transparent).

Opacity becomes an even more useful and relevant topic when we start animating. It's common to animate the opacity of something from 0 to 1 to cause it to fade in or from 1 to 0 to cause it to fade out.

Fonts and Text Styles

The majority of typography related properties (the preceding examples excluded) begin with text- or font-, and you'll see many of them now. The font properties are numerous enough that a shorthand property exists and is quite helpful. I'll introduce the individual properties before I talk about the shorthand syntax. A more extensive examination of what's possible with fonts will follow in a subsequent section.

font-style

The font-style property is primarily used to italicize your text. The values (besides the inherit value that all properties share) are actually normal, italic, and oblique. Using italic will choose the italicized version of whatever font is in use. Using oblique is awfully similar, though, and you may scratch your head wondering about the difference between them. The difference is that, while italic chooses the italicized version of the font, oblique only skews the normal version of the font. Often they look very much the same, but sometimes they are actually quite different.

Most typographers frown about the use of oblique rather than taking advantage of a proper italic face, but it will certainly work in a pinch. If you don't care so much about perfect typography then it will save you the hassle of embedding an additional italic subset font. The code in Listing 4-1 defines each of the three values for font-style and Figure 4-1 portrays the results.

Listing 4-1. Using the font-style property to make text italicized or oblique

```
<!-- HTML snippet -->
<div class="normal">Lorem ipsum dolor sit amet</div>
<div class="italic">Aenean cursus vehicula purus id sagittis</div>
<div class="oblique">Morbi tincidunt suscipit dignissim</div>

/* CSS snippet */
.normal { font-style: normal; }
.italic { font-style: italic; }
.oblique { font-style: oblique; }
```

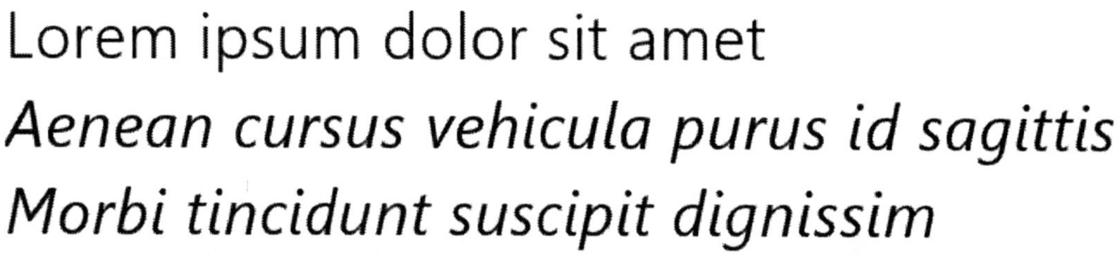

Lorem ipsum dolor sit amet

Aenean cursus vehicula purus id sagittis

Morbi tincidunt suscipit dignissim

Figure 4-1. *In most cases, oblique text appears the same as italic, but using it as a substitute for a font with an actual italic version may be frowned upon by serious typographers*

font-variant

The font-variant is a very simple one with only normal and smallcaps for values. Small caps can be an interesting and effective variant to standard capitalization. In small caps text, all letters are uppercase, but are rendered only slightly taller than the lowercase letters. You can see an example of the small caps variant in Listing 4-2 and Figure 4-2.

Listing 4-2. Using the font-variant property to turn text to small caps

```
<!-- HTML snippet -->
<div class="normal">Lorem ipsum dolor sit amet</div>
<div class="smallCaps">Aenean Cursus Vehicula Purus ID Sagittis</div>

/* CSS snippet */
.normal { font-variant: normal; }
.smallCaps { font-variant: small-caps; }
```

Lorem ipsum dolor sit amet
AENEAN CURSUS VEHICULA PURUS ID SAGITTIS

Figure 4-2. *Notice that all of the letters in the second line are uppercase, but the actual uppercase letters only only slightly taller than the lowercase letters*

font-weight

You'll likely use the font-weight property rather often to determine whether your text should be bold or not. A normal value will be normal and a bold value will be bold. The weight of the font can be set numerically by specifying any increment of 100 from 100–900. A value of 400 is the same as normal and a value of 700 is the same as bold. You can also use bolder or lighter to make the text incrementally bolder or lighter than the value it has inherited. Listing 4-3 and Figure 4-3 provide an example.

Listing 4-3. Using the font-weight property to make the text more or less bold

```
<!-- HTML snippet -->
<div class="normal">Lorem ipsum dolor sit amet</div>
<div class="bold">Lorem ipsum dolor sit amet</div>
<div class="_100">Lorem ipsum dolor sit amet</div>
<div class="_900">Lorem ipsum dolor sit amet</div>

/* CSS snippet */
.normal { font-weight: normal; }
.bold { font-weight: bold; }
._100 { font-weight: 100; }
._900 { font-weight: 900; }
```

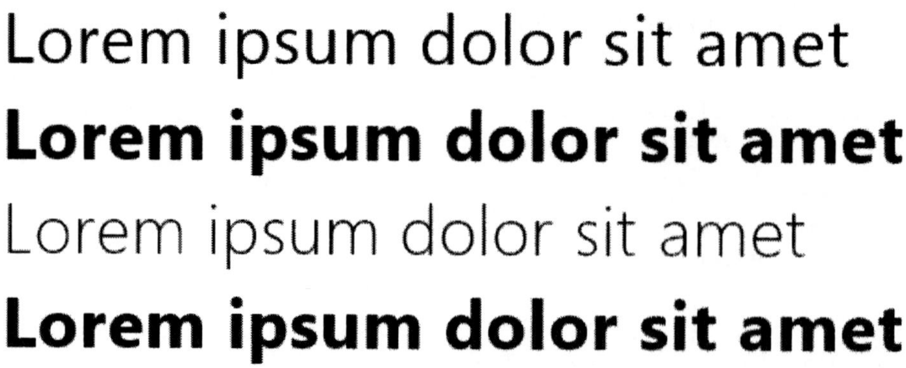

Lorem ipsum dolor sit amet

Lorem ipsum dolor sit amet

Lorem ipsum dolor sit amet

Lorem ipsum dolor sit amet

Figure 4-3. *The second line (bold) is obviously bolder than the first (normal), the third (100) is obviously lighter, and the last is hardly distinguishable though it is the maximum font weight*

font-size

You've got some options for specifying font sizes.

- **absolute sizes.** You can use absolute sizes: xx-small, x-small, small, medium, large, x-large, and xx-large. Specifying an absolute size leaves the user agent to decide what the actual size should be.

- **relative sizes.** You can specify a font size of larger or smaller, which will set the font size one increment larger or smaller than the value it has inherited.

- **length.** You can use a length value as a font size which will set the font size absolutely without consideration of the user agent.

- **percentage.** If you use a percentage for a font size, it will set the font's size relative to its parent's font size.

We'll be primarily concerned with pixels for Windows 8 apps - at least for elements that are to appear on the screen. Keep in mind that Windows 8 automatically scales up for higher resolution displays, so the developer does not need to modify font sizes dynamically. Listing 4-4 and Figure 4-4 show a variety of font sizes in use.

Listing 4-4. Using the font-size property to make text larger or smaller

```
<!-- HTML snippet -->
<div class="pt">Lorem ipsum dolor sit amet</div>
<div class="in">.Lorem ipsum dolor sit amet</div>
<div class="px1">Lorem ipsum dolor sit amet</div>
<div class="px2">Lorem ipsum dolor sit amet</div>

/* CSS snippet */
.pt { font-size: 12pt; }
.in { font-size: .5in; }
.px1 { font-size: 10px; }
.px2 { font-size: 30px; }
```

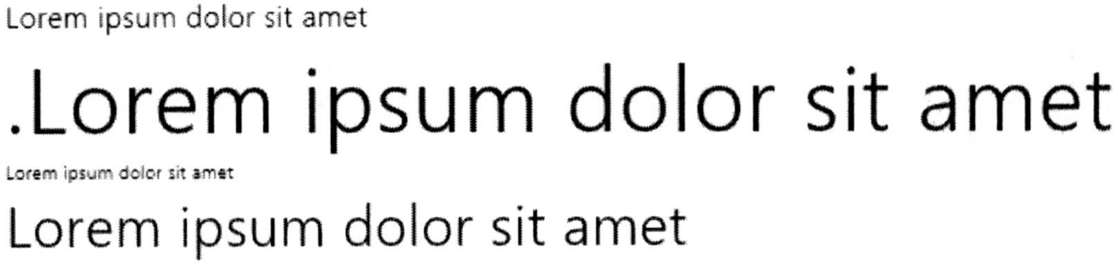

Lorem ipsum dolor sit amet

.Lorem ipsum dolor sit amet

Lorem ipsum dolor sit amet

Lorem ipsum dolor sit amet

Figure 4-4. *The differences in font size speak for themselves*

line-height

Similar and related to the font-size is the line-height (also known as leading), which controls the white space above and below each line of text. Values for line-height are also length values and a line-height of twice that of the font-size will effectively make for double spaced text. You can use a percentage value as well. Listing 4-5 and Figure 4-5 show a line height example.

Listing 4-5. Using the line-height property to set the vertical space taken by a line of text

```
<!-- HTML snippet -->
<div>Lorem ipsum dolor sit amet...</div>
<div class="doubleHeight">Lorem ipsum dolor sit amet...</div>

/* CSS snippet */
.doubleHeight { line-height:200%; }
```

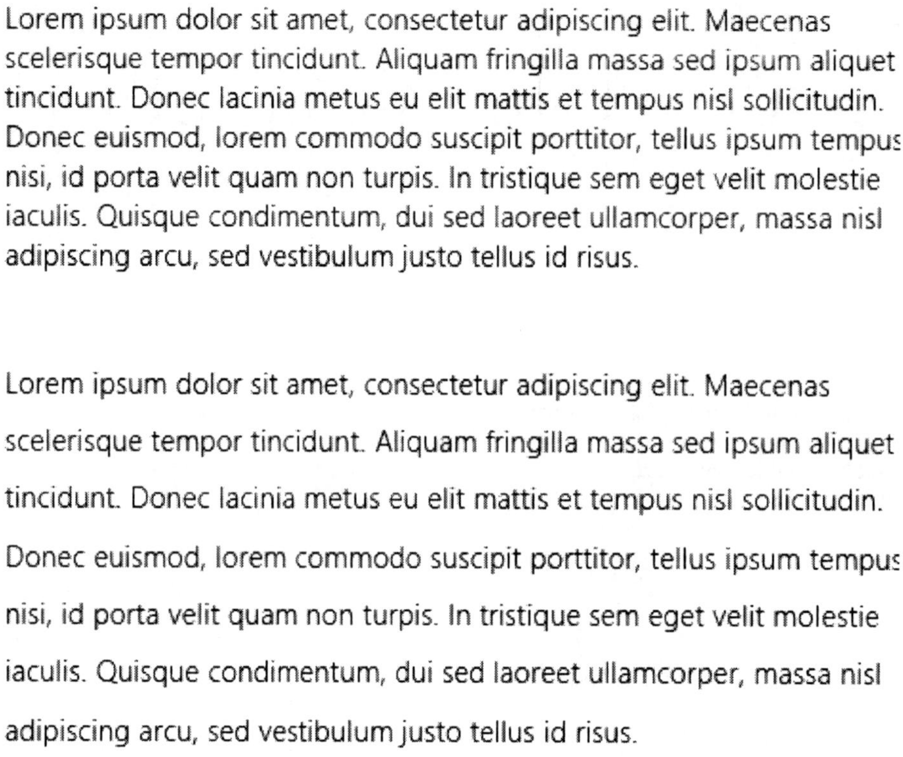

Lorem ipsum dolor sit amet, consectetur adipiscing elit. Maecenas scelerisque tempor tincidunt. Aliquam fringilla massa sed ipsum aliquet tincidunt. Donec lacinia metus eu elit mattis et tempus nisl sollicitudin. Donec euismod, lorem commodo suscipit porttitor, tellus ipsum tempus nisi, id porta velit quam non turpis. In tristique sem eget velit molestie iaculis. Quisque condimentum, dui sed laoreet ullamcorper, massa nisl adipiscing arcu, sed vestibulum justo tellus id risus.

Lorem ipsum dolor sit amet, consectetur adipiscing elit. Maecenas

scelerisque tempor tincidunt. Aliquam fringilla massa sed ipsum aliquet

tincidunt. Donec lacinia metus eu elit mattis et tempus nisl sollicitudin.

Donec euismod, lorem commodo suscipit porttitor, tellus ipsum tempus

nisi, id porta velit quam non turpis. In tristique sem eget velit molestie

iaculis. Quisque condimentum, dui sed laoreet ullamcorper, massa nisl

adipiscing arcu, sed vestibulum justo tellus id risus.

Figure 4-5. *The second paragraph is given a double line spacing by specifying 200% for the line-height*

font-family

The value of font-family determines which font is used to render the target element's text. It is a comma delimited list of system fonts and it's often referred to as the *font stack*. The user agent will continue to attempt to apply a font from the font stack until it succeeds at finding one that is actually installed on the user's system.

Besides actual font names, you can specify any of five generic font keywords: serif, sans-serif, monospace, cursive, and fantasy. If the user agent gets to a generic font in the font stack, it will choose a font from that generic type that is installed on the device. Some sample font-family values are illustrated in Listing 4-6 and Figure 4-6.

Listing 4-6. Using the font-family property to choose a font

```
<!-- HTML snippet -->
<div class="f1">Lorem ipsum dolor sit amet</div>
<div class="f2">Consectetur adipiscing elit</div>
<div class="f3">Maecenas scelerisque tempor tincidunt</div>
<div class="f4">Aliquam fringilla</div>
<div class="f5">Aliquet tincidunt donec lacinia</div>

/* CSS snippet */
.f1 { font-family: arial, sans-serif; }
.f2 { font-family: 'times new roman', serif; }
.f3 { font-family: trebuchet, helvetica, sans-serif; }
.f4 { font-family: wingdings; }
.f5 { font-family: garbage; }
```

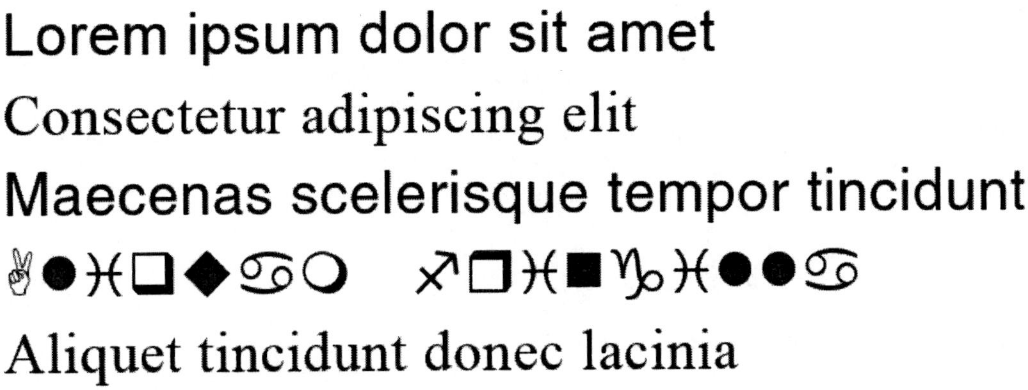

Lorem ipsum dolor sit amet

Consectetur adipiscing elit

Maecenas scelerisque tempor tincidunt

Aliquet tincidunt donec lacinia

Figure 4-6. *The first font available on the system is rendered. Notice the serif and sans-serif fallbacks and notice how the last font – "garbage" – is not found on the system and so the default font is used*

font shorthand property

All of the preceding font related properties can be encapsulated in the font shorthand property. The font property takes a lot of values, so it's important to get the syntax right. The most important thing is that they are provided in the right order.

Here is the order that the properties should be provided in: font-style, font-variant, font-weight, font-size, line-height, and then font-family. There are some caveats though.

- The font-style, font-variant, and font-weight are optional and it may work if they are out of order but they must come before the font-size and font-family.

- The font-size and line-height should be delimited with a slash (/) instead of a space.

- The line-height is optional and obviously you shouldn't include the slash if you don't include it.

- The font-size and font-family are mandatory. Without either the entire line will be ignored.

Listing 4-7 shows off a couple of font shorthand property values and Figure 4-7 shows the results.

Listing 4-7. Using the font shorthand property to set many font properties at once

```
<!-- HTML snippet -->
<div class="f1">Lorem ipsum dolor sit amet</div>
<div class="f2">Consectetur adipiscing elit</div>

/* CSS snippet */
.f1 { font: bold 36pt trebuchet; }
.f2 { font: italic small-caps bold 24pt/48pt 'times new roman'; }
```

Lorem ipsum dolor sit amet

CONSECTETUR ADIPISCING ELIT

Figure 4-7. *If you get the order of property values correct, they will all take effect*

text-transform

The text-transform property serves to manipulate the capitalization of your text. The capitalize value will capitalize the first letter of each word, the uppercase value will just capitalize the whole thing, and the lowercase value will turn all characters to lower case. The text-transform property is illustrated in Listing 4-8 and Figure 4-8.

Listing 4-8. Using the text-transform property to change the case of the text

```
<!-- HTML snippet -->
<div class="lowerCase">LOREM IPSUM DOLOR SIT AMET</div>
<div class="upperCase">lorem ipsum dolor sit amet</div>
<div class="capitalize">lorem ipsum dolor sit amet</div>

/* CSS snippet */
.lowerCase { text-transform: lowercase; }
.upperCase { text-transform: uppercase; }
.capitalize { text-transform: capitalize; }
```

lorem ipsum dolor sit amet
LOREM IPSUM DOLOR SIT AMET
Lorem Ipsum Dolor Sit Amet

Figure 4-8. The first line is transformed to lower, the second is transformed to upper, and the third is transformed to title case with the first letter of each word capitalized

---

■ **ALL CAPS!** You'll notice a number of places in Windows 8 where Microsoft chose to use all caps - menus are one of them. Contrary to what one might assume, using all caps is an effective way of reducing the relative significance of text. The human brain is trained to read lowercase or title case text, but uppercase text acts visually as more of a complimentary element and tends to be referenced more than read. Keep in mind that the same does not hold true for spans of paragraph text in all uppercase. Uppercase paragraph text will draw the reader's attention, but not in an appropriate way. The *Microsoft Manual of Style* says that one should "never use all uppercase for emphasis. Use sentence structure for emphasis instead. It's best to avoid formatting for emphasis, but if you must use formatting for emphasis, use italic formatting instead of all uppercase." (Microsoft Press, 2012)

Text Decoration

You can change the lines that appear over, under, and through your text using the text-decoration property. Actually, CSS3 calls for an expansion to the text-decoration property to allow for coloring and styling of the line that accompanies your text. The new standard turns the text-decoration property itself into a shorthand property for text-decoration-line, -color, and -style. Unfortunately, this new standard is not implemented yet by any modern browsers at the time of this writing. This includes the Trident engine that powers Internet Explorer 10 and Windows 8 apps.

Until the standards are implemented, just use the `text-decoration` property with values of `overline`, `line-through`, or `underline` to add scores over, through, or under your text as you can see in Listing 4-9 and Figure 4-9.

Listing 4-9. Values of text-decoration set to overline, line-through, and underline

```
<!-- HTML snippet -->
<div id="style1">Lorem ipsum dolor sit amet</div>
<div id="style2">Consectetur adipiscing elit</div>
<div id="style3">Maecenas scelerisque tempor tincidunt</div>

/* CSS snippet */
#style1 { text-decoration: overline; }
#style2 { text-decoration: line-through; }
#style3 { text-decoration: underline; }
```

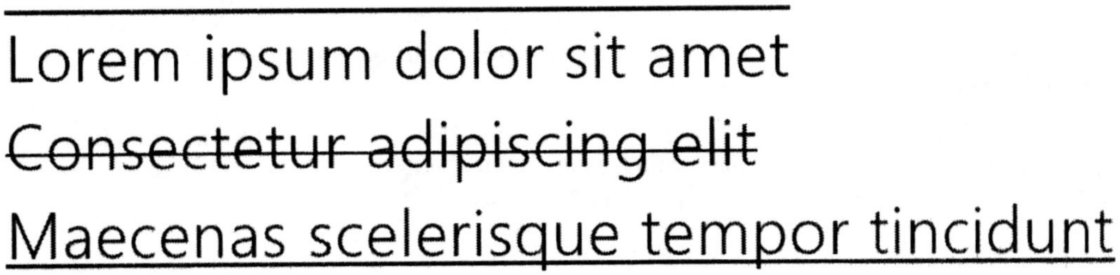

Lorem ipsum dolor sit amet
~~Consectetur adipiscing elit~~
Maecenas scelerisque tempor tincidunt

Figure 4-9. *Results in lines appearing over, through, and under the text*

font-face

We've discussed how you can specify the color, size, and even the family of your font, but there's one rather glaring caveat. If you specify `font-family: pickle;`, then the user has to have the *pickle* font installed on his machine to see it correctly.

Whether you're targeting the web or Windows 8, this is a significant problem. There are a few fonts that you can make a good bet will be on your users' systems, but none can be guaranteed. You can use the generic font types, but that doesn't assure that your typography is going to look the way you designed it. What you need is the ability to determine for certain that the user will be able to view your page with its intended typography by providing the font for them. That's where `@font-face` comes in. `@font-face` is a custom font definition. The @ syntax indicates that it's not a property or a value, but a special CSS entity much like the `@media` keyword.

The `@font-face` keyword allows us to define a custom font name and the URL to the source of the font. Likely your font will be in your project and I recommend you follow the convention of dropping your fonts into a folder called `type`. In that case, you can simply provide a root level URL like `/type/myfont.ttf`.

Listing 4-10 illustrates a simple `@font-face` definition and then the implementation of that font in HTML. Notice that the `font-family` value is being defined in the `@font-face` block and then referenced in the `.nifty` style rule. This name is your choosing, but the reference must match the definition.

Listing 4-10. A font-face definition referencing a font file stored in the projects type folder

```
<!-- HTML snippet -->
<span class="nifty">This is my nifty font!</span>
```

```
/* CSS snippet */
@font-face {
    font-family: "niftyfont";
    src: url("/type/nifty_n.woff") format(woff)
}

.nifty {
    font-family: niftyfont;
}
```

You can specify multiple values in the src property to create a compatibility stack, but when you're working on a Windows 8 app, you have the advantage of not having to worry about other browsers as targets. The format in the example is WOFF, but you may not have had experience with this font format.

WOFF (Web Open Font Format) is an open format standard proposed jointly by Opera, Microsoft, and Mozilla. The WOFF format is not actually a new font format, but rather just a wrapper around existing EOT, TTF, OTF fonts. Wrapping existing fonts in WOFF for use in your app has a couple of strong advantages:

- WOFF is compressed so wrapped fonts are smaller than their associated original fonts.

- Metadata can be included in the font package to deliver information about the font's origin and even its license information.

Whether you use a traditional font or one wrapped in WOFF, though, adding good typography is a good idea and defining a font (as opposed to just embedding your custom type in a bitmap) is a great one if you want your app to be accessible, adaptive, and searchable.

Microsoft vendor specific text properties

Microsoft offers a handful of vendor specific, text related CSS properties – namely: -ms-text-autospace, -ms-text-align-last, -ms-text-justify, -ms-text-kashida-space, -ms-text-overflow, and -ms-text-underline-position. These properties don't tend to be used broadly, but in certain situations they are in fact critical.

The -ms-text-autospace property allows the handling of spacing around ideographs - Asian characters that convey an idea.

The -ms-text-align-last property determines how to handle spacing for the very last line of a paragraph whose text is justified.

The -ms-text-kashida-space property controls kashida spacing which is the expansion of certain characters in Arabic writing systems.

Finally, the -ms-text-underline-position property can determine if the underline (if applied) of your text is displayed below or above the characters. The values are above and below, and auto is the default.

Alignment and justification

Alignment is a big part of text layout. Alignment controls the way that the rendering engine handles space before, after, and amid your text both horizontally and vertically. Likely, everyone has experience left aligning, centering, right aligning, and justifying text in a word processor. This is exactly the job of the text-align property.

You can set the text-align property to a value of left, right, center, or justify.

Besides setting the text's alignment horizontally, you can do a lot to control its vertical layout as well. The vertical-align property will take the following values: auto, baseline, sub, super, top, middle, bottom, text-top, and text-bottom. The default value, baseline, will align the bottom of a line of text (not counting descenders) with the baseline of its parent. The vertical-align property will also accept a length or a percentage value which will act as an offset.

The vertical-align property does not always behave as you might expect. In fact, it behaves a bit differently depending on the type of element it is applied to.

When you use vertical-align on an image tag, it acts like the old valign attribute and determines where the image sits relative to the text that contains it.

When you use the vertical-align property in the cell of a table, it affects the vertical alignment of the text (or other elements) in the cell as in Listing 4-11.

Listing 4-11. Vertical alignment in a simple table

```
<!-- HTML snippet -->
<table>
    <tr>
        <td colspan="3">I'm a table</td>
    </tr>
    <tr>
        <td>top</td>
        <td>middle</td>
        <td>bottom</td>
    </tr>
</table>

/* CSS snippet */
table { width: 300px; border-collapse:collapse; }
table tr:nth-of-type(2)  { height: 80px; }
table td { border: 1px solid; }
table tr:nth-of-type(2) td:nth-of-type(1) { vertical-align: top; }
table tr:nth-of-type(2) td:nth-of-type(2) { vertical-align: middle; }
table tr:nth-of-type(2) td:nth-of-type(3) { vertical-align: bottom; }
```

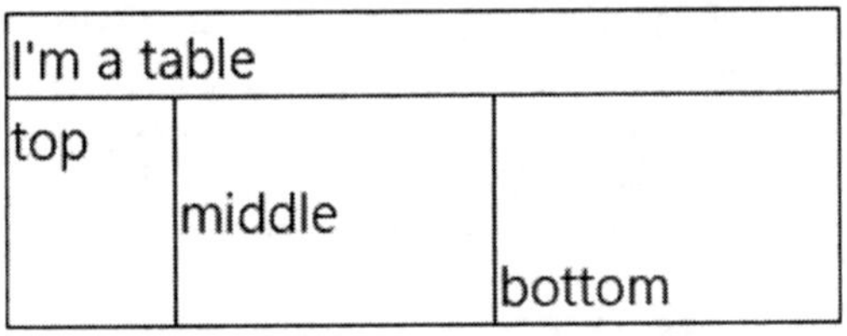

Figure 4-10. *The cell text is properly aligned vertically as defined*

There are a couple of off-topic things I want to point out about Listing 4-11:

- the border-collapse:collapse; property is used to remove the space that is inherent between cells in a table

- the :nth-of-type() selector is used to select table rows and cells by their position

In the table cells in Figure 4-10, you can see that the text has been vertically centered.

When you attempt to use vertical-align in a div, however, you might get a surprise. Notice in Listing 4-12 how we're attempting to instruct the div called va to align its text in the center horizontally and in the middle vertically.

Listing 4-12. *A common mistake regarding the use of vertical-align*

```html
<!-- HTML snippet -->
<div id="va">
    middle?
</div>
```

```css
/* CSS snippet */
div#va {
    height: 100px;
    width: 200px;
    vertical-align: middle;
    text-align: center;
    border: 1px solid black;
}
```

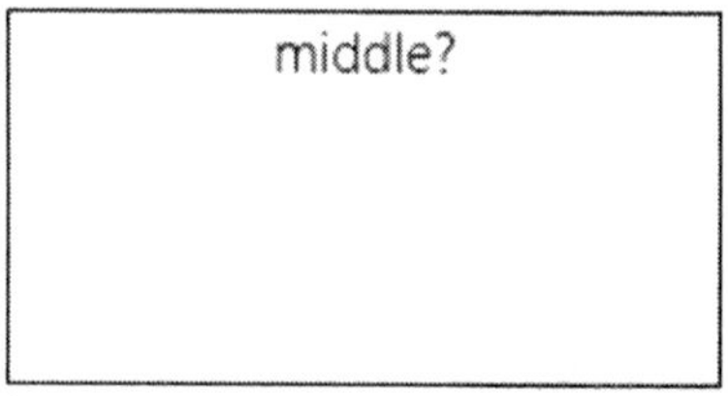

Figure 4-11. *The text we provided is not centered vertically*

It made it to the center horizontally, but it's obviously not in the middle vertically. Why is this property being ignored? The `vertical-align` property isn't just implemented weirdly in CSS. For table cells, it actually aligns vertically, but if our div contains inline elements (inline elements flow like text and wrap to the next line) the `vertical-align` does something completely different. It is equivalent to the old `valign` HTML attribute that adjusts the vertical position of elements relative to the baseline. It doesn't affect their position within their parent container at all.

This issue has plagued web designers for decades it seems and I know it's been the cause of some of my own sleepless nights. Web pages were never really designed to specify vertical behavior. The nature of HTML is to flex horizontally and flow contents vertically from top to bottom. The standards have evolved and made progress, but there are still remnants of the past.

A few workarounds have existed to help resolve this issue, but none of them are great, and that's why the new grid in Microsoft's implementation of CSS3 is very welcome. Chapter 6 will take you in-depth into the implementation of the grid for solving this significant issue.

Another great use for `vertical-align` is for setting text to be superscript or subscript. The `sub` and `super` values will perform this alignment for you. You'll often find this one inside a span element. The following, for instance, could be used to construct the equation $y = x^2$.

```html
<div>y = x<span style="vertical-align:super;">2</span></div>
```

Columns

Many modern HTML apps and sites rely heavily on large amounts of text, and CSS3 has brought these apps into the realm of feasibility with the introduction of multi-column text management. Support for multiple columns was not just snuck in with meager support either. It's rich and powerful and very full-featured.

Before the introduction of multi-columns, developers were forced to lay out columns manually or programmatically. The new multi-column CSS properties really make any kind of reader app not only possible, but expressive and fun.

Multi-column support is especially important for Windows 8 because the design language lays out content horizontally instead of vertically. I often hear people questioning why this is, so here are a few reasons...

- First of all, horizontal panning is unique and differentiating. It's yet another way that Windows 8 has reimagined user experience and another way that it stands apart from the competition.

- Most of the world's languages read left to right and thus the paradigm of panning from left to right is a natural one for humans.

- Apps with a lot of text laid out horizontally read like a magazine with new content being revealed from the right. This again makes it a familiar paradigm.

- The anatomy of the human arm and hand move more easily horizontally then vertically. Try swiping left and right and then up and down and you'll see that.

- Finally, screens have traditionally been in a landscape orientation and have gotten more exaggeratedly so with screen shifting from an aspect ratio of 4:3 to 16:9.

With a vertical layout, it's entirely possible to have one column the same width as the screen that goes on forever, but with a horizontal layout with new content being revealed from the right, columns become a necessity.

Be aware that one implication of changing from vertical scrolling to horizontal scrolling is that text will no longer be revealed line by line, but rather column by column (Figure 4-12). In Chapter 6, we'll learn about snap points. Snap points help to land the user at each column of text. The result is much like the turning of a page – a paradigm that e-book readers have been using for years and paper books have been using for centuries.

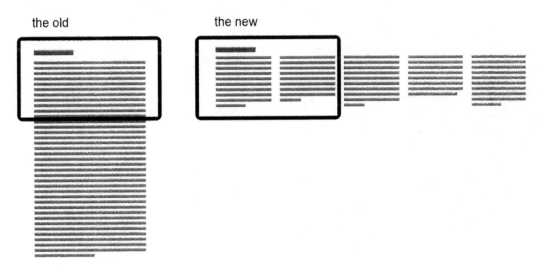

Figure 4-12. *Vertical text layout versus horizontal*

This difference between vertical and horizontal scrolling amounts to a pretty huge change of layout. Look at Figure 4-13 and Figure 4-14 to see an example of the same content - an article about the city of Paris - in each layout.

Figure 4-13. *A web article using vertical scrolling text running off the bottom of the screen*

Figure 4-14. *The same article laid out horizontally in a Windows 8 app inviting the user to pan to the right*

column-width and column-count

You can transform your text blocks into multi-column text blocks by choosing either a column count *or* a column width - only one needs to be set, and the other will be calculated. If you set a column count of 2 on a device that is 1366 pixels wide, then the columns will be calculated at 683 pixels (minus the width of margins and gutter). Use the column count when you know exactly how many columns you want to be rendered in a given container. Think about your user moving your text to a large screen format. If your user has two columns of text on their small screen and then moves your app to a large screen, do you still want two (now very wide) columns of text? Probably not. More likely, you'll want to set the column *width* and let as many columns as will fit be generated on the screen. Look at Figure 4-15 to see what I mean. Larger screens beg for more columns of text.

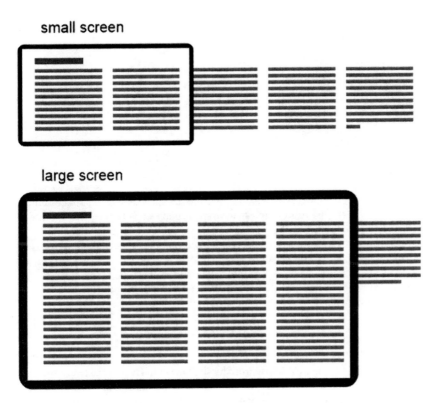

Figure 4-15. *Setting column width allows for more columns on a larger screen*

The properties themselves are `column-width` and `column-count`, and there's a shorthand property of `columns`. The interesting thing is that you will seldom need to use both the `column-width` and `column-count`, so you might just end up using the one shorthand method most or all of the time.

The shorthand property is called `columns`. It takes a width or a count or both. As I said, you'll likely choose one or the other, so usually your column properties will look something like those in Listing 4-13.

Listing 4-13. Typical properties for determining multiple columns

```
/* CSS snippet */
.columns {
    columns: 4;
}

.columns {
    columns: 200px;
}

.columns {
    columns: 400px;
}
```

column-gap and column-rule

The `column-gap` and `column-rule` properties give you control over what happens in the space between your columns.

The `column-gap` accepts a length value and determines how much space there is between columns. The Windows 8 design guidelines don't give a recommendation for the width of gaps between multi-column text, but it does recommend 40 pixels of space between columns in a list and that's what I would recommend for text columns too.

The `column-rule` is actually a shorthand property that encapsulates `column-rule-width`, `column-rule-style`, and `column-rule-color` easily all at once. A rule is simply a line to separate text columns. It can be helpful aesthetically, but it can also be a bit gaudy, so use column rules with caution. When two columns of text are unrelated to one another, it may be helpful to add a rule between them for clarity.

column-fill

There are two possible behaviors that the rendering engine can choose from for the flow of the text in the columns. If you have three columns and not quite enough text to fill up all three, the engine could either fill up the first and second columns and let the third come up short, or it could balance the amount of content (vertically) in all three columns.

The `column-fill` property is how you control which of these behaviors is used. The resulting behavior of the `auto` and `balance` values is displayed in Figure 4-16.

column-fill: auto;   column-fill: balance;

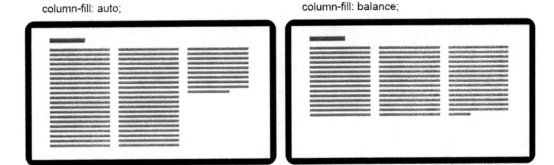

Figure 4-16. *The difference between a column-fill of auto and balance*

Samples of Multiple Columns

We'll look at a number of different multi-column configurations and for each we'll use the same HTML that you see in Listing 4-14.

Listing 4-14. A div with five good-sized paragraphs of text

```
<!-- HTML snippet -->
<div id="columns">
    <p>Lorem ipsum dolor sit amet ... </p>
    <p>Sed rhoncus, erat in eleifend ... </p>
    <p>Nam mollis iaculis neque ut ... </p>
    <p>In eleifend purus et leo ... </p>
    <p>Sed quis sapien vitae elit ... </p>
</div>
```

The div with an ID of columns contains five paragraphs of text. I have cropped the actual paragraph text for brevity, but each is actually of typical paragraph size. Let's look at a number of possible CSS style rules to format these five paragraphs into columns in a variety of ways.

Listing 4-15 and Figure 4-17 show the results of automatic column filling. Listing 4-16 and Figure 4-18, on the other hand, illustrate a balanced column fill.

Listing 4-15. Columns 400px in width with a column-fill of auto

```
/* CSS snippet */
#columns {
    columns: 400px;
    column-fill: auto;
    height: 600px;
}
```

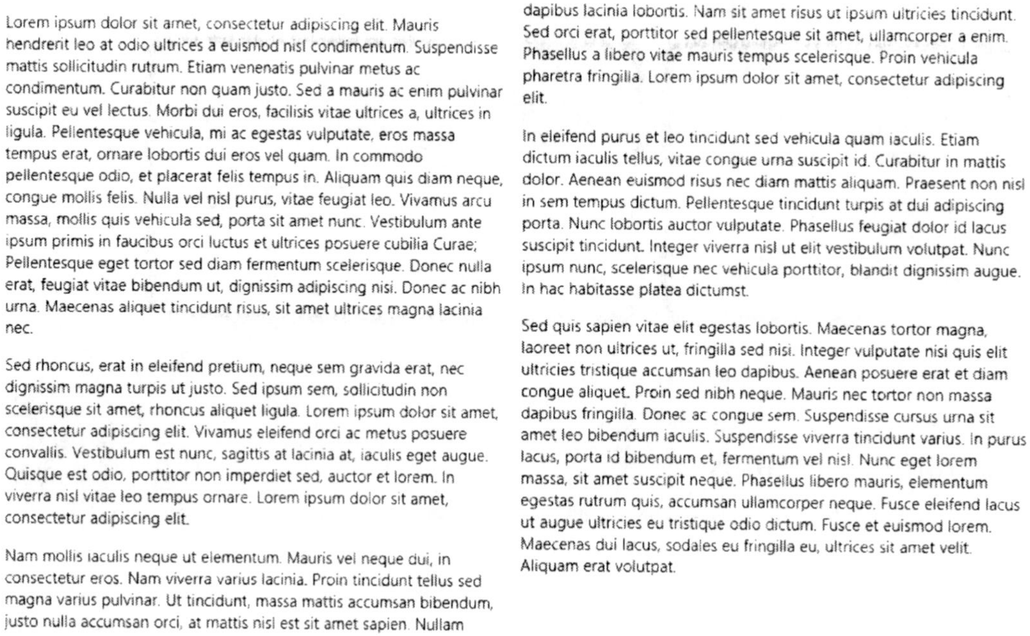

Lorem ipsum dolor sit amet, consectetur adipiscing elit. Mauris hendrerit leo at odio ultrices a euismod nisl condimentum. Suspendisse mattis sollicitudin rutrum. Etiam venenatis pulvinar metus ac condimentum. Curabitur non quam justo. Sed a mauris ac enim pulvinar suscipit eu vel lectus. Morbi dui eros, facilisis vitae ultrices a, ultrices in ligula. Pellentesque vehicula, mi ac egestas vulputate, eros massa tempus erat, ornare lobortis dui eros vel quam. In commodo pellentesque odio, et placerat felis tempus in. Aliquam quis diam neque, congue mollis felis. Nulla vel nisl purus, vitae feugiat leo. Vivamus arcu massa, mollis quis vehicula sed, porta sit amet nunc. Vestibulum ante ipsum primis in faucibus orci luctus et ultrices posuere cubilia Curae; Pellentesque eget tortor sed diam fermentum scelerisque. Donec nulla erat, feugiat vitae bibendum ut, dignissim adipiscing nisi. Donec ac nibh urna. Maecenas aliquet tincidunt risus, sit amet ultrices magna lacinia nec.

Sed rhoncus, erat in eleifend pretium, neque sem gravida erat, nec dignissim magna turpis ut justo. Sed ipsum sem, sollicitudin non scelerisque sit amet, rhoncus aliquet ligula. Lorem ipsum dolor sit amet, consectetur adipiscing elit. Vivamus eleifend orci ac metus posuere convallis. Vestibulum est nunc, sagittis at lacinia at, iaculis eget augue. Quisque est odio, porttitor non imperdiet sed, auctor et lorem. In viverra nisl vitae leo tempus ornare. Lorem ipsum dolor sit amet, consectetur adipiscing elit.

Nam mollis iaculis neque ut elementum. Mauris vel neque dui, in consectetur eros. Nam viverra varius lacinia. Proin tincidunt tellus sed magna varius pulvinar. Ut tincidunt, massa mattis accumsan bibendum, justo nulla accumsan orci, at mattis nisl est sit amet sapien. Nullam

dapibus lacinia lobortis. Nam sit amet risus ut ipsum ultricies tincidunt. Sed orci erat, porttitor sed pellentesque sit amet, ullamcorper a enim. Phasellus a libero vitae mauris tempus scelerisque. Proin vehicula pharetra fringilla. Lorem ipsum dolor sit amet, consectetur adipiscing elit.

In eleifend purus et leo tincidunt sed vehicula quam iaculis. Etiam dictum iaculis tellus, vitae congue urna suscipit id. Curabitur in mattis dolor. Aenean euismod risus nec diam mattis aliquam. Praesent non nisl in sem tempus dictum. Pellentesque tincidunt turpis at dui adipiscing porta. Nunc lobortis auctor vulputate. Phasellus feugiat dolor id lacus suscipit tincidunt. Integer viverra nisl ut elit vestibulum volutpat. Nunc ipsum nunc, scelerisque nec vehicula porttitor, blandit dignissim augue. In hac habitasse platea dictumst.

Sed quis sapien vitae elit egestas lobortis. Maecenas tortor magna, laoreet non ultrices ut, fringilla sed nisi. Integer vulputate nisl quis elit ultricies tristique accumsan leo dapibus. Aenean posuere erat et diam congue aliquet. Proin sed nibh neque. Mauris nec tortor non massa dapibus fringilla. Donec ac congue sem. Suspendisse cursus urna sit amet leo bibendum iaculis. Suspendisse viverra tincidunt varius. In purus lacus, porta id bibendum et, fermentum vel nisl. Nunc eget lorem massa, sit amet suscipit neque. Phasellus libero mauris, elementum egestas rutrum quis, accumsan ullamcorper neque. Fusce eleifend lacus ut augue ultricies eu tristique odio dictum. Fusce et euismod lorem. Maecenas dui lacus, sodales eu fringilla eu, ultrices sit amet velit. Aliquam erat volutpat.

Figure 4-17. *Two 400-pixel columns fit and the auto value for column-fill causes each to be is filled to the bottom before spilling into the next*

Let's see what we can do to balance the text vertically when we have multiple columns.

Listing 4-16. Three columns with a column-fill value of balance

```
/* CSS snippet */
#columns {
    columns: 3;
    column-fill: balance;
    height: 600px;
}
```

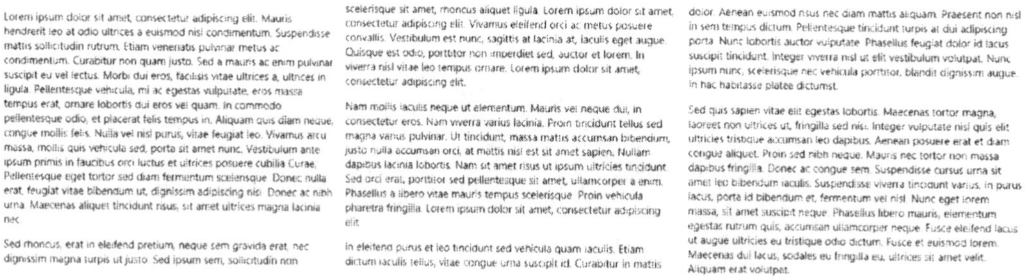

Figure 4-18. *Three columns are fit to the space and the text spills so that all have the same amount of text*

Certain types of content do well with narrow columns. I can imagine something like a dictionary that is primarily a list of short bits of content. When you're considering your design, you may determine that some column gap and some rules between columns can be helpful. Listing 4-17 shows off some narrow columns with a bit of a gap and a light gray rule between the columns.

Listing 4-17. As many 80-pixel columns as will fit with 40-pixel gaps and light gray rules in between

```
/* columns.css */
#columns {
    columns: 80px;
    column-gap: 40px;
    column-rule: 1px solid #ddd;
}
```

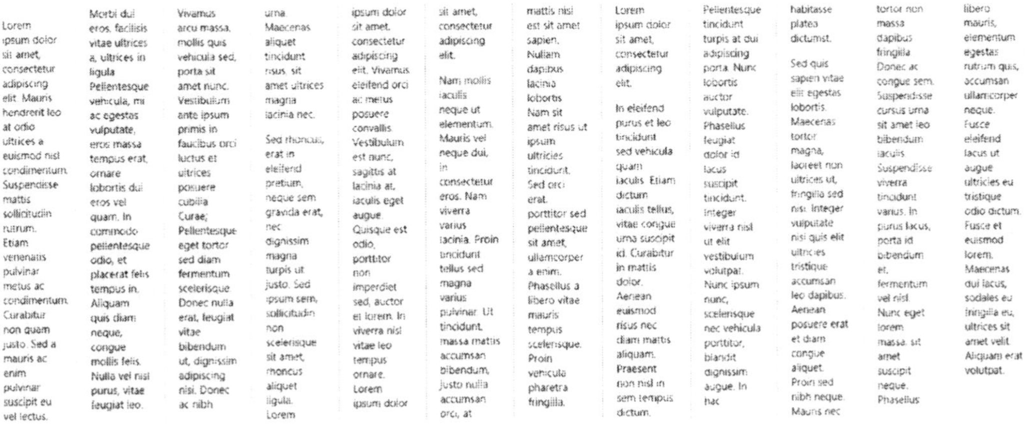

Figure 4-19. Narrow columns with rules looks pretty classy

■ **Widows and Orphans** When individual words or lines get stranded at the beginning or end of a column, they tend to look out of place and unintentional. We call these widows and orphans. The only way to avoid widows and orphans using CSS3 is to add `break-inside:avoid` to the paragraph elements. This will cause a paragraph to attempt to stay together instead of splitting itself between columns. It's not an ideal solution because it is all or nothing. If a paragraph doesn't fit by even one line, then the entire paragraph will jump to the next column and may leave a gaping hole that looks even more unintentional than a little widow.

List Styles

There are two kinds of lists: ordered and unordered. Ordered lists are typically marked with numbers or letters, and unordered lists are typically marked with bullets. You can control them both with the `list-style` properties: `list-style-type`, `list-style-position`, `list-style-image`, and the shorthand property `list-style`.

The `list-style-type` property is interesting because its values can convert a list into either an ordered list or an unordered list regardless of the markup. So if the HTML specifies a `ul` (unordered list) tag, you can simply apply a `list-style-type` and it will render as an ordered list as if you had used the `ol` tag.

Valid values for the list-style-type property are: none, circle, disc, square, Armenian, decimal, decimal-leading-zero, Georgian, lower-alpha, lower-greek, lower-latin, lower-roman, upper-alpha, upper-latin, and upper-roman.

The list-style-position property can be very handy when you're trying to get your lists to align correctly. A value of outside determines that the bullet is outside of the text and wrapping text indents so the bullet remains hanging on the left. A value of inside, on the other hand, determines that the bullet is within the text and wrapping text lines up with the bullet.

The list-style-image property allows you to specify a custom image to use for your list's bullets. The value should be in the form of url('folder/image.png').

Listing 4-18 and Figure 4-20 illustrate a standard, unordered list of fruit with no CSS modifications applied.

Listing 4-18. Standard unordered list with no styles applied

```
<!-- HTML snippet -->
<ul>
    <li>lorem</li>
    <li>ipsum</li>
    <li>dolor</li>
    <li>sit amet</li>
    <li>tempor</li>
</ul>
```

- lorem
- ipsum
- dolor
- sit amet
- tempor

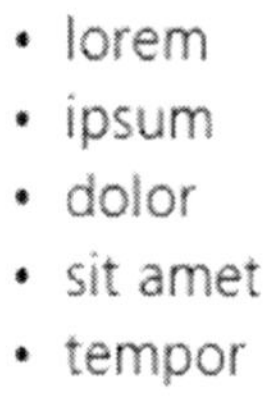

Figure 4-20. *There's nothing surprising about the simple bulleted list that's created*

Listing 4-19 adds a couple of styles to the list to transform the unordered list (which normally uses bullets) into an ordered one (using decimal numbers) and also assures that the numbers will be inside the list. I've limited the list to 200 pixels width and repeated the word mangoes just to illustrate that list-style-position property. You can see the result in Figure 4-21.

Listing 4-19. Standard unordered list now with styles being applied

```
<!-- HTML snippet -->
<ul>
    <li>lorem</li>
    <li>ipsum</li>
    <li>dolor</li>
    <li>sit amet</li>
    <li>Maecenas scelerisque tempor tincidunt</li>
</ul>

/* CSS snippet */
ul {
```

```
    list-style-type: decimal;
    list-style-position: inside;
    width: 200px;
}
```

1. lorem
2. ipsum
3. dolor
4. sit amet
5. Maecenas scelerisque
tempor tincidunt

Figure 4-21. *An ordered list is created (with numbered values 1–5) even though the markup defines it to be an unordered list. Also, notice the way the 5th item wraps all the way to the level of the numbers*

It's very easy to style lists using CSS, so lists are a good, semantic way to indicate any repeating list of items or entities in your UI. You could, for instance, transform a list of items into a list, a menu, or a bunch of tiles.

Hyphenation

Hyphenation is the breaking of words in the wrapping of a text block for the purpose of improved justification. If the rendering engine is forced to keep entire words together, it can make for some awkwardly large spans of whitespace in a text column. If the engine is, however, allowed to break a word in the middle and continue it on the next line and indicate this with a hyphen then it can have more control over the wrapping of the text.

Until recently, there was no hyphenation in web pages. CSS3 has defined the hyphens property, but it has not been implemented by very many browsers. IE10 and Windows 8 actually do not recognize the standard hyphens property, but they do also support a vendor specific version of the same property. The syntax is the same too with the exception of the vendor specific prefix. The property, then, is `-ms-hyphens`. Like all of the other vendor specific properties and property values, Microsoft is committed to the CSS standards and as soon as possible, Microsoft will switch over to the standard property by dropping the vendor prefix. Today you use `-ms-hyphens`, but eventually, you'll just use hyphens.

-ms-hyphens

Directing a block of text to be hyphenated is extremely simple. Listing 4-20 does so with this single `-ms-hyphens` property with a value of `auto`. The `-ms-hyphens` property can have one of three valid values (besides `inherit`): `none`, `auto`, and `manual`. A `none` value will obviously disallow any hyphenation being done. A `manual` value will only allow hyphenation breaks where break points have been explicitly suggested in the content – indicated either by the presence of a hard hyphen (–) or a soft hyphen (­). A soft hyphen indicates that the word is okay to break at a given point, but the hyphen doesn't appear unless it actually has to break. An `auto` value, on the other hand, will allow the rendering engine to break at those suggested points and also in the middle of words where no suggestion has been made.

Listing 4-20. Using -ms-hyphens: auto to turn on hyphenation

```
<!-- HTML snippet -->
<p>Lorem ipsum dolor sit amet...</p>
```

```
/* CSS snippet */
p {
    width: 500px;
    -ms-hyphens: auto;
}
```

Lorem ipsum dolor sit amet, consectetur adipiscing elit. Mauris hendrerit leo at odio ultrices a euismod nisl condimentum. Suspendisse mattis sollici-tudin rutrum. Etiam venenatis pulvinar metus ac condimentum. Curabitur non quam justo. Sed a mauris ac enim pulvinar suscipit eu vel lectus. Morbi dui eros, facilisis vitae ultrices a, ultrices in ligula. Pellentesque vehicula, mi ac egestas vulputate, eros massa tempus erat, ornare lobortis dui eros vel quam. In commodo pellentesque odio, et placerat felis tempus in. Aliquam quis diam neque, congue mollis felis. Nulla vel nisl purus, vitae feugiat leo. Vivamus arcu massa, mollis quis vehicula sed, porta sit amet nunc. Vestibu-lum ante ipsum primis in faucibus orci luctus et ultrices posuere cubilia Curae; Pellentesque eget tortor sed diam fermentum scelerisque. Donec nulla erat, feugiat vitae bibendum ut, dignissim adipiscing nisi. Donec ac nibh urna. Maecenas aliquet tincidunt risus, sit amet ultrices magna lacinia nec.

Figure 4-22. *Hyphens are used to make the text's right margin less jagged*

In most cases, that will be all you need to do, but if you need a bit more control over the way the hyphenation is rendered then you'll need to look into the other properties.

-ms-hyphenate-limit-zone

The `-ms-hyphenate-limit-zone` property determines the minimum amount of whitespace that can be left at the end of a line. If you specify a zone of 50px and before justification occurs there would be any more than 50 pixels of whitespace left on a single line, then words from the next line will be hyphenated and pulled up to fill in some of that space. A smaller number will result in less allowance for whitespace and thus more hyphenation. If the zone is too large no hyphenation will occur at all.

If the CSS in Listing 4-21 and Figure 4-23 were to be applied to the same HTML from Listing 4-20, then we'll end up with one hyphenated line - the one that ends with *adipis-*. Had that fraction of the word *adipiscing* not been pulled up and hyphenated, the whitespace after the word *dignissim* would have exceeded 50 pixels.

Listing 4-21. Setting the hyphenation zone with -ms-hyphenate-limit-zone

```
/* CSS snippet */
p {
    width: 500px;
    -ms-hyphens: auto;
    -ms-hyphenate-limit-zone: 50px;
}
```

Lorem ipsum dolor sit amet, consectetur adipiscing elit. Mauris hendrerit leo at odio ultrices a euismod nisl condimentum. Suspendisse mattis sollicitudin rutrum. Etiam venenatis pulvinar metus ac condimentum. Curabitur non quam justo. Sed a mauris ac enim pulvinar suscipit eu vel lectus. Morbi dui eros, facilisis vitae ultrices a, ultrices in ligula. Pellentesque vehicula, mi ac egestas vulputate, eros massa tempus erat, ornare lobortis dui eros vel quam. In commodo pellentesque odio, et placerat felis tempus in. Aliquam quis diam neque, congue mollis felis. Nulla vel nisl purus, vitae feugiat leo. Vivamus arcu massa, mollis quis vehicula sed, porta sit amet nunc. Vestibulum ante ipsum primis in faucibus orci luctus et ultrices posuere cubilia Curae; Pellentesque eget tortor sed diam fermentum scelerisque. Donec nulla erat, feugiat vitae bibendum ut, dignissim adipiscing nisi. Donec ac nibh urna. Maecenas aliquet tincidunt risus, sit amet ultrices magna lacinia nec.

Figure 4-23. *The behavior of the hyphenation is affected as you can see if you compare this figure to Figure 4-22*

-ms-hyphenate-limit-chars

The next of the -ms-hyphenate properties is -ms-hyphenate-limit-chars. This property sets a minimum size for words that can be hyphenated. You can specify a minimum size for the entire word in question, a minimum size for the part of it that would land before the hyphen, and a minimum size for the part that would land after the hyphen. These three values are separated by spaces. A value of 5 2 2 then would indicate that hyphenated words must have a minimum of 5 total characters, and after hyphenation there must be at least 2 characters before the hyphen and 2 characters after it.

You can use the keyword auto in place of any of the three values. The default value for auto is 5 2 2, so if auto replaces the first value then it will represent a 5, the second 2, and the third 2 again. A value of 8 4 4 would be very conservative and would only allow large words to break and would require that at least 4 characters remain on one line and at least 4 characters make it down to the next.

The CSS in Listing 4-22 uses a value of 7 3 3 as an example and notice in Figure 4-24 how the word *sollicitudin* was allowed to break since it's greater than 7 characters (and at least 3 of them were able to remain before the hyphen), but *Curae* was not allowed to break since it only contains 5 characters.

Listing 4-22. Setting how large a word must be to be broken and hyphenated

```
/* CSS snippet */
p {
    width: 500px;
    -ms-hyphens: auto;
    -ms-hyphenate-limit-chars: 7 3 3;
}
```

Lorem ipsum dolor sit amet, consectetur adipiscing elit. Mauris hendrerit leo at odio ultrices a euismod nisl condimentum. Suspendisse mattis sollicitudin rutrum. Etiam venenatis pulvinar metus ac condimentum. Curabitur non quam justo. Sed a mauris ac enim pulvinar suscipit eu vel lectus. Morbi dui eros, facilisis vitae ultrices a, ultrices in ligula. Pellentesque vehicula, mi ac egestas vulputate, eros massa tempus erat, ornare lobortis dui eros vel quam. In commodo pellentesque odio, et placerat felis tempus in. Aliquam quis diam neque, congue mollis felis. Nulla vel nisl purus, vitae feugiat leo. Vivamus arcu massa, mollis quis vehicula sed, porta sit amet nunc. Vestibulum ante ipsum primis in faucibus orci luctus et ultrices posuere cubilia Curae; Pellentesque eget tortor sed diam fermentum scelerisque. Donec nulla erat, feugiat vitae bibendum ut, dignissim adipiscing nisi. Donec ac nibh urna. Maecenas aliquet tincidunt risus, sit amet ultrices magna lacinia nec.

Figure 4-24. *Again, the hyphenation behavior has changed from previous examples*

-ms-hyphenate-limit-lines

The final member of the -ms-hyphenate family is -ms-hyphenate-limit-lines. This property will make sure that there are no more than the designated number of sequential hyphenated lines. In Listing 4-23, the -ms-hyphenate-limit-zone is set to 3px which is going to result in a lot of hyphenation, but the -ms-hyphenate-limit-lines is set to 2 which means that no more than 2 lines in a row can be hyphenated. If you look at the result in Figure 4-25, you'll notice that the line that ends with *Donec* is a candidate for hyphenation with at least 3 pixels of whitespace before the end of the line, but the preceding two lines (ending with *Vestibu-* and *Pel-*) are already hyphenated and so it must not be.

Listing 4-23. Using -ms-hyphenate-limit-lines to set how many sequential hyphenated lines are allowed

```
/* CSS snippet */
p {
    width: 500px;
    -ms-hyphens: auto;
    -ms-hyphenate-limit-zone: 3px;
    -ms-hyphenate-limit-lines: 2;
}
```

Lorem ipsum dolor sit amet, consectetur adipiscing elit. Mauris hendrerit leo at odio ultrices a euismod nisl condimentum. Suspendisse mattis sollici-tudin rutrum. Etiam venenatis pulvinar metus ac condimentum. Curabitur non quam justo. Sed a mauris ac enim pulvinar suscipit eu vel lectus. Morbi dui eros, facilisis vitae ultrices a, ultrices in ligula. Pellentesque vehicula, mi ac egestas vulputate, eros massa tempus erat, ornare lobortis dui eros vel quam. In commodo pellentesque odio, et placerat felis tempus in. Aliquam quis diam neque, congue mollis felis. Nulla vel nisl purus, vitae feugiat leo. Vivamus arcu massa, mollis quis vehicula sed, porta sit amet nunc. Vestibu-lum ante ipsum primis in faucibus orci luctus et ultrices posuere cubilia Pel-lentesque; Curae eget tortor sed diam fermentum scelerisque. Donec adipiscing erat, feugiat vitae bibendum ut, dignissim nulla nisi. Donec ac nibh urna. Maecenas aliquet tincidunt risus, sit amet ultrices magna lacinia nec.

Figure 4-25. *The -ms-hyphenate-limit-lines limits the number of contiguous hyphenated lines and can keep your text from looking too chopped up*

Summary

We've covered a lot of ground related to styling text in this chapter. We've covered the CSS properties that you can use to customize your text's color and opacity, the variety of ways to affect your fonts, and we've covered multiple columns and hyphenation for some powerful text layout control that's rather new to the CSS world.

The importance of sharp, clean, and purposeful typography in your app really can't be overstated. It's a critical tool in the effort to make a Windows 8 app's design something compelling enough that users are going to love it, talk about it with their friends, and bless your app with a high rating.

CHAPTER 5

■ ■ ■

Box Properties

■ **Note** Everything in HTML fits in a box and knowing how to control the format and layout of these boxes is paramount to a solid understanding of CSS.

Box properties are the properties of an HTML element that describe things like its size, fill, border, and spacing.

We'll look into element size and spacing as well as all the fill and border colors that make these elements look good and make them act as they should when the view state changes. It's one thing to get a single view working just right, but what happens when the user rotates their device to a portrait orientation? If an elements' box properties aren't set right then the whole layout can be adversely affected. The properties that we're going to look at in this chapter are critical to getting your Windows 8 app to look as it should. Figure 5-1 shows some Windows 8 apps designed according to the Microsoft design principles.

Figure 5-1. *A few Windows 8 apps designed according to the Microsoft design principles*

A whole lot of design, thought, and testing went in to the design language that guides the look and feel of Windows 8. Everything from the size of the touch targets to the spacing between them has a place in the design principles. In Figure 5-1, notice the consistent space above, below, and to the left of the content. Notice that the content is not packed on the screen but granted a bit of breathing room. And notice how there are very few visual elements for interaction or navigation besides the content itself. All of these are part of the design language and a ton more.

To implement these principles you will have to rely heavily on the box model and on various layout techniques. This chapter covers the box model and Chapter 7 will cover layout. To get a thorough understanding of the box model, you'll have to understand sizing, margins, borders, and padding. We'll take some more time to cover gradients and shadows since they can sometimes complement your core graphics and add value to your design.

The Box Model

You must understand the box model if you are to understand the margin, border, padding, and background properties on their own. Be sure the terms shown in Figure 5-2 are committed to memory.

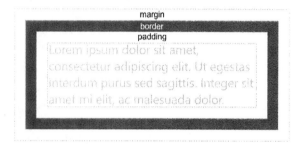

Figure 5-2. *The HTML/CSS box model*

The space labeled *margin* is space between the element and everything around it. The *border* is shown here as a gray line, but it can actually be any of a variety of styles, colors, and thicknesses. The space between the border and the actual content inside the box is called the *padding.*

The content is represented here as text, but keep in mind that your content may be text or it may be more elements nested as children.

I need to define some more terms that are based on this box model. The border box is the area of the diagram that includes the border area, the padding area, and the content, but excludes the margin. The padding box is the rectangular area that includes the padding area and the content area (excludes the margin and the border). And the content box is just the content area. You'll see why these terms are significant in just a moment.

Sizing

HTML container elements can be defined with no sizing information specified and left to react to the size of their parents or the size of their content, but you can also explicitly declare what size they should be. It's especially helpful in a Windows 8 app to specify the size because the visual artifacts will show up on a variety of devices and some of the devices will actually have system-level scaling applied to maintain a consistent and touchable user experience. In other words, unlike existing iterations of Windows design environments, things like buttons will not get smaller as the user cranks their resolution up.

Most HTML elements can have width and height properties specified to determine their explicit size. Besides this absolute value, it is also possible to specify minimum and maximum values for each. Here's a list of the properties available: width, min-width, max-width, height, min-height, max-height.

The minimum and maximum properties are extremely helpful in creating good adaptive layout. A min-width value of 80px will allow the target element to grow larger than 80 pixels in width (if a user is typing into the element, for instance) but never narrower.

Before setting a width and height on an element always ask yourself if you should be using a minimum or maximum property instead. Should your element be an absolute size or should it be able to adapt and get either smaller or larger in certain circumstances? Values of both properties should be a standard unit of length, as we've discussed already. Listing 5-1 shows you how element sizing can be specified in a variety of units.

Listing 5-1. A div with five children of varying widths

```
<!-- HTML snippet -->
<div id="parent">
    <div></div>
    <div></div>
    <div></div>
    <div></div>
    <div></div>
</div>

/* CSS snippet */
#parent { width:200px; border: 1px solid black;}
    #parent > div { background:green; height: 20px; margin:2px; color:white; }
    #parent div:nth-of-type(1) { width: 10px; }
    #parent div:nth-of-type(2) { width: 50%; }
    #parent div:nth-of-type(3) { width: 100px; }
    #parent div:nth-of-type(4) { width: calc(100% - 10px); }
    #parent div:nth-of-type(5) { width: 1in; }
```

There are some things you should note about Listing 5-1.

- Notice the indentation of all but the first line. This is an example of the convention mentioned earlier for indicating hierarchy.

- Notice the fourth child's width uses the calc() function to indicate that the width should be "10 pixels short of 100%".

- Notice the use of the :nth-of-type() pseudo-class. This is a great way to define style rules for a sequence of like elements in order. Because the :nth-of-type() is used instead of :nth-child, we could add a header above the sequence of div elements at a later time and not have any effect on their style.

Listing 5-1 results in rendered HTML that looks like Figure 5-3. You can see the different widths relative to one another.

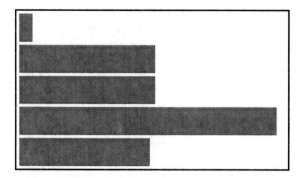

Figure 5-3. *Various sized rectangles illustrate the width properties*

Until CSS3, when the width and height of an object were set, the specified value affected the width and height of the content area (see the box model). This may be an intuitive approach in some cases, but it is also cause for some consternation. As one example, setting the width of a div to 100% would cause it to take the width of its parent, but then adding some padding and border would cause it to appear wider than its parent. So even though this method of measuring a box is often frustrating, it has remained the W3C standard.

CSS3 also introduced two enhancements that drastically improve our sizing scenarios. The first we've already discussed, which is the calc() method for specifying widths like calc(100% - 20px). The second is the box-sizing property. The box-sizing property takes a value of either border-box or content-box (default). Specifying border-box indicates that width and height should be translated to be the width and height of the entire box (including padding and border) and not just the content.

Let's look at the example in Listing 5-2 to be sure we're clear on this behavior.

Listing 5-2. A 200-pixel box using the default content-box sizing method

```
<!-- HTML snipppet -->
<div id="box"></div>

/* CSS snippet */
#box {
    margin: 50px;
    padding: 50px;
    border: 50px solid gray;
    width: 200px;
    height: 200px;
}
```

Figure 5-4. *A div with a 50-pixel border that clearly appears more than 200 pixels overall in width*

Now, if I told you that the border in that resulting box is 50 pixels thick, would you believe that the entire box is 200 pixels wide by 200 pixels tall? It would seem to add up to more. Using the standard sizing method, the content is 200 pixels wide and the padding and borders of 50 pixels each add the entire apparent width of the box up to 400 pixels!

Listing 5-3 repeats the same CSS but introduces one more property and look at the dramatically different result.

Listing 5-3. A 200 pixel box using the border-box sizing method

```
<!-- HTML snipppet -->
<div id="box"></div>

/* CSS snippet */
#box {
    margin: 50px;
    padding: 50px;
    border: 50px solid gray;
    width: 100px;
    height: 100px;
    box-sizing: border-box;
}
```

Figure 5-5. *A div that has set its sizing method via box-sizing and truly appears to be 200 pixels overall in width now*

Overflow

The box model with its sizing, its margin, and its padding gives you good control over the shape of all the containers on the page. The whole point of these containers on the page is to contain your app's content and very often that content will be too large or too long to fit. The container's behavior in this case is what we call overflow.

If a div element, for example, is tall enough to show 10 lines of text, and there are more than 10 lines of text in it, then we have some overflow.

You use the overflow property to control this behavior. Valid values are visible (and that one is the default), hidden, scroll, and auto.

- visible determines that the overflowing content should be visible. Even though it is visible, it does not affect the layout of any elements it may collide with.

- hidden makes any overflowing content invisible.

- scroll adds a scrollbar to the element so the user can choose to scroll to the overflowing content.

- auto only adds the scrollbars if there is reason to do so.

The overflow property is actually a shorthand property for overflow-x and overflow-y, so you can control the way the container behaves in both axes independently.

Listing 5-4 shows the example I mentioned of a div that is sized to show 10 lines of text but contains more. The overflow property has not been set, so the default value of visible is being used, and in fact the extra text is clearly visible in the result. One interesting behavior of this overflowing text that may or may not be intuitive to you is that it does not push other content around. The containing div acts as a block level element pushing subsequent content down, but its overflowing text has no further effect on the position of anything else on the page.

Listing 5-4. A div with overflowing content does not specify its overflow

```
<!-- HTML snippet -->
<div id="container">
    <p>Lorem ipsum dolor sit amet ... </p>
</div>
```

```
/* CSS snippet */
#container {
    height: 220px;
    width: 300px;
    border: 1px solid gray;
    margin: 10px;
    padding: 10px;
}
```

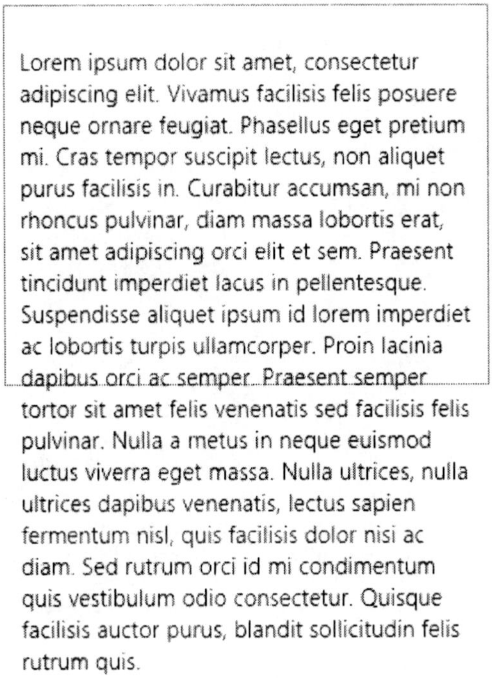

Lorem ipsum dolor sit amet, consectetur
adipiscing elit. Vivamus facilisis felis posuere
neque ornare feugiat. Phasellus eget pretium
mi. Cras tempor suscipit lectus, non aliquet
purus facilisis in. Curabitur accumsan, mi non
rhoncus pulvinar, diam massa lobortis erat,
sit amet adipiscing orci elit et sem. Praesent
tincidunt imperdiet lacus in pellentesque.
Suspendisse aliquet ipsum id lorem imperdiet
ac lobortis turpis ullamcorper. Proin lacinia
dapibus orci ac semper. Praesent semper
tortor sit amet felis venenatis sed facilisis felis
pulvinar. Nulla a metus in neque euismod
luctus viverra eget massa. Nulla ultrices, nulla
ultrices dapibus venenatis, lectus sapien
fermentum nisl, quis facilisis dolor nisi ac
diam. Sed rutrum orci id mi condimentum
quis vestibulum odio consectetur. Quisque
facilisis auctor purus, blandit sollicitudin felis
rutrum quis.

Figure 5-6. *By default overflow is visible as you can see*

Let's have a look at that same HTML with different values of overflow applied. In Listing 5-5 you can see that we can eliminate this visible overflow by setting the overflow property to hidden.

Listing 5-5. An overflow value of "hidden" should change the behavior

```
<!-- HTML snippet -->
<div id="container">
    <p>Lorem ipsum dolor sit amet ... </p>
</div>

/* CSS snippet */
#container {
    height: 220px;
    width: 300px;
    border: 1px solid gray;
```

```
    margin: 10px;
    padding: 10px;
    overflow: hidden;
}
```

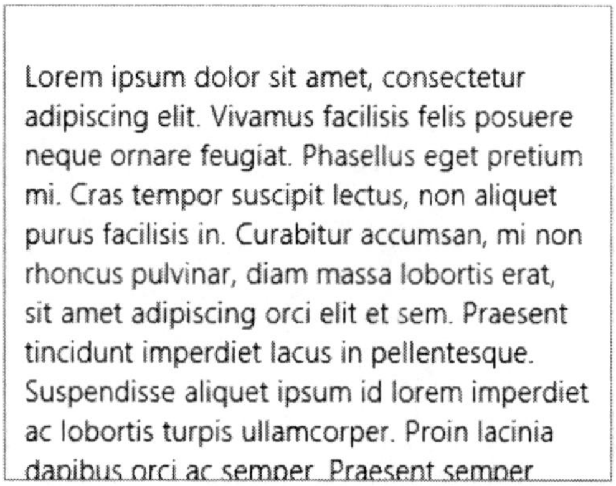

Lorem ipsum dolor sit amet, consectetur
adipiscing elit. Vivamus facilisis felis posuere
neque ornare feugiat. Phasellus eget pretium
mi. Cras tempor suscipit lectus, non aliquet
purus facilisis in. Curabitur accumsan, mi non
rhoncus pulvinar, diam massa lobortis erat,
sit amet adipiscing orci elit et sem. Praesent
tincidunt imperdiet lacus in pellentesque.
Suspendisse aliquet ipsum id lorem imperdiet
ac lobortis turpis ullamcorper. Proin lacinia
dapibus orci ac semper. Praesent semper

Figure 5-7. Overflowing content is now hidden, but there is no way to access it

That leaves us with no way to view the hidden text, though. Listing 5-6 improves on this by setting the
`overflow-y` to `auto`, which results in the `div` remaining the same size but suddenly taking on the ability to scroll.
You might wonder why I didn't choose the `scroll` value instead of `auto`. The `scroll` value forces the container to
always be in scroll mode, but the `auto` value is intelligent enough to only render the scroll bar when there is actually
overflowing content that needs scrolling. Note that in Windows 8, the system determines whether the user is currently
working with a mouse or with touch and renders the scrollbar accordingly. When using the mouse, a user will
see a traditional scrollbar, but when using touch, a user will see a cleaner, smaller scroll position indicator that is
informative without having to be interactive.

Listing 5-6. Setting overflow to "auto" causes content to be scrollable

```
<!-- HTML snippet -->
<div id="container">
    <p>Lorem ipsum dolor sit amet ... </p>
</div>

/* CSS snippet */
#container {
    height: 220px;
    width: 300px;
    border: 1px solid gray;
    margin: 10px;
    padding: 10px;
    overflow-y: auto;
}
```

Adding that one property `overflow-y: auto;` will cause a container to render a vertical scroll bar when its
content overflows. Figure 5-8 illustrates this and highlights the difference in the look of the scroll bar when the user is
using mouse versus touch.

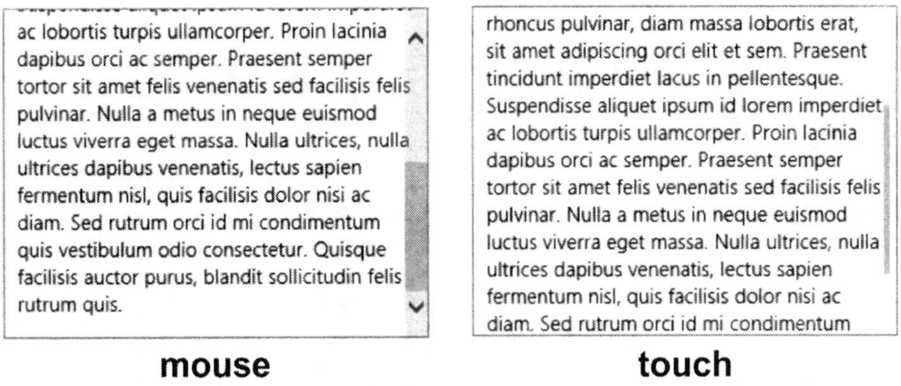

ac lobortis turpis ullamcorper. Proin lacinia
dapibus orci ac semper. Praesent semper
tortor sit amet felis venenatis sed facilisis felis
pulvinar. Nulla a metus in neque euismod
luctus viverra eget massa. Nulla ultrices, nulla
ultrices dapibus venenatis, lectus sapien
fermentum nisl, quis facilisis dolor nisi ac
diam. Sed rutrum orci id mi condimentum
quis vestibulum odio consectetur. Quisque
facilisis auctor purus, blandit sollicitudin felis
rutrum quis.

rhoncus pulvinar, diam massa lobortis erat,
sit amet adipiscing orci elit et sem. Praesent
tincidunt imperdiet lacus in pellentesque.
Suspendisse aliquet ipsum id lorem imperdiet
ac lobortis turpis ullamcorper. Proin lacinia
dapibus orci ac semper. Praesent semper
tortor sit amet felis venenatis sed facilisis felis
pulvinar. Nulla a metus in neque euismod
luctus viverra eget massa. Nulla ultrices, nulla
ultrices dapibus venenatis, lectus sapien
fermentum nisl, quis facilisis dolor nisi ac
diam. Sed rutrum orci id mi condimentum

mouse   **touch**

Figure 5-8. *The scrollbars are rendered differently when using a touch versus a mouse*

Visibility

The visibility of an element can be modified to determine whether the element appears or not.

There are two different style properties that affect an element's visibility: `visibility` and `display`.

The `visibility` property can be set to `visible`, `hidden`, or `collapse`. The default value is `visible` and obviously sets an element to appear. The `hidden` value makes the element completely invisible. Even when an element is hidden, it will still affect layout, so if you set it to be 100 pixels high, then it's still going to take up 100 pixels of vertical space. Finally, the `collapse` value works much like the `hidden` value except that for table rows and columns it also collapses the row or column so it doesn't take up the space it otherwise would.

The `display` property can be set to a lot of different things, but most of them have more to do with the target element's layout than its visibility. One of the possible values, however, is `none`. Setting `display` to `none` will not only hide the target element, but will effectively pull it out of the DOM so that it no longer affects the layout.

Some libraries such as jQuery provide functions (in jQuery they are `show()` and `hide()`) that make modifying these properties and showing or hiding elements much easier. In Appendix A, I'll discuss a number of CSS related libraries and how they can be used in your Windows 8 app.

Margin

An element's margin is the amount of space outside and around the element. Elements are rectangular and have properties for each side, so we have the following properties: `margin-top`, `margin-right`, `margin-bottom`, and `margin-left`.

To illustrate margins, let's create three elements one on top of the other and then apply some margins to them to see the effect. Listing 5-7 contains the HTML and the initial CSS without any styles that pertain to margin.

Listing 5-7. Some div elements with no margins applied

```
<!-- HTML snippet -->
<div id="parent">
    <div></div>
    <div></div>
    <div></div>
</div>
```

```
/* CSS snippet */
#parent > div {
    width: 200px;
    height: 80px;
    border: 1px solid black;
}
```

These three div elements placed one after another result in the three boxes in Figure 5-9 which are also placed one after another.

Figure 5-9. *The div elements butt right up to each other and may look crowded*

You can see that the div elements are immediately next to one another. In fact they even appear to share the same border. Now let's put a little bit of space between these elements. To do so, we can add some margin to the bottom of each, to the top of each, or a little bit of both. According to the Windows 8 design principles, we should have 10 pixels of space between tiles, let's just add a 5-pixel margin all the way around each of our elements. Listing 5-8 shows how to accomplish this using CSS. The HTML would be the same as the previous listing.

Listing 5-8. Some div elements with a 5-pixel margin applied

```
/* default.css */
#parent > div {
    width: 200px;
    height: 80px;
    border: 1px solid black;
    margin: 5px;
}
```

Figure 5-10. *The div elements now have a little bit of room in between*

That's what 10 pixels between elements looks like. There's nothing difficult about that. Just for fun, Listing 5-9 adds varying levels of left margin to those elements.

Listing 5-9. The same 5-pixel margin still specified and now some extra left margin

```
/* default.css */
#parent > div {
    width: 200px;
    height: 80px;
    border: 1px solid black;
    margin: 5px;
}

    #parent > div:nth-child(1) {
        margin-left: 5px;
    }

    #parent > div:nth-child(2) {
        margin-left: 50px;
    }

    #parent > div:nth-child(3) {
        margin-left: 100px;
    }
```

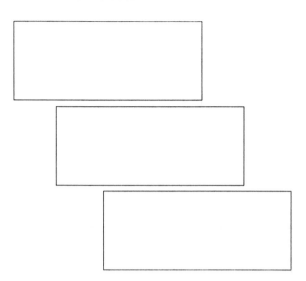

Figure 5-11. *The margin between elements is still visible; as is the extra left margin*

The margin shorthand property makes the setting of all four at once a bit easier though. The shorthand property will take any of the following forms.

- Margins on all four sides can be indicated by specifying each of the top, right, bottom, and left margins in that order and separated by spaces as in margin: 10px 8px 7px 2px;

- Margins that are symmetrical horizontally and vertically can take a single value that represents the top and bottom and another that represents the left and right as in margin: 20px 5px; In that case, the top and bottom margins would be set to 20px and the left and right to 5px.

- Finally, margins that are the same all the way around can take a single value as in margin: 10px; which would create 10px of space on all four sides.

The margin property is an extremely useful one for spacing of all kinds. It's used to control spacing above or below paragraphs in a text block and between groups of tiles in a list. It's also used to follow the Windows 8 design principles and add 120 pixels of space on the left side of each view. In fact, to accommodate this left margin, if you use the Navigation App project template to create your project then every time you create a new page, your CSS file will look something like the style rule in Listing 5-10.

Listing 5-10. The default style sheet for a new Page Control in Visual Studio

```
/* CSS snippet */
.pageTitle p {
    margin-left: 120px;
}
```

This rule sets 120 pixels of left margin for the "content goes here" paragraph that a page gets by default. I don't find this too helpful, since I quickly replace that stock paragraph and seldom end up with a single p tag in my main section! So replacing this rule with the following works quite well by setting a left margin for anything I drop in the main section (that is, the section with a role of main) as in Listing 5-11.

Listing 5-11. A better way to set the standard left margin to affect everything in the main section

```
/* CSS snippet */
.pageTitle section[role=main] > * {
    margin-left: 120px;
}
```

If you create a new Windows 8 project using the grid project template, your app looks like Figure 5-12 right away, and you can already see the characteristic 120 pixels of left margin already programmed into that project template.

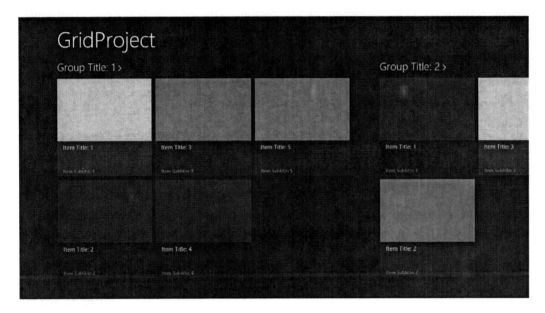

Figure 5-12. *The 120-pixel left margin that's typical of Windows 8 app is apparent in the grip project template. Recommended, standard margins also delineate list items and groups*

Borders

Borders are the lines that surround an element. Again, we get a shorthand property of border–this time to give us a break from typing border-width, border-style, and border-color each time. Listing 5-12 shows how to create a thin, black border around a div.

Listing 5-12. A thin, black border around a div

```
/* CSS snippet */
div {
    border: 1px solid black;
}
```

You can use any unit of length you wish for the border-width. The border-style has values of dashed, dotted, double, groove, hidden, inset, none, outset, ridge, and solid. The border-color can take any of the myriad ways to define a color that I laid out in Chapter 3.

Listing 5-13 shows a few more combinations of border properties.

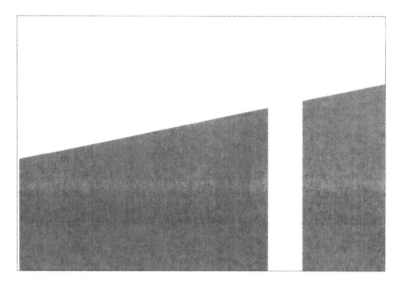

Figure 5-14. *The image appears in the background of the div element, but as you can tell it's too big*

background-size

The background-size property value can be a pair of lengths or percentages that represent the width and height. In place of a width or height value the keyword auto can be used to let the length value be determined based on the images' aspect ratio and the other dimension, and specifying auto for both width and height is the same as not setting the property at all.

In addition to specifying the size of the background image explicitly, the cover or contain values can be used to resize the image in a clever and helpful way. The cover value shrinks the image to fit perfectly into the container, and the contain value grows it to fit. In either case, the image is resized, but its aspect ratio is maintained.

If more than one background image exists then the size affects all of them alike. Let's use this property in Listing 5-16 to resize our Windows 8 logo to fit better in our div element.

Listing 5-16. A background-size property is added to control the size of the background image

```
<!-HTML snippet -->
<div id="container"></div>

/* CSS snippet */
div#container {
    width:600px;
    height:400px;
    border:1px solid gray;
    background-image: url("/images/win8logo.png");
    background-size: auto 100px;
}
```

Figure 5-15 shows the effect of adding the background-size property.

Figure 5-15. *The background image has been properly resized, but it's not exactly the effect we had in mind*

The image in Figure 5-15 is 100 pixels tall as we specified, but it is repeating and tiling the entire background. This is the default behavior of background images, and to override it we need to use the `background-repeat` property.

■ **Tip** The functionality that the `cover` and `contain` values provide for fitting a background image to its container is expanded in a WinJS control called the ViewBox. A ViewBox affects any single element even if that element contains a complex hierarchy of content. This is a tremendously powerful implement for adapting content dynamically to the size and shape of the screen it's currently on. You will read more about ViewBox controls in Chapter 7.

---

background-repeat

Repeating backgrounds by default makes sense considering their original and primary intent was to wallpaper the background with continuous image tiles. This behavior is very customizable, however. The `background-repeat` property offers some pretty slick functionality. It can take the values of `no-repeat`, `repeat`, `repeat-x`, `repeat-y`, `round`, or `space`.

The default value is `repeat` and to turn that behavior off entirely you would use `no-repeat`. If you want the image to repeat just in the x direction then use `repeat-x` and likewise with `repeat-y`. The `round` value will actually repeat the image in both directions but will not allow clipping if the element size is not a clean multiple in size. The images that do fit are then scaled up to fit the element. The `space` value is similar but instead of scaling the resulting images up it adds space between them to fill the space.

Listing 5-17. A background-repeat property is added with a value of no-repeat

```
<!—HTML snippet -->
<div id="container"></div>

/* CSS snippet */
div#container {
    width:600px;
```

```
    height:400px;
    border:1px solid gray;
    background-image: url('/images/win8logo.png');
    background-size: auto 100px;
    background-repeat: no-repeat;
}
```

Figure 5-16. *The background image no longer repeats*

background-position

CSS also gives us control over where in the containing element the background image should be rendered. If you turn the repeating off and just have a single image, you can use the background-position property with value combinations like left top, right center, or center bottom. You can also use a pair of length units or percentages to indicate the position in the x and y directions respectively.

Using this technique to set a relatively dim image to appear in the lower-right corner of your view is an excellent way to add your brand. Regardless of how the user scrolls the content, the image will remain in that corner.

Listing 5-18 adds the background-position property to our container.

Listing 5-18. A background-repeat property is added with a value of no-repeat

```
<!—HTML snippet -->
<div id="container"></div>

/* CSS snippet */
div#container {
    width:600px;
    height:400px;
    border:1px solid gray;
    background-image: url('/images/win8logo.png');
    background-size: auto 100px;
```

```
    background-repeat: no-repeat;
    background-position: center center;
}
```

The result that you see in Figure 5-17 is starting to actually look like something we meant to do!

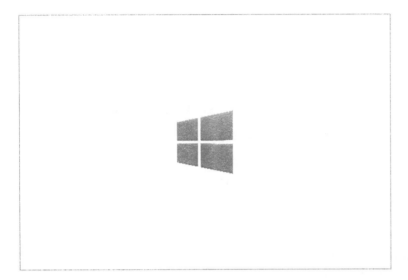

Figure 5-17. *The background image is centered both horizontally and vertically*

Here, we've opted to center the image using the center keywords, but we could just as easily have placed the image absolutely using something like background-position: 100px 100px, which would have set the logo 100 pixels from the top and left of the container.

background-origin

The background-origin is used to determine where the background-position coordinates originate. The default value is padding-box, so a background-position of 0% 0% or 0px 0px or left top would mean that the background image originates aligned with the top and left side of the padding (even though by default the background image actually extends underneath the border as well).

background-clip

I mentioned earlier that an element's background affects the area under the content, the padding, and the border, but the background-clip property gives us a bit of control over that. This property takes the same values as background-origin: border-box, padding-box, and content-box. Omitting it will mean it is using its default value which is border-box. Clipping to the border box means that the background sits underneath that entire area under the content, the padding, and the border. Setting the background-clip property to a value of padding-box, however, will effectively clip the portion under the border so that the background is only visible under the padding and the content. Finally, a value of content-box will clip it inside even the padding so that it sits only under the content.

 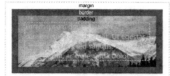 

| background-clip:border-box | background-clip:padding-box | background-clip:content-box |

Figure 5-18. *The background image is clipped to a specific area of the box model*

background-attachment

The background-attachment property determines how your background image should behave when the foreground contents are scrolling.

A value of fixed attaches the background image to the viewport (usually the entire window) which has the effect of keeping it fixed to the page.

A value of scroll affixes the background image to the document, so if the entire contents of the body overflow the page and forces scrolling, then a background image will scroll along with it.

A third value of local was introduced in CSS3 which attaches the background image of an element to the content in that element. Only with the introduction of this value are we able to scroll a background image with the content of a scrolling div.

As an example, look at Listing 5-19. A div containing three sizeable paragraphs of text is assigned a CSS style rule that, among other things, sets it to have a small background image rendered in its center. The overflow-y makes it scrollable, but we'll discuss that property soon. The property to note is the background-attachment of local. This will cause the background image to be scrolled with the rest of the content, as you can see in the results.

Listing 5-19. A background-attachment value of local is used to stick the background image to the scrolling container that it's inside of

```
<!-HTML snippet -->
<div>
    <p>Lorem ipsum dolor sit amet... </p>
    <p>Sed rhoncus, erat in eleifend... </p>
    <p>Nam mollis iaculis neque ut... </p>
    <p>In eleifend purus et leo... </p>
    <p>Sed quis sapien vitae elit... </p>
</div>

/* CSS snippet */
div {
    padding: 10px;
    border: 1px solid gray;
    width: 500px;
    height: 500px;
    background: url('/images/win8logo.png') no-repeat;
    background-position: center center;
    background-attachment: local;
    background-size: 80px 80px;
    overflow-y: scroll;
}
```

Adding this single property to our target element effectively pins the background image to the scrolling portion of the containing element.

Figure 5-19. *A scrollable div with a locally attached background image will scroll the image as well as its content*

Gradients

If you come from a web-development background, you know full well the hack that's been used to give a document a color gradient across its width or height. The hack I'm referring to is an image containing the desired gradient that is only one pixel in the direction perpendicular to the gradient. The image is then set as the background image and allowed to repeat across the page. It works, but it's not elegant and it has some drawbacks. One that I'm thinking of is the case where a user scrolls to the edge of the gradient or upgrades to a higher resolution screen and is presented with the abrupt edge of the gradient. It's embarrassing for the web designer, but the issue is gone now with the advent of CSS3 gradients.

I'd like to include a soft caution here against using gradients without consideration. Gradients can be helpful, but subtlety is the key. Superfluous graphical artifacts in general tend to violate the Microsoft design principles that use things like color and shape as information and not just eye candy. That said, a subtle gradiated background can be just right in some cases.

Gradients are implemented within the `background-image` property by using either the `linear-gradient()` function for a linear gradient or the `radial-gradient()` function for a radial gradient.

The `linear-gradient()` function accepts the gradient direction and then at least two color stops. Listing 5-20 shows a gradient that goes from black to white from left to right.

Listing 5-20. A linear gradient defined as the background to a div

```
<!-- HTML snippet -->
<div class="gradient"></div>


/* CSS snippet */
.gradient {
```

```
    width:400px;
    height:400px;
    background-image: linear-gradient(to right, black 0%, white 100%)
}
```

Figure 5-20. *A smooth gradient is rendered from black to white*

Adding color stops is easy too. Listing 5-21 alternates between black and white every 20%.

Listing 5-21. A linear gradient with alternating color stops

```
<!-- HTML snippet -->
<div class="gradient"></div>

/* CSS snippet */
.gradient {
    width:400px;
    height:400px;
    background-image: linear-gradient(to right, black 0%, white 20%, black 40%,
        white 60%, black 80%, white 100%);
}
```

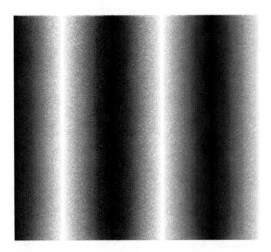

Figure 5-21. *A more complex linear gradient*

The first argument that indicates the direction can accept a side (left, right, top, bottom), a corner (top left, top right, bottom left, bottom right), or a custom degree like 45deg or 320deg.

You can find a lot more information on the implementation of the linear gradient on Microsoft's site by visiting http://msdn.microsoft.com/en-us/library/windows/apps/hh453527.aspx.

The function for creating a radial gradient is a bit more involved, and I'm only going to show an example and encourage you once again to visit Microsoft's documentation on the subject at http://msdn.microsoft.com/en-us/library/windows/apps/hh453718(v=vs.85).aspx when you're ready to implement it yourself. Listing 5-22 will create a gradient that starts in the center with black and radiates out to the farthest corner as white.

Listing 5-22. Radial gradient from center to farthest corner

```
<!-- HTML snippet -->
<div class="gradient"></div>

/* CSS snippet */
.gradient {
    width:400px;
    height:400px;
    background-image: radial-gradient(circle at 50% 50%, black 0%, white 100%);
}
```

Figure 5-22. A radial gradient from black in the middle to white on the outside

Shadow

Web designers have come up with all sorts of tricks for creating drop shadows over the years, because no provisions have existed in the standard-until now. Now implementing a drop shadow is easy, but better even than that is the fact that it's standard.

I would issue the same soft caution against the use of drop shadows as I would for gradients. It is a visual adornment. A shadow is a skeuemorphic artifact in that it attempts to make some element in your app look like it's in the real world. But it's not in the real world, is it? It's in the digital world and the design principles in Windows 8 suggest that we design our apps to be authentically digital without taking all of the dependencies and constraints that real world effects can bring.

Recommended or not, box shadows are very easy to implement. Listing 5-23 shows a small white box with a simple drop shadow. The values represent the horizontal offset, vertical offset, blur radius, spread distance, and shadow color.

Listing 5-23. A box-shadow definition on a div element

```
<!-- HTML snippet -->
<div class="shadow"></div>

/* CSS snippet */
.shadow {
    width: 100px;
    height: 100px;
    background-color: white;
    border: 1px solid black;
    box-shadow: 10px 10px 10px 0px hsla(0,0%,0%,.5);
}
```

Figure 5-23. *A simple box shadow under a white box*

One interesting thing about shadows is that they can be used to create more than just shadows. Listing 5-24 shows two examples. In the first, a shadow is added with no horizontal or vertical offset to create a glow effect. In the second, a solid shadow is used to apparently extend the box out and under a dashed border to make it appear that the element has sewing stitches around it.

Listing 5-24. Two alternative uses for the box -shadow property

```
<!-- HTML snippet -->
<div class="flex">
    <div class="glowBox"></div>
    <div class="stitches"></div>
</div>

/* CSS snippet */
.flex {
    display:-ms-flexbox;
    -ms-flex-pack:distribute;
    -ms-flex-align:center;
    height:200px;
    width:600px;
}

.glowBox {
    border:1px solid gray;
    width:100px;
    height:100px;
    box-shadow: 0px 0px 40px 10px hsla(0,0%,0%,.5);
}

.stitches {
    background-color: lightgray;
    border:2px dashed black;
    box-shadow: 0 0 0 4px lightgray;
    color: black;
    padding: 10px;
    border-radius: 4px;
    width:100px;
    height:100px;
}
```

Figure 5-24. *Two div elements-one glowing and the other apparently stitched all the way around*

Summary

In this chapter, we've learned all about the properties that affect the rectangular model of any HTML element (what we call *the box*). We define CSS properties that affect the size (width and height), the margin (space outside), the border, the padding (space inside), and more. We learned about setting relative or absolute values for width and height for content to determine its rendered size. We also learned how to handle element contents that are too large big for their space and overflow. We learned about defining the left, right, top, and bottom margins of an element separately or all together. We learned about using line style, size, and color to determine what the border of our element might look like. We learned about defining padding to give our content a little bit of breathing room inside its frame.

We also looked at setting backgrounds within an element that may be a solid color, an image, or even a linear or radial gradient. Finally, we learned about box shadows and using them to give our elements some apparent depth and a little bit of creative interest. It's important to understand these concepts before biting off subsequent concepts, especially the advanced layout concepts in Chapter 7.

Now that we have a basic understanding of the box properties, we'll move on to the transformation and animation of elements. Instead of determining the static appearance of elements, we'll determine their transitions and animations and really bring our Windows 8 apps to life.

■ ■ ■

CHAPTER 6

Transforms, Transitions, and Animation Properties

■ **Note**   Animation is much more than an embellishment in a successful Windows 8 app; rather, it makes itself essential by engaging the user and bringing the app to life. And an engaging and lively app is a successful app.

A Windows 8 app without enough animation is going to leave the user with at least a subconscious sense that something is lacking or something is dead. Too much animation threatens to detract, distract, and possibly even annoy. So animation should be just enough to make your app's visual artifacts come to life, and no more.

The right amount of animation is a core tenet to Windows 8 design. One of the principles that cover Windows 8 design is to be authentically digital—that is, to embrace the capabilities and liberties of a modern digital system and shake the constraints of physical ones. Animations and transitions that accentuate the users' tasks fall in line with this principle.

There's another principle that relates to the subject—that your UI should be fast and fluid. Not only should your interface never have hiccups in performance or in contact with the user, but it should flow from one screen to the next. There's good reason to animate a UI, and there's even better reason not to animate too much.

In animations, Microsoft has again embraced and implemented the W3C standards and then extended them where necessary to enable the demands of modern applications. And since your animations are running native in Windows 8, they'll have the tremendous advantage of the operating system's hardware acceleration. You don't have to accept a performance penalty for working with the web stack.

In this chapter, we'll discuss all things related to CSS and animation. We'll cover transforms, transitions, and animation both in two dimensions as well as in three. Many more pages could easily be dedicated to these broad subjects than we have time and space for now, but I hope to convey the concept and get you excited about what's possible.

Transforms

Transforms are simply changes. It might be a change of width, a change of color, or some other property. You know already, though, that these properties' changes can be done by simply modifying property values, so why would you want to add a transform, for instance, to move an element some pixels to the right, when you could simply adjust its position properties and see the same effect? Or why would you apply a scale transform to cause something to grow, when you could just increase its width and height properties?

The answer is that a transform is easy to apply and remove (programmatically even). It affects the target element after it has already been rendered, and it affects the entire target element, children included.

Additionally, transforms allow you to affect your elements in ways that are not possible with properties alone. You cannot add rotation to an element without a transform, for instance. In fact, there is an entire subset of CSS transforms that affect the element with 3D-like effects, and these effects would certainly not be possible with standard properties.

There are many transformational effects available, and yet there are only about six CSS properties to remember, and they are perspective, perspective-origin, backface-visibility, transform-origin, transform-style, and transform. There are many more details about these properties. You can see a full list at http://www.w3.org/TR/css3-transforms/#transform-property.

Transform functions

The most interesting property by far is the transform property. For its value it expects a list of one or many *transform functions*. I'll describe each of the transform-related properties first and then focus in great detail on the transform property.

perspective

Don't get confused about the difference between this property value and the perspective() function that will be discussed soon. They have the same visual effect, but this one (the perspective value for the transform function) affects the transforms of all of its children, whereas the perspective() function only affects the transform of the element it's on. I'll wait until the next section to describe the actual effect of the perspective() function. The perspective property value only affects 3D transformed elements.

perspective-origin

The perspective-origin property is the virtual camera's deviation (using x and y coordinates) from directly in front of the target element. If you're looking at the wall of a square building and you step to the right far enough, the wall will change shape from your perspective, and this is exactly what you should think of when you're modifying this property. Like perspective, perspective-origin affects the transforms of its children's transforms, but not its own.

backface-visibility

The backface-visibility property determines what happens to an element's contents when we spin it around and see the back of it. Set it to visible if you should see the back of the content in that case or to hidden if you should not.

transform-origin

If you stuck a pin near one corner of a square and rotated it, you would get a different result than if you stuck your pin in the square's center. This is what the transform-origin property does for you. It indicates which part of an element the transformation should originate at. It behaves a bit differently depending on the transform.

transform-style

You can specify either flat or preserve-3d as values for the transform-style property. If you choose preserve-3d, then nested elements will preserve their location relative to each other in their 3D space. If you choose flat, however, then all elements collapse to a shared plane.

transform

The transform function is the one that does most of the heavy lifting. Its value can be quite large because it's composed of one to perhaps many of the available transform functions (separated by spaces). There's a lot of complexity involved in the transform property and all of its many functions. You are welcome to go to w3c.org and get your fill of the formulas and theories, but I'm going to keep all of my descriptions and examples rather simple and pragmatic. I'll talk more about the reasons you might choose to use transforms for your application than I will the math and theory behind doing it.

2D transform functions

There are a lot of transform functions to choose from. You can affect your target element with any of the following two dimensional transforms: rotate(), scale(), scaleX(), scaleY(), skew(), skewX(), skewY(), translate(), translateX(), translateY(), or matrix().

rotate()

There's nothing obscure about the purpose of the rotate function. It rotates the target element in a clockwise direction by a specified number of degrees. The degree unit is deg and follows a value from negative infinity to positive. Negative values will rotate the target element in the counter-clockwise direction and positive values in the clockwise direction.

The rotate() function is perfectly willing to accept numbers greater than a 360-degree, full rotation, with which it will just continue rotating. A value of 440deg, therefore, will rotate the target one and a half times in the clockwise direction and will end up being equivalent to a value of 180deg.

Listing 6-1 demonstrates identical div elements with three different rotation values.

■ **Note**   You may notice in the code listings in this chapter that the parent container may have its display **value** set to either -ms-flexbox or -ms-grid. For now, just know that these are layout techniques. The flexbox is great for lining its children up next to each other, and the grid is used in this case to stack them on top of each other. We'll talk much more about these and other layout techniques in Chapter 7.

Listing 6-1. A text block at 5deg, -45deg, and 180deg respectively

```
<!-- HTML snippet -->
<div class="parent">
    <div>Lorem ipsum dolor sit amet...</div>
    <div>Lorem ipsum dolor sit amet...</div>
    <div>Lorem ipsum dolor sit amet...</div>
</div>

/* CSS snippet */
.parent {
    display: -ms-flexbox;
}

.parent div {
    border: 2px solid gray;
    width: 200px;
    height: 200px;
```

```
    padding: 5px;
    margin: 5px;
}

.parent div:nth-of-type(1) {
    transform: rotate(5deg);
}

.parent div:nth-of-type(2) {
    transform: rotate(-45deg);
}

.parent div:nth-of-type(3) {
    transform: rotate(180deg);
}
```

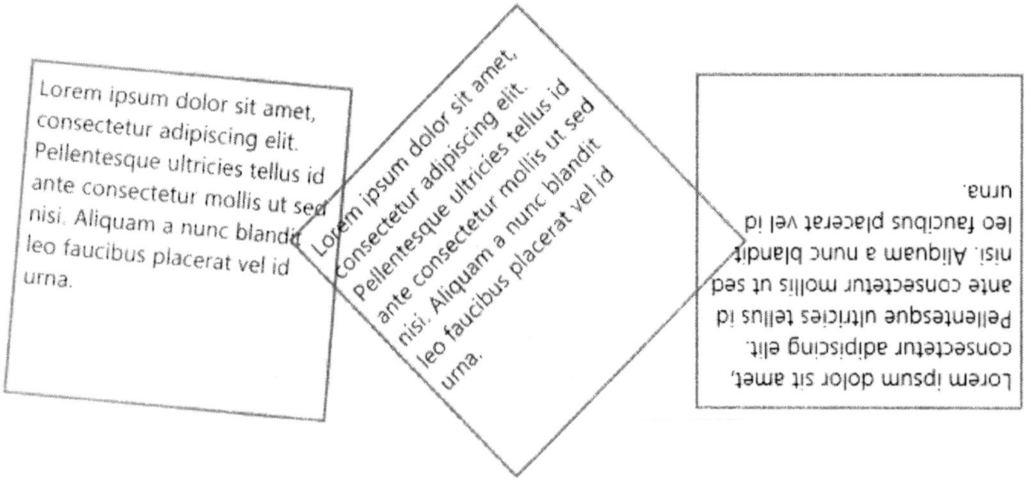

Figure 6-1. *Transformed elements with various levels of rotation*

scale()

Scaling is the resizing of the target element and all of its contents, and it takes effect after the target has been rendered. This means that child content of the element is not going to be laid out based on the resizing of its parent element, but rather scaled along with it.

The scale() function asks for a multiplier for a value. A value of 0.5 would scale an object to half its original size, 1 would leave it unchanged in size, and 2 would double it. Listing 6-2 goes through that exact scenario.

Listing 6-2. Scaling an object to half and then to twice its original size

```
<!-- HTML snippet -->
<div class="parent">
    <div>Lorem ipsum dolor sit amet...</div>
    <div>Lorem ipsum dolor sit amet...</div>
    <div>Lorem ipsum dolor sit amet...</div>
</div>
```

```
/* CSS snippet */
.parent {
    display: -ms-flexbox;
}

.parent div {
    border: 2px solid gray;
    width: 200px;
    height: 200px;
    padding: 5px;
    margin: 5px;
}

.parent div:nth-of-type(1) {
    transform: scale(1);
}

.parent div:nth-of-type(2) {
    transform: scale(0.5);
}

.parent div:nth-of-type(3) {
    transform: scale(2);
}
```

Notice how after being scaled, the divs in Figure 6-2 are actually overlapping. This doesn't seem possible based solely on legacy HTML experience. The fact that the scaling occurs only after the target element has been fully rendered means that it's quite a different effect than simply specifying alternate values for the width and height properties.

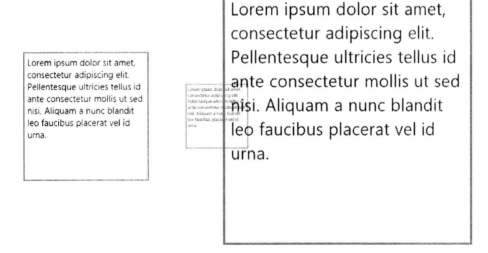

Figure 6-2. *Three levels of scale*

Consider the div element in Listing 6-3. It has a paragraph for its contents, and its dimensions are 400 pixels wide by 200 pixels high.

Listing 6-3. A 400 pixel by 200 pixel div element with text content

```
<!-- HTML snippet -->
<div id="textDiv">
    <p>Lorem ipsum dolor sit amet...</p>
</div>

/* CSS snippet */
#textDiv {
    width: 400px;
    height: 200px;
}
```

Lorem ipsum dolor sit amet, consectetur
adipiscing elit. Pellentesque ultricies tellus
id ante consectetur mollis ut sed nisi.
Aliquam a nunc blandit leo faucibus
placerat vel id urna. Praesent lacinia, ligula
non bibendum faucibus, purus libero
pellentesque nunc, nec cursus elit velit sit
amet sapien. Donec vulputate faucibus
tortor eget pulvinar. Nam porttitor leo et
elit volutpat quis sagittis massa tincidunt.

Figure 6-3. *The text wraps according to the width of its container*

Now let's look at Listing 6-4, wherein we resize the div using the width and height properties. You'll notice that the paragraph text has reacted to the change in size of its parent.

Listing 6-4. Resizing the div to 800 pixels by 400 pixels by manipulating the style properties

```
/* CSS snippet */
#textDiv {
    width: 800px;
    height: 400px;
}
```

Lorem ipsum dolor sit amet, consectetur adipiscing elit. Pellentesque ultricies tellus id ante consectetur
mollis ut sed nisi. Aliquam a nunc blandit leo faucibus placerat vel id urna. Praesent lacinia, ligula non
bibendum faucibus, purus libero pellentesque nunc, nec cursus elit velit sit amet sapien. Donec
vulputate faucibus tortor eget pulvinar. Nam porttitor leo et elit volutpat quis sagittis massa tincidunt.

Figure 6-4. *The div text has been layed out to fit its larger container*

And now, in contrast, Listing 6-5 scales the element instead. You'll notice that the paragraph text has not changed its layout but remains the same shape, albeit at twice the size.

Listing 6-5. Scaling up the div using a transform instead of sizing

```
/* CSS snippet */
#textDiv {
    width: 200px;
    height: 100px;
    transform: scale(2,2);
}
```

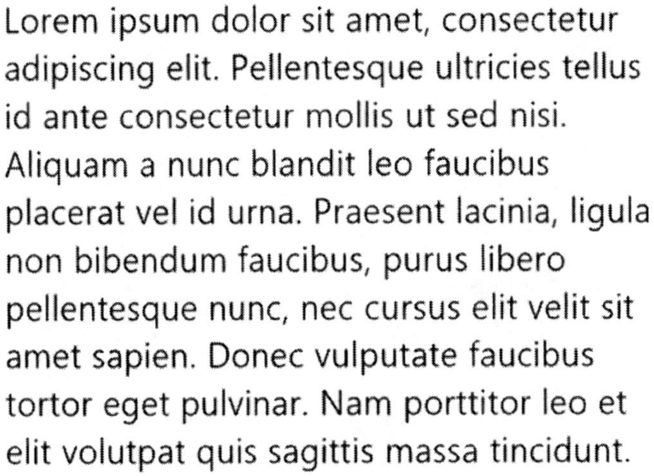

Lorem ipsum dolor sit amet, consectetur adipiscing elit. Pellentesque ultricies tellus id ante consectetur mollis ut sed nisi. Aliquam a nunc blandit leo faucibus placerat vel id urna. Praesent lacinia, ligula non bibendum faucibus, purus libero pellentesque nunc, nec cursus elit velit sit amet sapien. Donec vulputate faucibus tortor eget pulvinar. Nam porttitor leo et elit volutpat quis sagittis massa tincidunt.

Figure 6-5. *The text is laid out exactly as it was in the smaller container and only scaled afterward*

Scaling can be done on both the x and y axes uniformly or to one of the axes independently of the other. The functions scaleX() and scaleY() exist and will transform only the appropriate axis, but the same thing can be accomplished by simply providing two values to the scale method and being sure to set one of them to a value of 1. The two expressions in Listing 6-6, then, are identical.

Listing 6-6. Two alternate ways to double the width of the target element

```
/* CSS snippet */
div {
    transform: scale(2,1);
}

div {
    transform: scaleX(2);
}
```

skew()

The skew() function translates opposite sides of the target element in opposite directions, distorting the shape of the element and its contents. It can be used to create a variety of effects.

A skew can be used to show perspective. Also, a skew can be used to show acceleration and deceleration of elements if you're animating them on the screen, but that's an animation. The skew transform on its own is static.

Listing 6-7 shows a basic skew transform, this time again affecting a paragraph of text.

Listing 6-7. A basic skew of text along a single axis

```
<!-- HTML snippet -->
<div class="parent">
    <div>Lorem ipsum dolor sit amet...</div>
    <div>Lorem ipsum dolor sit amet...</div>
    <div>Lorem ipsum dolor sit amet...</div>
</div>

/* CSS snippet */
.parent {
    display: -ms-flexbox;
}

.parent div {
    border: 2px solid gray;
    width: 200px;
    height: 200px;
    padding: 5px;
    margin: 5px;
}

.parent div:nth-of-type(1) {
    transform: skew(0deg,10deg);
}

.parent div:nth-of-type(2) {
    transform: skew(-5deg,0deg);
}

.parent div:nth-of-type(3) {
    transform: skew(15deg,15deg);
}
```

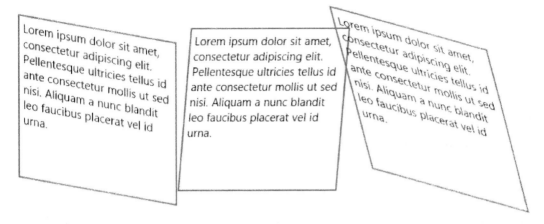

Figure 6-6. *A vertical skew, a horizontal skew, and then a combination of the two*

Like the scale transform, the skew transform comes in the `skewX()` and `skewY()` variety as well, but again, I don't personally find it worthwhile to use them because it's just as easy to use `skew(n,n)` and pass in two values.

translate()

Like its cousins scale and skew, translate is available in independent axis versions, which are, as you might guess, `translateX()` and `translateY()`. Did I mention that I don't personally find them worthwhile?

The translate transform is a very important one. To translate means simply to move. The `translateX()` function moves its target left and right along the x axis, and the `translateY()` function moves it up and down along the y axis. The `translate()` function then takes two values and can move its target anywhere along the xy plane. You can likely imagine how many uses there might be for such a function.

Listing 6-8 uses a flexbox to lay 5 `div` elements out next to each other. They're all give a predetermined size of 75 pixels square, some margin, and a white border to differentiate. The highlighted block, then, picks out the 5th `div` and applies a transform to knock it out of place by 20 pixels to the right and down.

Listing 6-8. A combination of rotate(), scale(), and translate() give the first letter some pizazz

```
<!-- HTML snippet -->
<div class="parent">
    <div>Lorem ipsum dolor sit amet...</div>
    <div>Lorem ipsum dolor sit amet...</div>
    <div>Lorem ipsum dolor sit amet...</div>
</div>

/* CSS snippet */
.parent {
    display: -ms-flexbox;
}

.parent div {
    border: 2px solid gray;
    width: 200px;
    height: 200px;
```

```
    padding: 5px;
    margin: 5px;
}

.parent div:nth-of-type(1){
    transform: translate(0,0)
}

.parent div:nth-of-type(2){
    transform: translate(20px,20px);
}

.parent div:nth-of-type(3){
    transform: translate(0,0);
}
```

Lorem ipsum dolor sit amet, consectetur adipiscing elit. Pellentesque ultricies tellus id ante consectetur mollis ut sed nisi. Aliquam a nunc blandit leo faucibus placerat vel id urna.		Lorem ipsum dolor sit amet, consectetur adipiscing elit. Pellentesque ultricies tellus id ante consectetur mollis ut sed nisi. Aliquam a nunc blandit leo faucibus placerat vel id urna.
	Lorem ipsum dolor sit amet, consectetur adipiscing elit. Pellentesque ultricies tellus id ante consectetur mollis ut sed nisi. Aliquam a nunc blandit leo faucibus placerat vel id urna.	

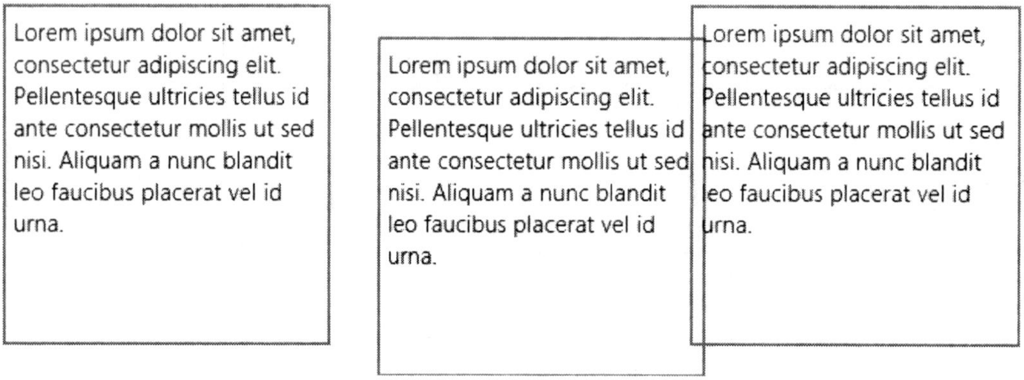

Figure 6-7. The div in the center has been moved from its original location 20 pixels to the right and 20 pixels down

matrix()

All of the functionality behind the functions we've looked at already and a lot more are available with the matrix function. The matrix function is not for the faint of heart. It's tedious and it's complex, but when you need to get under the hood and make your transforms look just so, then this function (along with a little review of that linear algebra book on your shelf) will get you there.

3D transform functions

First of all, the term 3D is a bit of a misdirection. These so-called three-dimensional transforms are no more three dimensional than anything else that happens on your two-dimensional computer screen, but the thing that defines 3D techniques on the computer is the 3D space that objects are rendered in before being projected to your two-dimensional screen. The effect gives a 3D appearance at best.

There are many available three dimensional transform functions. You can choose from perspective(), perspective-origin(), rotate3d(), rotateX(), rotateY(), rotateZ(), scale3d(), scaleZ(), translate3d(), and translateZ(),and matrix3d().

For all of the 3D transforms, you should imagine your flat, rendered elements standing up in 3D space with a virtual camera pointed at them. Some of the properties are going to manipulate the position of this virtual camera, and others are going to manipulate the position of the rendered elements.

138

perspective()

The perspective() function manipulates the virtual camera of the element being transformed. It takes a length value with higher values, meaning that the virtual camera is further from the object and the element will appear more flat, and lower values, meaning that the virtual camera is closer to the object and the element will appear to have more depth.

It's easy to notice the dramatic depth introduced as the perspective() function is configured to bring the camera closer to the object. Listing 6-9 shows the visual effect of reducing the perspective.

Listing 6-9. Three divs all rotated the same with perspective values of none, 400px, and 200px

```
<!-- HTML snippet -->
<div class="parent">
    <div>Lorem ipsum dolor sit amet...</div>
    <div>Lorem ipsum dolor sit amet...</div>
    <div>Lorem ipsum dolor sit amet...</div>
</div>

/* CSS snippet */
.parent {
    display: -ms-flexbox;
}

.parent div {
    border: 2px solid gray;
    width: 200px;
    height: 200px;
    padding: 5px;
    margin: 5px;
}

.parent div:nth-of-type(1) {
    transform: rotate3d(1,1,1,45deg);
}

.parent div:nth-of-type(2) {
    transform: perspective(400px) rotate3d(1,1,1,45deg);
}

.parent div:nth-of-type(3) {
    transform: perspective(200px) rotate3d(1,1,1,45deg);
}
```

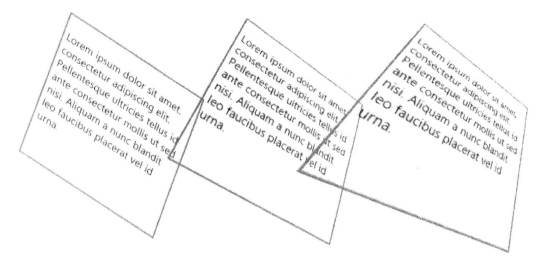

Figure 6-8. *Decreasing perspective values causes an increase in the apparent depth*

As I mentioned previously, you should be careful not to confuse this `perspective()` function with the `perspective` property. Again, the function affects the transform of the elements that it's applied to. Also keep in mind that `perspective` will not have any effect on an object that doesn't have any other 3D transform functions applied to it.

rotate3d()

Of course, rotation was available to us when we were looking at the 2D transforms as well, but you might expect some additional capability in the 3D environment, and you'd be right. In our new space, we'll be able to rotate about all three axes using `rotate3d()`, `rotateX()`, `rotateY()`, and `rotateZ()`. There's nothing the latter three functions can do that the first can't. The `rotate3d()` function takes four arguments. The first three are the x, y, and z coordinates of a vector, which will be normalized to a unit vector, and the fourth is the number of degrees (clockwise) about which to rotate the element around that vector.

Calling `rotate3d(1,0,0,45deg)`, then, will rotate the element 45 degrees clockwise about the x-axis; `rotate3d(0,1,0,45deg)` will rotate it the same 45 degrees clockwise about the y-axis; and `rotate3d(1,1,0,45deg)` will rotate it 45 degrees about a vector that starts at the origin and projects directly in between the x and y axes on the xy plane.

In any of the rotation functions, a positive angle value will rotate the element clockwise around the axis or unit vector, and a negative value will rotate it counter-clockwise.

Listing 6-10 rotates a flat element in 3D.

Listing 6-10. The rotate3d() function used to rotate a div around the x-axis, the y-axis, and then a combination of both

```
<!-- HTML snippet -->
<div class="parent">
    <div>Lorem ipsum dolor sit amet...</div>
    <div>Lorem ipsum dolor sit amet...</div>
    <div>Lorem ipsum dolor sit amet...</div>
</div>
```

```css
/* CSS snippet */
.parent {
    display: -ms-flexbox;
}

.parent div {
    border: 2px solid gray;
    width: 200px;
    height: 200px;
    padding: 5px;
    margin: 5px;
}

.parent div:nth-of-type(1) {
    transform: rotate3d(1,0,0,45deg);
}

.parent div:nth-of-type(2) {
    transform: rotate3d(0,1,0,45deg);
}

.parent div:nth-of-type(3) {
    transform: rotate3d(1,1,0,45deg);
}
```

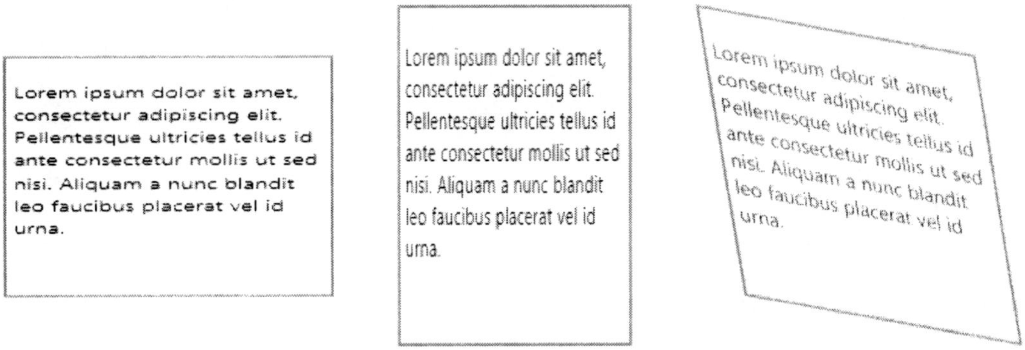

Figure 6-9. A rotation around the x-axis just looks like the element is being squished vertically, around the y-axis looks like it's being squished horizontally, and with the combination it starts to look like it's actually 3D

■ **Note** Technically, any of the three transformations above could have been achieved using just the right two-dimensional transform functions, but that requires a coordinate system mapping. In other words, let's imagine you're trying to cause a square visual element to appear as though it were opening toward the user like a saloon door. To do this using two-dimensional transforms would require you to figure out what combination of skewing, scaling, and translating would cause this effect. Using three-dimensional transforms, however, would only require a single rotateY() function call and almost no thought at all!

scale3d()

Once you've brought your elements into three dimensions, all of the major transformation functions—rotate, scale, and translate—must be implemented. The scale3d() function, like its counterparts, is accompanied by scaleX(), scaleY(), and scaleZ() functions, and again, the scale3d() function can perform any function the others can. Are you detecting a pattern?

The scale3d() function asks us for three arguments, which are the scale factors along the x, y, and z axes. Listing 6-11 uses three subsequent scale3d() function calls to best illustrate the difference.

Listing 6-11. One div configured not to scale (1,1,1), a second configured to scale down (0.8,0.8,0.8), and a third scaling up in the y and z axes and scaling down in the x-axis

```
<!-- HTML snippet -->
<div class="parent">
    <div>Lorem ipsum dolor sit amet...</div>
    <div>Lorem ipsum dolor sit amet...</div>
    <div>Lorem ipsum dolor sit amet...</div>
</div>

/* CSS snippet */
.parent {
    display: -ms-flexbox;
    perspective: 800px;
}

.parent div {
    border: 2px solid gray;
    width: 200px;
    height: 200px;
    padding: 5px;
    margin: 5px;
}

.parent div:nth-of-type(1) {
    transform: rotate3d(1,1,0,45deg) scale3d(1,1,1)
}

.parent div:nth-of-type(2) {
    transform: rotate3d(1,1,0,45deg) scale3d(0.8,0.8,0.8)
}

.parent div:nth-of-type(3) {
    transform: rotate3d(1,1,0,45deg) scale3d(0.5,1.2,1.2);
}
```

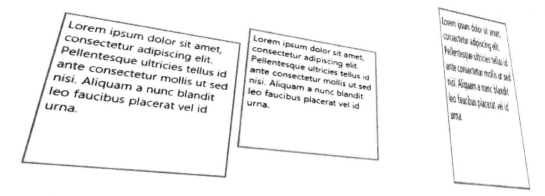

Figure 6-10. *The results of three dimensional scaling*

translate3d()

When it comes to moving your element around in two dimensions, the translateX() and translateY() functions cover the bases, but with the third dimension comes demand for a translateZ(), and so it is. The translateZ() function moves things closer to and further from the viewer (assuming the viewer is still in his or her original location of perspective-origin: 50% 50%).

Listing 6-12 shows an example with three opaque elements stacked directly on top of each other. Some distance has been added between the stacked elements using a 3D translation along the z axis. The entire scene has been rotated to reveal the hidden elements.

Listing 6-12. Style rules to rotate and translate three elements. The .parent rule is overridden to use a grid to cause the elements to stack on top of one another

```
<!-- HTML snippet -->
<div class="parent">
    <div>Lorem ipsum dolor sit amet...</div>
    <div>Lorem ipsum dolor sit amet...</div>
    <div>Lorem ipsum dolor sit amet...</div>
</div>

/* CSS snippet */
.parent {
    display: -ms-grid;
}

.parent div {
    border: 2px solid gray;
    background-color: white;
    width: 200px;
    height: 200px;
    padding: 5px;
    margin: 5px;
}

.parent div:nth-of-type(1) {
    transform: rotate3d(1, -1, 0, 45deg) translate3d(0, 0, 0);
}
```

```
.parent div:nth-of-type(2) {
    transform: rotate3d(1, -1, 0, 45deg) translate3d(0, 0, 60px);
}
```

```
.parent div:nth-of-type(3) {
    transform: rotate3d(1, -1, 0, 45deg) translate3d(0, 0, 120px);
}
```

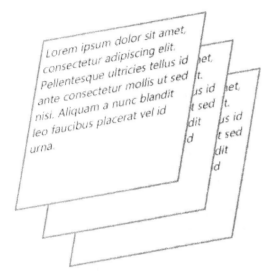

Figure 6-11. *The rotation of the scene and the varying levels of translation of each element enable us to see each element even though they are stacked*

matrix3d()

The matrix3d() function is the mother of all of the other transformation functions. All of the others are based on it, so it's capable of doing everything the other functions can do and much more. The only drawback is that it's rather difficult to figure out how to use it unless you have an advanced math degree.

I only have a minor in mathematics, so Listing 6-13 borrows an example of the matrix3d function from the MSDN website (http://msdn.microsoft.com/en-us/library/windows/apps/jj193609.aspx).

Listing 6-13. Sixteen values for the matrix3d() function cause a combination of transformations to occur to the target element

```
<!-- HTML snippet -->
<div class="parent">
    <div>Lorem ipsum dolor sit amet...</div>
</div>

/* CSS snippet */
.parent {
    display: -ms-flexbox;
}
```

```
.parent div {
    border: 2px solid gray;
    width: 200px;
    height: 200px;
    padding: 5px;
    margin: 5px;
}

.parent div:nth-of-type(1) {
    transform: matrix3d(
        0.359127,   -0.469472, 0.806613, 0,
        0.190951,    0.882948, 0.428884, 0,
        -0.913545,   0,        0.406737, 0,
        0,           0,        0,        1
    );
}
```

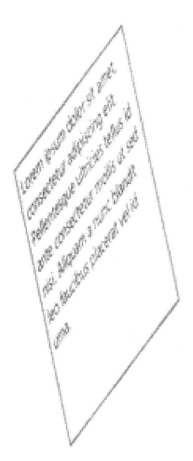

Figure 6-12. *A combination of transformations done using the matrix3d() function*

A transform is a change, but it's a static one that's applied when your app's view is rendered and remains as long as the view does. What we really need to do is to get things moving. When switching from one page to the next, for instance, we may need the subtlest of animations to indicate that one flies in and the other flies out. When we change the font from normal to bold, we may wish for the text to embolden instead of merely becoming bold in an indiscernible instant.

To get things moving, we're going to need to use transitions.

Transitions

You may consider animations to be a scripting function and wonder what they're doing in CSS instead of JavaScript. Transitions and animations are all about style, though. The only difference is that they take into account not only the static state of styles but also the dynamic in-between.

Transitions offer an implementation for the style in between the styles. They are the description of what should happen from here to there. When an element is suddenly added to the screen, how should it get there? When it's removed, how should it leave?

Just like transforms, there aren't a large number of CSS properties that apply to transitions—just four, actually, plus a shorthand. You can choose from `transition-property`, `transition-duration`, `transition-timing-function`, and `transition-delay`, or you can skip the long property names and roll them all together into the `transition` shorthand method. This is the more common approach.

Transitions take effect, and their animation begins once an element is targeted by a style rule. In the examples below, you'll see that our transition is in a style rule with a :hover pseudo-class in the selector. This means the user will hover over an element and at that point will become a target of the style rule that contains a transition; therefore, instead of simply changing the style properties from what they were to what the new rule says they should be, they will be transitioned.

If a transition is the in-between of two states, then we are obviously dealing with some starting state and some ending state. Transitions are always defined by the ending state. If we're transitioning a `div` from short to somewhat taller, then the transition is defined by the style rule that defines the taller state.

Listing 6-14 and Figure 6-13 show a very simple transition. A `div` element starts off with a size of 100 pixels on each side. It has a white background and a gray border for visibility. A second style rule is defined that applies to the box when it is in its hover state—that is, when the user hovers their mouse over the div. The second frame represents the moment the user hovers.

In that second rule, we specify two properties and then an extremely simple transition property that simply indicates that it should take two seconds for all of the properties in this style rule to take effect. This means that the five frames represents two seconds, and that's how long it will take for the white box to become gray and for the square edges to acquire a border radius.

Listing 6-14. A very simple transition configured to take two seconds and apply to the background-color and border-radius properties when the target element is hovered

```
<!-- HTML snippet -->
<div id="box">
</div>

/* CSS snippet */
#box {
    width: 100px;
    height: 100px;
    border: 2px solid hsl(0,0%,70%);
}
```

```
#box:hover {
    background-color: gray;
    border-radius: 25px;
    transition: 2s;
}
```

Figure 6-13. *Five frames of the transition attempting to illustrate the resulting animation*

In the last example, we created a transition that omitted any properties and consequently applied to them all. If you want to limit what properties the transition actually applies to, you must specify them. Listing 6-15 shows an alternate version of the #box:hover style rule from the previous example, and Figure 6-14 shows the result. The difference, of course, is that while the border-radius appears to be animating just as before, the background-color is no longer taken into consideration by the transition property because an explicit list of properties exists and background-color wasn't invited. The div, therefore, turns gray the moment the user hovers over it, and in our Figure 6-14, the second and subsequent frames depict exactly that.

Listing 6-15. The border-radius property being included explicitly in the transtion property

```
#box:hover {
    background-color: gray;
    border-radius: 25px;
    transition: border-radius 2s;
}
```

Figure 6-14. *Results in an exlusion of background-color from the translation properties and an obvious immediate application of the background-color in the second frame*

Specifying that the transition should take two seconds assumes that the progressive changes to the object should occur according to the ease function. The ease function acts a bit more the way that a real object—constrained by gravity—would in our world, in that it starts off a bit more slowly and finishes a bit more slowly too. The ease function is easy on the eyes, since even if it's subconscious, it looks like what our human brains are used to seeing.

We don't have to follow this function, though. In Listing 6-16, notice that the shorthand property is still in use, but we now have specified that the linear function should be used. The change to the animation would be too subtle to detect in my 5-frame animation, so you'll just have to try this on your own. The valid values for a timing function are linear, ease, ease-in, ease-out, ease-in-out, cubic-bezier(), step-start, step-end, or steps().

Listing 6-16. The linear timing function added to the transition shorthand property

```css
/* CSS snippet */
#box:hover {
    background-color: gray;
    border-radius: 25px;
    transition: border-radius linear 2s;
}
```

The linear, ease, ease-in, ease-out, and ease-in-out values are convenient, and cubic-bezier() allows you to specify any continuous function you wish. The step-start and step-end values and the steps() function allow non-continuous timing so that the transition takes effect in stairstep fashion.

Finally, if you don't specify a value for the transition-delay property, then there will be no delay and the transition will begin the moment the CSS style rule takes effect. Adding a delay value of 2s would begin transitioning a full two seconds after the state change.

You can also apply multiple transition properties, but you don't do so by adding multiple style properties. Instead, you put the multiple properties into the same transition property and separate them with commas.

Listing 6-17 will animate both the background-color and the border-radius of our div, but the background-color will not begin for 2 seconds and will take 10 long seconds to complete. Hopefully, this example sets your imagination running on the possibilities of CSS transitions.

Listing 6-17. Different timing specified for the two properties

```css
/* CSS snippet */
#box:hover {
    background-color: gray;
    border-radius: 25px;
    transition: border-radius 2s, background-color 10s;
}
```

Not every CSS property is a candidate for transitioning, but nearly so. The actual list of transitionable properties, according to the W3C, contains background-image, background-position, border-color, border-width, border-spacing, bottom, color, crop, font-size, font-weight, grid-*, height, left, letter-spacing, line-height, margin, max-height, max-width, min-height, min-width, opacity, outline-color, outline-offset, outline-width, padding, right, text-indent, text-shadow, top, vertical-align, visibility, width, word-spacing, z-index, and zoom.

Transitions give us some good control over what happens to an element as it goes from one state to another. If we're really going to get a grip on how things move around our app, though, we'll need to dive into the subject of proper CSS animations.

Animations

CSS animations give us a lot more control over their target elements than transitions do. Transitions allow us to define a single transition from a start state to an end state, but animations allow the definition of an arbitrary number of keyframes that the entire animation can sequence through. With a transition I could change my div from white to gray, but with an animation I could change it from white to red to green to purple and then to gray, and I'd have control over the timing at each and every one of those steps along the way.

Animations are a little more complicated than transitions but, like most CSS concepts, are certainly not too much to understand. Animations are done in two separate steps.

The first step is to define your animation itself apart from any target elements that it might eventually apply to. This is done using a similar syntax to the definition of media queries and the definition of font faces. An animation definition looks like Listing 6-18.

Listing 6-18. The basic structure of an animation definition

```
@keyframes myAnimation {
    {keyframe1} {
        {properties}
    }
    {keyframe1} {
        {properties}
    }
    ...
    {keyframeN} {
        {properties}
    }
}
```

Animations can have any number of keyframes. The identifier for each keyframe can be either `from`, `to`, or a numeric percentage value. The `from` value is equivalent to 0% and the `to` value is equivalent to 100%. You don't have to specify a starting keyframe (`from`) or an ending keyframe (`to`). If you leave either off, it will get the property values of the target element back to where they were before the animation was applied.

Listing 6-19 defines an animation that will turn its target element from whatever color it was to gray, and then back again.

Listing 6-19. A single mid-point keyframe (start and end keyframes would be implicitly assumed)

```
/* CSS snippet */
@keyframes toGrayAndBack {
    50% {
        background-color: gray;
    }
}
```

The second step is to apply your animation to an element. This is done simply by adding the `animation-name` property to an elements style collection (or applying a class to an element which contains the `animation-name` property).

Like transitions, animations begin the moment this application takes effect. If an element is defined with an animation-name property, then the animation will begin the moment the page is loaded. To trigger an animation using JavaScript, you can apply the animation to a style and then programmatically add that style to the element you wish to animate.

The animation properties are `animation-name`, `animation-duration`, `animation-timing-function`, `animation-iteration-count`, `animation-direction`, `animation-play-state`, `animation-delay`, `animation-fill-mode`, and the `animation` shorthand property. I recommend using the `animation` shorthand property since it makes for much more readable code.

An animation application might look like Listing 6-20, which would determine the animation called `myAnimation` to wait for a one second delay, then follow an ease timing function for five seconds, and repeat that three times.

Listing 6-20. The application of the myAnimation animation to the element called myElement

```
#myElement {
    animation: myAnimation 5s ease 1s 3;
}
```

Notice the way the name myAnimation was defined in Listing 6-19 and the fact that the same exact animation name was used in Listing 6-20 to apply it. If these names don't match exactly, then the animation will not apply.

In Listing 6-21, then, we'll bring the definition and the application together. The code takes the toGrayAndBack animation that we created and applies it to a div element. You can see the div in Figure 6-15 taking four seconds to turn from white to gray and then back again. Notice that the first (from) and last (to) states are not defined in this animation. Only the middle (50%) is defined. The div is therefore white because no other background-color has ever been applied to it, and that's the state that the animation defaults to.

Listing 6-21. The animation definition and application together

```
<!-- HTML snippet -->
<div id="box"></div>

/* CSS snippet */
@keyframes toGrayAndBack {
    50% {
        background-color: gray;
    }
}

#box { animation: toGrayAndBack 4s; }
```

Figure 6-15. *Five frames showing the animation of the element's background color from white to gray and back to white again*

Now we'll progress some by defining more than a single keyframe. Listing 6-22 includes three keyframes in which the first and the last are not assumed from the object but specified explicitly. Keep in mind that if your first and last keyframes are not identical, then you'll have a hard time creating a looping animation without introducing a jarring transition.

Listing 6-22. The start and end keyframes included explicitly

```
<!-- HTML snippet -->
<div id="box">
</div>
```

```
/* CSS snippet */
@keyframes toBlackToGray {
    start {
        background-color: white;
    }
    50% {
        background-color: black;
    }
    end {
        background-color: gray;
    }
}

#box {
    animation: toBlackToGray 4s;
}
```

Figure 6-16. *Five frames illustrating the animation of the background from white to black and then to gray*

I should note a convenient shortcut here. The keyframe names such as start, 50%, and end can be combined and separated with commas if the block definitions are identical. Many times you'll start and end with the same set of properties, and you can shorthand that with this method. Listing 6-23 offers an example of this technique for taking its target element from white to black and back again to white.

Listing 6-23. Two keyframes being defined together. It is fine to define keyframes out of order.

```
/* CSS snippet */
@keyframes toBlackAndBack {
    start, end {
        background-color: white;
    }
    50% {
        background-color: black;
    }
}
```

Finally, Listing 6-24 progresses us even further by using three intermediate keyframes to move one div in orbit around another.

Listing 6-24. HTML and CSS to create two div elements and animation, the orbiting of one around the other

```
<!-- HTML snippet -->
<div id="fixed"></div>
<div id="orbit"></div>

/* CSS snippet */
#fixed {
    background-color: black;
    width: 100px;
    height: 100px;
    position: relative;
    left: 150px;
    top: 250px;
}

#orbit {
    background-color: gray;
    width: 100px;
    height: 100px;
    position: relative;
    left: 0px;
    top: 0px;
    animation: orbit 10s linear infinite;
}

@keyframes orbit {
    25% {
            left: 300px;
            top: 0px;
        }
    50% {
            left: 300px;
            top: 300px;
        }
    75% {
            left: 0px;
            top: 300px;
        }
}
```

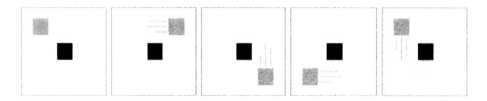

Figure 6-17. *The gray div follows a linear timing path around the black one*

Besides just a list of properties that should take effect, a keyframe can also specify a timing function. This means that you can either specify one timing function for all of your keyframes to adopt by putting it in the animation application on the target element, or you can specify multiple timing functions inside each keyframe and have them each work however you would like, even if they're different from one another.

It's impressive that so much animation can be done with declarative CSS alone, but it's quite likely you'll need to incorporate some logic into the animation of your visual assets, and you'll need to use JavaScript for that. In a card game, for instance, you don't know what choices a user is going to make until he or she makes them, and you'll need to respond and animate accordingly.

One of the first provisions you get for CSS animations is the ability to capture animation-based events. The available events are animationstart, animationiteration, and animationend, and the function of each is quite likely evident from its name, so I'll spare you the explanation. These events are fired on the target element, so you can wire up your event handler like Listing 6-25.

Listing 6-25. Implementation of an event handler for the animationstart event

```
ready: function (element, options) {
    document.querySelector("#myElement").addEventListener("animationstart", function(e) {
        // do something
    });
}
```

The animation events are certainly very helpful when you need to react logically to the state of animation on some element. As an example, you may wish to trigger the start of an animation when another animation ends. That code might look like Listing 6-26, in which a class is added to elementB when elementA has completed its animation.

Listing 6-26. Addition of a class to an element to trigger an animation when another ends

```
ready: function (element, options) {
    var elementA = document.querySelector("#elementA");
    var elementB = document.querySelector("#elementB");
    elementA.addEventListener("animationend", function(e) {
        elementB.classList.add("flash");
    });
}
```

MSCSSMatrix Object

We've discussed a myriad of ways you can apply CSS properties to improve your app with transforms, but the discussion would be incomplete without an introduction to the MSCSSMatrix object. Besides all of these properties that you specify in your CSS file, the MSCSSMatrix JavaScript object allows you to apply all of the transformations we've discussed so far *in your script*. This implies that you can add logic and more complex timing to them.

A simple example should make it clear. Listing 6-27 includes no CSS at all, but only HTML and JavaScript. Assume the JavaScript exists inside of a ready method that fires when the DOM is ready.

Listing 6-27. *A simple div with text instructed by JavaScript to rotate ten degrees counter-clockwise about the z-axis*

```
<!-- HTML snippet -->
<div class="parent">
    Hello world
</div>

// JavaScript snippet
var d = document.querySelector(".parent");
d.style.transform = new MSCSSMatrix(d.style.transform).rotate(0, 0, -10);
```

Hello world

Figure 6-18. *The resulting, rotated text, accomplished with no explicit CSS written*

In this example we've utilized the `rotate` function, but all of the other transformation functions are available, and of course, you can still set your matrix values manually too.

It's exciting to imagine what can be done with the power of the CSS transformations available to us in JavaScript. You can find much more information about the MSCSSMatrix object on the Microsoft MSDN website at `http://msdn.microsoft.com/en-us/library/windows/apps/hh453593.aspx`.

The introduction of transforms, transitions, and animations in CSS3 are just some of the reasons why the web stack is one of the world's most powerful (as well as ubiquitous) user-interface technologies in existence.

Summary

So far, we've been looking at examples that include only a handful of basic elements. In a real app scenario, you would be required to get more visual assets on the screen and to lay them out in a way that has meaning and implements good design.

The layout elements and techniques that you'll get in CSS, as well as some assistance from the WinJS library, will give you the power you need to turn your design into a working model, and we'll look at those layout techniques in the next chapter.

CHAPTER 7

Layout Properties

■ **Note**   CSS's ability to drive layout without driving developers crazy has been a long time coming. It's pretty much always been a sore spot.

The web stack's long history of somewhat less than stellar layout support is caused by a few things, in my opinion. First, we had tables, and tables sufficed to some degree. Sure, they were never the right place to define your layout, but were sufficient. Second, web development targets many browsers on a variety of devices, and attempts to define a document that adapts to its display. Contrast this to the print world where a standard sheet of paper never changes size and visual artifacts can be positioned anywhere.

Layout is still challenging in HTML, but gone are the days where developers are mourning their lack of options. Today we see more developers arguing constructively about which of the many options works best in a particular scenario.

Legacy layout

Tables are a very early element in HTML. Chances are good that you've had some experience with HTML tables, but if you haven't, then just know that they've been used for much more than tabular data. They've been used for layout as well.

The only HTML implement I would consider to be as rudimentary as tables (or perhaps even more so) is framesets. Websites have been laid out with navigation panes and header and footer panes, and framesets were the means to achieve them with different HTML files loading in each pane. Framesets brought their own set of pains both for the developers and the users, so the recommendation became the use of tables with all content defined in a single HTML file.

Besides tables, the topic of legacy layout should also include the use of plain old div elements with display and position properties used to wrangle them into place.

Table layout

Table layout is actually quite flexible and effective and I would imagine that a number of site designers are still relying on it today. I also bet those designers are keeping the fact a secret from their peers, because tables are by no means the current recommendation. They're not recommended because they're cross purpose to maintaining a separation of concerns and because they're not adaptable - two core principles in web design.

Remember that HTML defines the structure and CSS defines the style? The HTML allows you to define the elements in use and their hierarchical relationship to each other, but should say nothing of the positioning of those elements. Layout, rather, is a style and it belongs in CSS. Putting your layout into your HTML in the form of tables may get the job done, but it results in a site that is not capable of being as adaptable as modern apps and devices need it to be.

Defining layout with a table makes certain assertions like "this content must be below this content" or "this content must be contained in this area," and they lock the site into those assertions.

Listing 7-1 shows a table that may very well define the layout of a document.

Listing 7-1. The table element used as layout

```
<!-- HTML snippet -->
<table>
    <tr><td rowspan="3" id="nav"></td><td rowspan="3"></td><td></td></tr>
    <tr><td></td></tr>
    <tr><td></td></tr>
    <tr><td colspan="3" id="footer"></td></tr>
</table>

/* CSS snippet */
table{
    width:1100px;
    height: 560px;
    border-collapse: collapse;
}

table td {
    border: 2px solid black;
    padding: 5px;
}

#nav {
    width:180px;
}

#footer {
    height:80px;
}
```

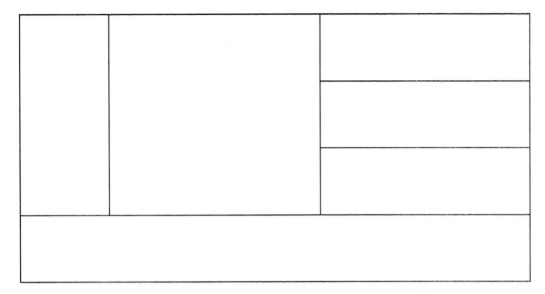

Figure 7-1. *This sample layout looks pretty good, but using tables to define layout is never a good idea*

Display and Position

If tables are taboo in layout, then what? The next more elegant solution is to use div elements with display and position properties to manually send them where they should go on the screen. A div (short for division) is an abstract element that is generally meant to separate bits of content from one another. It's rendered in block mode which means that preceding and succeeding elements render above and below it. This is in contrast to inline elements, which flow like text in a word processor.

These div elements can be formatted and positioned with styling properties, which makes them a good replacement for tables in layout. They are ubiquitous on the web today, but that's not to say they are a delight for a developer to deal with! The techniques that have been available for using div elements as layout have brought their own pains and that's why web developers everywhere are excited about the advent of new formatting capabilities that are either here already or coming soon. Nevertheless, we'll discuss classic div positioning in good detail here, because it's foundational and because you're sure to see it in the "wild."

The display property determines how its target is going to be displayed and becomes a very important property in the subject of layout. The valid values for the display property (including the Microsoft vendor-specific values) are inline, block, list-item, run-in, inline-block, table, inline-table, table-row-group, table-header-group, table-footer-group, table-row, table-column-group, table-column, table-cell, table-caption, -ms-flexbox, -ms-inline-flexbox, -ms-grid, -ms-inline-grid, and none.

Display Properties

There are a lot of values, so I think we need at least a cursory introduction to some of the display properties to get a full understanding of layout.

inline

When an element is inline, it acts like text in a word processor—that is, it renders horizontal to its previous sibling element, it flows from one line to the next, and it affects its own line-height. Inline elements are not affected by attempts to size them with width and height.

block

Block elements take up as much width as they can, which forces them to be on their own line. Specifying multiple block elements results in the elements being stacked vertically when rendered. Block elements can be sized.

inline-block

Elements set to display as `inline-block` act like an inline element from its parent's point of view, but they render themselves and their children as a block element. This is an effective way to create multiple `div` elements that show up next to one another like text does.

list-item

An element set to `display: list-item` renders as if it were an item in a list. A *marker box* and a *block box* are created for the element giving it a bullet and a left margin that you would expect.

run-in

The `run-in` value is an interesting and rather artistic single-use value that is often used for headers. If a header is set to display as `run-in` then it will render on the same line as a paragraph of text immediately below it and force the text to scoot over to make room.

inline-table and table-*

All of the behavior of the various components of a table (a row, a cell, etc.) can be emulated by setting an elements display to the various table properties. The reason, you'll recall, that using tables in your HTML is bad practice is because layout is not the job for HTML. If you implement your tables using these style properties, though, then you get all of the layout benefits of tables without the drawbacks. I still don't recommend it though.

-ms-flexbox and -ms-inline-flexbox

A flexbox is a really powerful element for laying out content. Flexboxes are intelligent about the way their children are rendered and give you the ability to flow, wrap, stretch, align, and do even more. There's a whole section dedicated to flexboxes coming up. Using the `-ms-flexbox` value will create a block style element and using `-ms-inline-flexbox` will create an inline flexbox.

-ms-grid and -ms-inline-grid

Grids also give you some excellent control over how child elements are laid out. Grids allow specific placement of content in a way that can still adapt to changes in size and position. Just like flexbox there is a block and an inline version.

Once you have chosen the appropriate display value for your element, you should know your options for positioning it.

Position Properties

Positioning is done by way of the `position` property and the values are `static`, `absolute`, `relative`, and `fixed`. The value of `static` is the default. The benefits of the position values are described in the following sections.

static

The default static value doesn't do any extra work to position the object. Whether it's an inline or a block element, its position is determined by its position in the HTML file.

absolute

An absolute value sets an element up to be placed anywhere relative to its parent if its parent is positioned. If its parent is not positioned then it will be relative to the document body. Elements that are positioned absolutely are taken out of the document flow and stop affecting it. They no longer push other elements around or get pushed around by them.

relative

Like the absolute value, the relative value sets you up to explicitly place your element, but placement values are taken to be relative to where the element would have rendered if it were static. It's a great way to move an element a little to the left.

fixed

The fixed value works similar to absolute, but it takes into account the viewport that it is in, so if it is rendered in a scrolling div, it can be placed relative to that div.

Every position value except for static sets you up to determine the placement of your element and you do so by specifying values for left, right, top, and bottom. For absolute and fixed positions, these properties determine the placement of the four edges of your element relative to another element, but for the relative position, they determine the placement of that edge relative to where the element would have been rendered if static.

Listing 7-2 shows an example of a simple row of square div elements (laid out using a flexbox which we'll discuss soon). The third element is told to have a position value of relative (as opposed to the default of static) and then is told to scoot 15 pixels to the right and down. The effect is to displace the box from its place as you can see in Figure 7-2.

Listing 7-2. Setting an element's position to relative and its left and top to 15 pixels

```
<!-- HTML snippet -->
<div id="dpFlexbox">
    <div></div>
    <div></div>
    <div></div>
    <div></div>
    <div></div>
</div>

/* CSS snippet */
#dpFlexbox {
    display: -ms-flexbox;
}

#dpFlexbox > div {
    border: 1px solid black;
    width: 100px;
    height: 100px;
    margin: 5px;
}
```

```
#dpFlexbox > div:nth-of-type(3) {
    position: relative;
    background-color: gray;
    left: 15px;
    top: 15px;
}
```

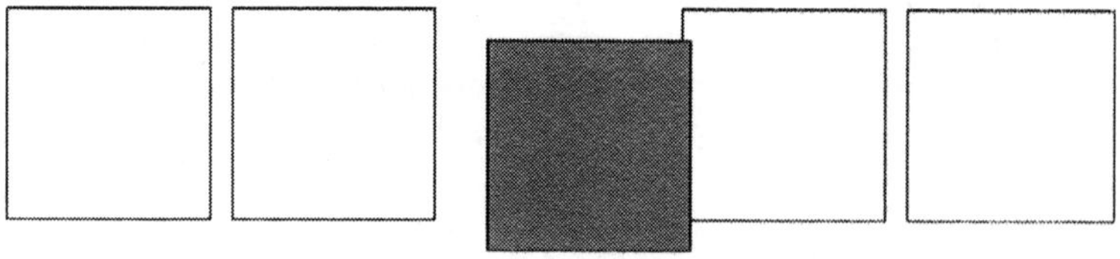

Figure 7-2. *The element is offset from the space it would have occupied*

Listing 7-3 shows the same five boxes with the third one again given values of 15 pixels for the left and top, but this time the position is set to absolute. As you can see, the gray box has now been moved to 15 pixels from the top-left corner of the document. Notice too in Figure 7-3 that the other div elements have collapsed together, since the third one was pulled out of the flow.

Listing 7-3. Setting the position to absolute this time

```
<!-- HTML snippet -->
<div id="dpFlexbox">
    <div></div>
    <div></div>
    <div></div>
    <div></div>
    <div></div>
</div>

/* CSS snippet */
#dpFlexbox {
    display: -ms-flexbox;
}

#dpFlexbox > div {
    border: 1px solid black;
    width: 100px;
    height: 100px;
    margin: 5px;
}

#dpFlexbox > div:nth-of-type(3) {
    position: absolute;
    background-color: gray;
    left: 15px;
    top: 15px;
}
```

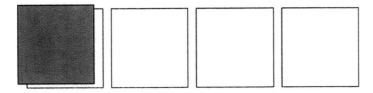

Figure 7-3. *The element goes to the top-left corner of the document and loses its place in the list of div elements*

We discussed the margin, border, and padding properties already, but I want to bring to your attention that they do play a big role in content layout. One of the core principles in Windows 8 design is that *Less is More*. It means that we aren't trying to pack as much information on the screen as we can. We aren't trying to keep the user one click from everything as seems to be the trend in website design. So we're not afraid to add some intentional, purposeful breathing room to our content's layout. This usually takes the form of a margin or a padding, so be ready to use them.

Floating

Block-level elements can be told to *float* using the float property. A floating element allows subsequent inline content to render next to itself (instead of below). You can provide values of left or right to determine which side of the block-level element content should populate.

When used as it was intended, floating works quite well, but web developers have been using it for some time to get block-level elements to facilitate layout.

Using float for layout though reminds you that it's not so comfortable in its imposed role.

Modern Layout

Luckily, we're not restricted to the old way of laying out content. We have more modern facilities now that are expectedly simpler and more powerful at the same time. The particularly painful parts of web development have a way of provoking enough demand for something new.

Flexbox

There's still quite a bit of tumult in the standards recommendations and implementations for flexboxes, but IE10 and Windows 8 has a good, solid implementation of this extremely helpful layout technique.

Flexboxes solve an old problem. The abstract div elements that we've been using for so long for laying out our content were designed as block elements. Modern user interfaces and especially the interface in Windows 8 are full of flowing lists of products, friends' pictures, and pictures.

While it was rarely impossible to implement the necessary layout using classic div positioning and floating, it's very often painful. Flexboxes alleviate most or all of that pain.

Directing a list of elements to lay out as a flexbox is as easy as setting display: -ms-flexbox; on its parent. The default layout direction is horizontal, so as soon as this one property is added, child elements will begin flowing from left to right. This is helpful on its own, but it's only the start. Flexboxes also enable you to size the items and the space along the axis of layout and also perpendicular to the axis of layout. They also allow you to control the layout direction and order of your content regardless of how it is specified in the HTML.

Flexbox Properties

Let me introduce you to the remainder of the flexbox related properties and values and explain their function. The following properties would be added to the parent element (the one we added `display: -ms-flexbox;` to).

-ms-flex-direction

Determines the direction that child elements flow. You would use the default value of `row` to lay items out left to right or `column` to lay items out top to bottom. You can also use `row-reverse` for right to left or `column-reverse` for bottom to top.

-ms-flex-align

The `-ms-flex-align` property handles the spacing *perpendicular* to the direction that items are laid out. Assuming we have a flexbox with a direction set to `row`, a value of `start` would line child elements up along the top of the row, `center` would line them up in the center, and `end` would line them up along the bottom. Additionally, `baseline` would line up the leading edges and `stretch` (which is the default) would grow each element to fit the space. And the inverse is true for flexboxes with a direction set to `column`.

-ms-flex-pack

Similar to how `-ms-flex-align` handles spacing perpendicular to the direction, `-ms-flex-pack` handles spacing *inline* with the direction. With a value of `start`, you can direct all child elements to pack into the left side (still assuming a flexbox with a direction of `row`), with `center` to pack into the center, with `end` to pack into the right, and with `justify` you can direct the child elements to equalize their spacing so they fit nicely from start to end in their allotted space.

-ms-flex-wrap

The `-ms-flex-wrap` property gives you control over what happens when the child elements reach the end of the flexbox. Wrapping is a great way to lay out content. Use `wrap` to turn on wrapping or leave it set to its default value of `none` to turn it off.

-ms-flex-flow

The `-ms-flex-direction` and `-ms-flex-wrap` are common properties and a shorthand property of `-ms-flex-flow` has been provided to encapsulate them.

Again, the properties mentioned so far should be applied to the *parent* element—the flexbox itself. The following properties, on the other hand, should be added to the *child* elements:

-ms-flex

The `-ms-flex` property is a rather important one. It takes up to three values (separated by spaces as you might guess) which are the amount of *positive flex*, the amount of *negative flex*, and the *preferred size*. You can also use the value of `none` which is equivalent to a value of `0 0 auto`. An item's positive flex is its ability to grow along the axis of direction, and its negative flex is its ability to shrink. The integer value you set for flex determines the relative (relative to other flex items, that is) size change. If this isn't clear, then see the example in Listing 7-7.

-ms-flex-order

Finally, the -ms-flex-order is also an integer value and specifies the group that the child item belongs to. Setting a group may not seem related to ordering at first, but if you gave every item its own group number (0,1,2,3,...), then the flex order would arrange your items accordingly. If you don't provide values for the flex order or if you put all of the items in the same group then their order will not change from how it is specified in the DOM.

That's the breakdown on the properties, but let's take a look at some flexboxes in action to get a good feel for when and how we should use them.

Listing 7-4 defines a very simple flexbox. This one requires a single line of CSS and effectively lays out the child elements horizontally.

Listing 7-4. Setting a parent div's display property to -ms-flexbox

```
<!-- HTML snippet -->
<div id="flexbox">
    <div></div>
    <div></div>
    <div></div>
    <div></div>
    <div></div>
</div>

/* CSS snippet */
#flexbox {
    display: -ms-flexbox;
}

#flexbox > div {
    border: 1px solid black;
    width: 100px;
    height: 100px;
    margin: 5px;
}
```

The flexbox value is lightweight and easy to define and you'll find great uses for it all over the place once you start looking.

The flexbox in Figure 7-4 did not have a size specified, so it just conformed to the size of its contents. Note in Listing 7-5, how the contents are laid out when we add width and height properties (and add a border for visibility) to the flexbox.

Figure 7-4. *The flexbox is horizontal by default and lays our div elements out nicely*

Listing 7-5. Adding some dimensions and a border to the flexbox

```
<!-- HTML snippet -->
<div id="flexbox">
    <div></div>
    <div></div>
    <div></div>
    <div></div>
    <div></div>
</div>

/* CSS snippet */
#flexbox {
    display: -ms-flexbox;
    width: 800px;
    height: 300px;
    border: 3px solid lightgray;
}

#flexbox > div {
    border: 1px solid black;
    width: 100px;
    height: 100px;
    margin: 5px;
}
```

Figure 7-5. *The child elements are all aligned to the top and left by default*

The contents take the top and the left. All of the functionality that you see so far only involves a single flexbox-related property: the display: -ms-flexbox. The layout is being controlled by a number of default values. Let me bring those to light.

First, the direction property is defaulted to row, and that's why the contents are laid out horizontally. Also, the pack and align properties are defaulted to start which puts the contents in the upper-left corner of the flexbox. We can get creative with these properties, however, and really control how these boxes behave.

In Listing 7-6, we set the pack of the flexbox to distribute. We also change the width and height of the boxes to be minimums and set them free to grow. The default value for the items to align property is stretch. Remember that the pack is the spacing along the direction of layout—horizontal in this case, and align is the spacing perpendicular to the direction of layout—vertical in this case.

Listing 7-6. Packing is set to distribute and alignment will adopt its default value of stretch

```
<!-- HTML snippet -->
<div id="flexbox">
    <div></div>
    <div></div>
    <div></div>
    <div></div>
    <div></div>
</div>

/* CSS snippet */
#flexbox {
    display: -ms-flexbox;
    -ms-flex-pack: distribute;
    width: 800px;
    height: 300px;
    border: 3px solid lightgray;
}

#flexbox > div {
    border: 1px solid black;
    min-width: 100px;
    min-height: 100px;
    margin: 5px;
}
```

Figure 7-6. The child elements are spaced out evenly and stretch vertically to fill their container

Never before have we seen such simple control over item layout in HTML, and it doesn't end here.

These elements have all been stretched to be the same height, but if they weren't, then our align property would be able to handle many different configurations for lining them up.

Besides the alignment (-ms-flex-align) and packing (-ms-flex-pack) control, we also have some say in how the items *flex*. Flexing happens along the direction of layout and is the expanding or shrinking of an item to fill the void space. The properties we've set so far have been at the flexbox level, but the flex properties work on the items themselves since they all may be different values.

In Listing 7-7, we've removed the min-width value from the items, instructed the second and fourth items (the even items) to flex with a relative value of two, and told the first, third, and fifth items (the odd items) to flex with a relative value of one. In the result in Figure 7-7, you can see that the items have done just as we've asked and adopted their relative width values to fill all space in the flexbox. Tremendous!

Listing 7-7. Instructing the child items to "flex" with different relative flex values

```
<!-- HTML snippet -->
<div id="flexbox">
    <div></div>
    <div></div>
    <div></div>
    <div></div>
    <div></div>
</div>

/* CSS snippet */
#flexbox {
    display: -ms-flexbox;
    width: 800px;
    height: 300px;
    border: 3px solid lightgray;
}

#flexbox > div {
    border: 1px solid black;
    min-height: 100px;
    margin: 5px;
}

    flexbox > div:nth-child(odd) {
        -ms-flex: 1;
    }

    #flexbox > div:nth-child(even) {
        -ms-flex: 2;
    }
```

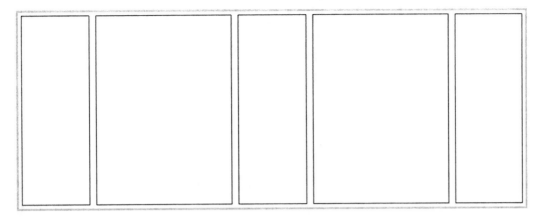

Figure 7-7. *All items are flexing, but the even items are taking up twice the horizontal space*

There's one more flexbox talent that you should see before we move on to study the grid.

If a flexbox's items do have explicit sizing and they overrun the flexbox, the flexbox handles them like any other `div` with overflow—by default it would show the overflow escaping its bounds. It would look something like Figure 7-8.

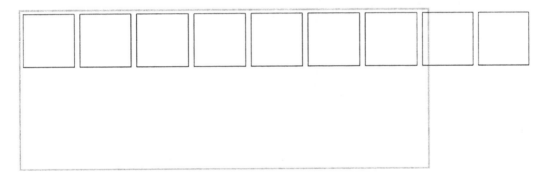

Figure 7-8. *A flexbox with too many child items and no wrapping will overflow its bounds*

Regular `div` elements allow us to hide or scroll the overflowing content, but a flexbox goes a step further and allows you to wrap the contents as you can see in Listing 7-8. Voila!

Listing 7-8. Add wrapping to the flexbox

```
<!-- HTML snippet -->
<div id="flexbox">
    <div></div>
    <div></div>
    <div></div>
    <div></div>
    <div></div>
    <div></div>
    <div></div>
    <div></div>
    <div></div>
</div>
```

```
/* CSS snippet */
#flexbox {
    display: -ms-flexbox;
    -ms-flex-wrap: wrap;
    width: 800px;
    height: 300px;
    border: 3px solid lightgray;
    -ms-flex-pack: start;
}

#flexbox > div {
    border: 1px solid black;
    width: 100px;
    height: 100px;
    margin: 5px;
}
```

Figure 7-9. *The items are wrapped to the next line*

Using a Flexbox in a Windows 8 App

I've shown you technically what the various properties and features of a flexbox are, but I think it will help to see a flexbox in action in a Windows 8 app.

The goal in this example will be to create a container in which a single child item is in view and the subsequent child item is peeking in from the right, inviting the user to swipe to reveal it. Snap points should help the user bring the scroll position to exactly the next item. Flexboxes are very good at this scenario, so let's see how we would implement this. Listing 7-9 shows a simple and effective solution that takes advantage of our friend the flexbox.

Listing 7-9. The complete HTML, CSS, and JavaScript to create a container with swipeable content

```
<!-- HTML snippet -->
<div class="swiper">
    <div>
        <h3>Lorem Ipsum</h3>
```

```
        <p>Lorem ipsum dolor sit amet, consectetur adipiscing...</p>
        <p>Donec dignissim tempor risus, in iaculis odio...</p>
    </div>
    <div>
        <h3>Maecenas velit</h3>
        <p>In hac habitasse platea dictumst. Quisque facilisis...</p>
        <p>Maecenas velit nisi, accumsan tempor tincidunt vel...</p>
    </div>
    <div>
        <h3>Nisl augue</h3>
        <p>Nulla rhoncus, nulla at convallis pretium, nisl augue...</p>
        <p>Donec tempor urna venenatis neque ornare congue...</p>
    </div>
</div>

/* CSS snippet */
.swiper {
    border:2px solid gray;
    display:-ms-flexbox;
    height:400px;
    width:600px;
    overflow-x:auto;
    -ms-scroll-snap-x:mandatory snapInterval(0%,80%);
}

.swiper > div {
    width: 80%;
    padding-left:40px;
    box-sizing: border-box;
    overflow-y:auto;
    margin-bottom:16px; /* room for vertical scrollbar */
    padding-right:16px; /* room for vertical scrollbar */
}

.swiper > div:last-child {
    width:100%;
}
```

This solution in Listing 7-9 does demand an explanation.

First, the HTML defines a simple div element with three child div elements, each containing its own content. The containing div has been assigned a class of swiper. Using a class to add this functionality is a smart way to do it because it means it will be simple to add this functionality to any element we wish by simply adding the class.

The first style rule targets elements with that swiper class. For this rule, we use the all-important display:-ms-flexbox; property. This property alone sets up all of the child elements to layout next to one another. The border and height and width properties are somewhat arbitrary and just used for visibility. The last two properties are important, though.

The overflow-x:auto; property sets the element to scroll horizontally if its content is wider than the container. The last property, -ms-scroll-snap-x:mandatory snapInterval(0%,80%);, is responsible for halting the user's pan gestures at sensible increments, namely when an item's edge is at the left side of the container. Notice that the second parameter to the snapInterval in that property value is 80%. The reason for that will be clear after seeing the determined width of child elements in the next style rule.

The next style rule's selector is `.swiper > div`. You'll recognize the child combinatory which makes the style rule that uses this selector target *every div element that is a direct child of an element with a class of swiper*.

The children of the flexbox should be 80% wide (and should match the value of the `-ms-scroll-snap` property of the containing element. This allows 20% of the content of the next child item to "peek" into the frame eluding to content to come and inviting the user to request it. Furthermore, each child should have 40 pixels of padding on the left side to separate them from each other, but that 80% width we selected should use a `box-sizing` value of `border-box` to include the padding value with the overall width.

It's not ideal to allow any of the child items to overflow vertically. Doing so opens the user up to getting confused between the two different scroll directions. Nevertheless, the `overflow-y: auto;` property will assure that if content does get too tall at least it won't spill over the bottom, but will render a scroll bar instead.

The last two properties for that rule provide bottom margin and right padding to allow room for the scroll bars to render without covering up the content.

The last style rule is a simple one that only states that the last child should not be 80% wide, but rather 100%. Without this property applying to the last child, the mandatory snap points will not allow you to navigate to the last element.

You can see the results of this code in Figure 7-10, but better yet you should explore the behavior of this solution by looking at the source code.

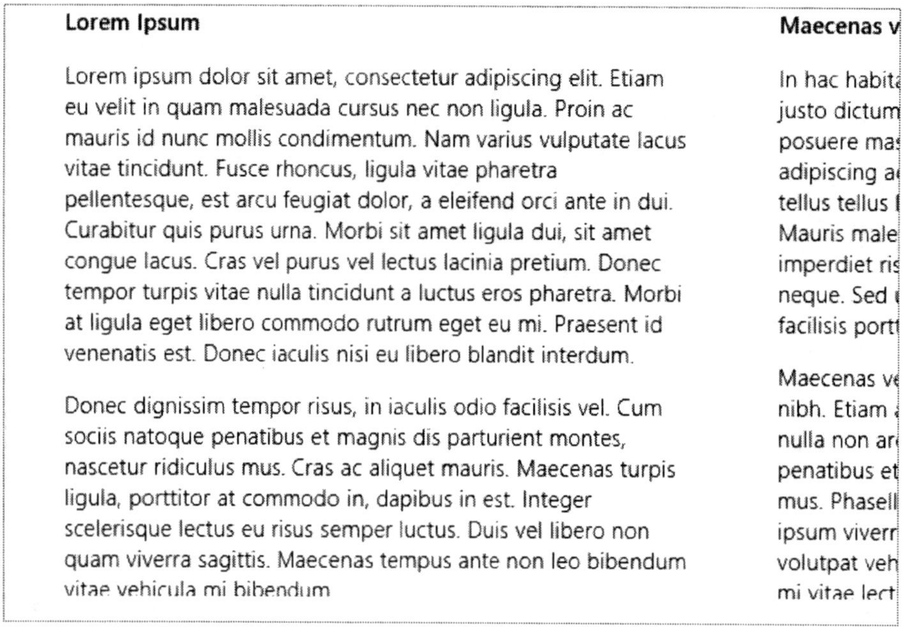

Lorem Ipsum

Lorem ipsum dolor sit amet, consectetur adipiscing elit. Etiam eu velit in quam malesuada cursus nec non ligula. Proin ac mauris id nunc mollis condimentum. Nam varius vulputate lacus vitae tincidunt. Fusce rhoncus, ligula vitae pharetra pellentesque, est arcu feugiat dolor, a eleifend orci ante in dui. Curabitur quis purus urna. Morbi sit amet ligula dui, sit amet congue lacus. Cras vel purus vel lectus lacinia pretium. Donec tempor turpis vitae nulla tincidunt a luctus eros pharetra. Morbi at ligula eget libero commodo rutrum eget eu mi. Praesent id venenatis est. Donec iaculis nisi eu libero blandit interdum.

Donec dignissim tempor risus, in iaculis odio facilisis vel. Cum sociis natoque penatibus et magnis dis parturient montes, nascetur ridiculus mus. Cras ac aliquet mauris. Maecenas turpis ligula, porttitor at commodo in, dapibus in est. Integer scelerisque lectus eu risus semper luctus. Duis vel libero non quam viverra sagittis. Maecenas tempus ante non leo bibendum vitae vehicula mi bibendum

Maecenas v

In hac habit
justo dictum
posuere mas
adipiscing a
tellus tellus l
Mauris male
imperdiet ris
neque. Sed
facilisis port

Maecenas ve
nibh. Etiam
nulla non ar
penatibus et
mus. Phasell
ipsum viverr
volutpat veh
mi vitae lect

Figure 7-10. Subsequent content is available to the right and makes itself known by showing just a teaser

The flexbox is an exciting addition to the CSS family, but its primary function involves laying out data that should flow, flex, or form to the space it's allotted. To take a bit more structured approach, take a look at the new CSS grid.

Grid

The grid serves a very different purpose than the flexbox. The flexbox would help you make a list of products for a catalog as an example, but the grid would layout your whole UI and strongly contribute to its adaptability as well.

An element is turned into a grid by simply adding the display property to it with a value of -ms-grid. Look at what happens to the stack of div elements in Listing 7-10 when the only change we make is to direct their parent to be a grid.

Listing 7-10. Set a div to have a display value of -ms-grid

```
<!-- HTML snippet -->
<div id="grid">
    <div id="a">A</div>
    <div id="b">B</div>
    <div id="c">C</div>
    <div id="d">D</div>
</div>

/* CSS snippet */
#grid {
    display: -ms-grid;
    width: 800px;
    height: 300px;
    border: 3px solid lightgray;
}

#grid > div {
    border: 1px solid black;
    width: 100px;
    height: 100px;
    margin: 5px;
}
```

Figure 7-11. *The child items are stacked one on top of another*

That seems a little odd at first. All of the items are stacked right on top of each other. It doesn't seem like much of a layout tool yet. To remedy this, we should also define some rows and columns. Listing 7-11 does just that, defining a simple two by two grid so that each of our boxes can have its own space. Besides defining the rows, however, we also have to tell each element which row and column it belongs in. Any child elements of a grid that are not assigned a row or column take the default value of 1 and show up in the first row or column.

Listing 7-11. Add column and row assignments for each child item

```
<!-- HTML snippet -->
<div id="grid">
    <div id="a">A</div>
    <div id="b">B</div>
    <div id="c">C</div>
    <div id="d">D</div>
</div>

/* CSS snippet */
#grid {
    display: -ms-grid;
    -ms-grid-rows: 1fr 1fr;
    -ms-grid-columns: 1fr 1fr;
    width: 800px;
    height: 300px;
    border: 3px solid lightgray;
}

#grid > div {
    border: 1px solid black;
    width: 100px;
    height: 100px;
    margin: 5px;
}

#a { -ms-grid-row: 1; -ms-grid-column: 1; }
#b { -ms-grid-row: 1; -ms-grid-column: 2; }
#c { -ms-grid-row: 2; -ms-grid-column: 1; }
#d { -ms-grid-row: 2; -ms-grid-column: 2; }
```

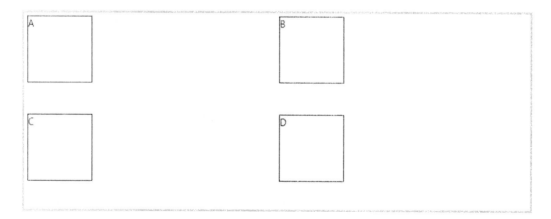

Figure 7-12. The child items go to their assigned cells

The rows for the grid have been defined as 1fr 1fr. This is a space-delimited list of the row height for all rows. In this case, we employ the `fr` unit designator, which stands for `fraction`. If all rows are given a fractional value of 1, then each will be granted an equal part of the available grid height.

It is also possible to define some rows to have an absolute height, in which case the fractional values determine each row's part of the total height minus all absolute value definitions. A grid row definition of 100px 1fr 100px would create a grid with a 100-pixel row on the top and bottom with the remaining space given to the middle row.

The fractional parts apply to the fraction *of the remaining space* after all of the absolute lengths are applied. For example, a 1000-pixel wide grid with a column value of 200px 1fr 3fr would get a column of 200 pixels (absolutely defined) plus a column of 200 pixels (1/4 of the remaining 800 pixels) plus a column of 600 pixels (3/4 of the remaining 800 pixels).

Let's say now that we want to define an app layout that includes a fixed header, some fixed space on the left, and then the remaining space divided equally in half (vertically). Take a look at Listing 7-12 to see how this would be done.

Listing 7-12. Set up an app layout using a grid

```
<!-- HTML snippet -->
<div id="grid">
    <div id="header">header</div>
    <div id="left">left</div>
    <div id="firstHalf">first half</div>
    <div id="secondHalf">second half</div>
</div>

/* CSS snippet */
#grid {
    display: -ms-grid;
    -ms-grid-rows: 120px 1fr;
    -ms-grid-columns: 120px 1fr 1fr;
    width: 1000px;
    height: 540px;
    border: 3px solid lightgray;
}

#grid > div {
    border: 1px solid black;
    margin: 5px;
    padding: 10px;
}

#header { -ms-grid-row: 1; -ms-grid-column: 1; }
#left { -ms-grid-row: 2; -ms-grid-column: 1; }
#firstHalf { -ms-grid-row: 2; -ms-grid-column: 2; }
#secondHalf { -ms-grid-row: 2; -ms-grid-column: 3; }
```

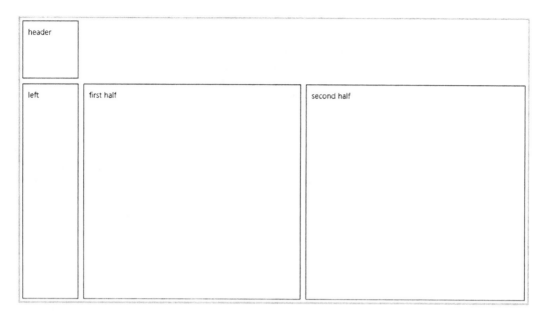

Figure 7-13. *The layout is implemented with just one small problem*

That layout looks pretty good, but we've got one small problem: the header item is only taking the first column. Another way the grid resembles its old table ancestor is in its ability to span rows or columns. In the previous example, we added a split in our main content session, but likely we would not want that to affect our header. The solution in Listing 7-13 simply defines our #header element to span three columns taking up the entire top of the layout. These span definitions apply to individual grid children, so it's perfectly valid to instruct one element to land in a single cell and another to span multiple. This is a considerable advantage over tables.

Listing 7-13. Add cell spanning to the header child item

```html
<!-- HTML snippet -->
<div id="grid">
    <div id="header">header</div>
    <div id="left">left</div>
    <div id="firstHalf">first half</div>
    <div id="secondHalf">second half</div>
</div>
```

```css
/* CSS snippet */
#grid {
    display: -ms-grid;
    -ms-grid-rows: 120px 1fr;
    -ms-grid-columns: 120px 1fr 1fr;
    width: 1000px;
    height: 540px;
    border: 3px solid lightgray;
}
```

```
#grid > div {
    border: 1px solid black;
    margin: 5px;
    padding: 10px;
}

#header { -ms-grid-row: 1; -ms-grid-column: 1; -ms-grid-column-span: 3; }
#left { -ms-grid-row: 2; -ms-grid-column: 1; }
#firstHalf { -ms-grid-row: 2; -ms-grid-column: 2; }
#secondHalf { -ms-grid-row: 2; -ms-grid-column: 3; }
```

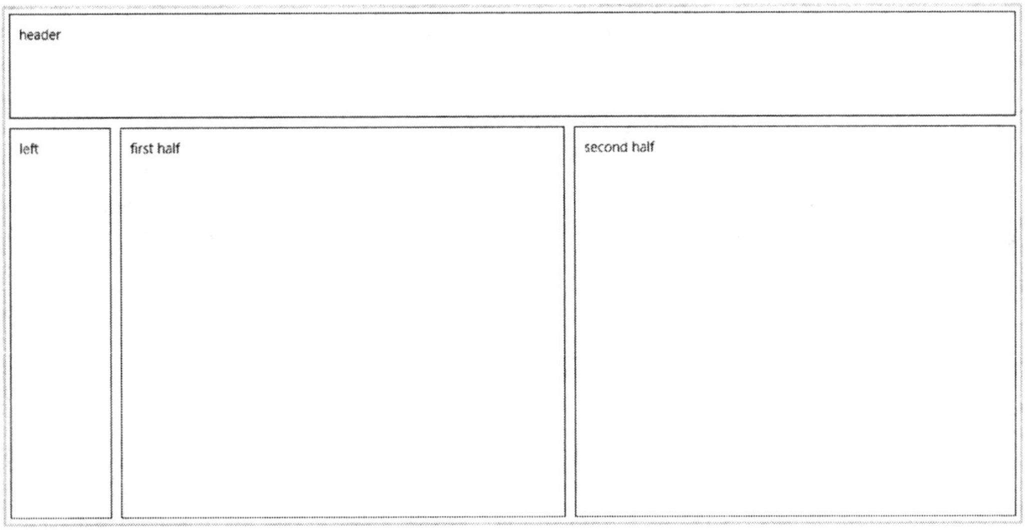

Figure 7-14. *The header spans three columns and takes up the entire top of our app layout*

Using a Grid in a Windows 8 App

Just like we did with the flexbox, we'll look at an example of using a grid in a real live Windows 8 app.

Let's imagine we're displaying a user's profile which includes his mug shot and a number of areas of information about him that form a layout something like what you see in Figure 7-15.

Figure 7-15. *A rough depiction of the desired profile layout*

This is a perfect candidate for a CSS grid. First, notice that our layout is arranged already into three columns. Next, notice that although our content does not form nice rows, we can achieve the same affect using three rows and then doing some spanning.

Figure 7-16. *The profile layout with some overlaid lines depicting how our grid should be setup*

Now let's dive into the solution.

Listing 7-14. A grid is defined and individual elements are placed and spanned accordingly

```html
<!-- HTML snippet -->
<div class="profile">
    <div class="image">image</div>
    <div class="section1">section 1</div>
    <div class="section2">section 2</div>
    <div class="section3">section 3</div>
    <div class="section4">section 4</div>
</div>
```

```css
/* CSS snippet */
.profile {
    display:-ms-grid;
    width:1025px;
    height:576px;
    -ms-grid-columns: 7fr 14fr 9fr;
    -ms-grid-rows: 120px 2fr 3fr;
}

.profile > div {
    border: 1px solid black;
    margin: 5px;
    padding: 5px;
    font-size:x-large;
}

.image {
    -ms-grid-row-span: 2;
}

.section1 {
    -ms-grid-row: 3;
}

.section2 {
    -ms-grid-column: 2;
    -ms-grid-row-span: 3;
}

.section3 {
    -ms-grid-column: 3;
}

.section4 {
    -ms-grid-column: 3;
    -ms-grid-row: 2;
    -ms-grid-row-span: 2;
}
```

Figure 7-17 is the result and is roughly equivalent to the initial diagram. I hope this convinces you that custom layouts for your Windows 8 views are easy to achieve using the CSS grid functionality.

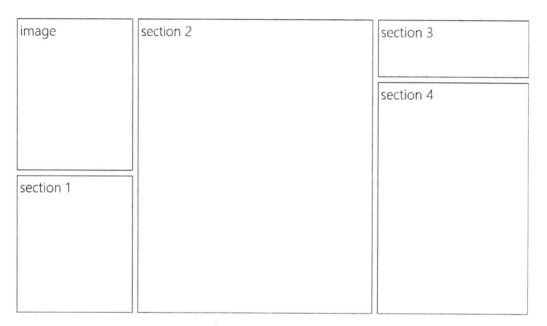

Figure 7-17. *The end result looks much like the profile layout we were after*

ViewBox and ListView

We've covered the legacy and modern layout implements offered to us by CSS, but when you're working on a Windows 8 app, you have the Windows Library for JavaScript (WinJS) available and you're provided some more modern layout control by WinJS. Even though they're not CSS properties, they're worth having a look at in the context of this book.

The first is the `WinJS.UI.ViewBox`. The ViewBox is a control that you can add content to when you want that content to scale automatically to changes in the app's view state. If an app is running on a tablet, for instance, it might be rotated to a portrait orientation, and in that case, it may be desirable to scale up or down the content within. I'm not talking about a re-rendering of its contents based on new dimensions. I'm talking about a straight scaling of the content exactly as it would have been rendered before the intervention of the ViewBox.

This scaling is made possible thanks to the scaling and translate transform functions that we already learned in Chapter 6. The ViewBox is happy to apply this effect for you, and the only thing it asks is that you give it no more than a single child item. This doesn't turn out to be much of a problem since even if you do have multiple child items all you really have to do is wrap them in a container like a simple div.

The ViewBox fits the child item without changing its aspect ratio as you can see in Figure 7-18. In a landscape orientation the height will constrain the child's size and in a portrait orientation the width will be the constraint.

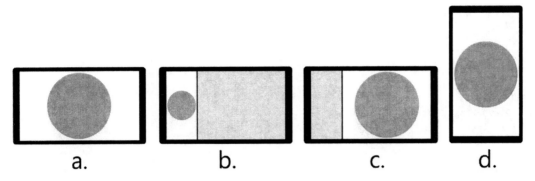

Figure 7-18. *How a simple shape would be rendered in a ViewBox in the full (a), snapped (b), fill (c), and portrait (d) view states*

Another WinJS provision on the topic of content layout is the very powerful `WinJS.UI.ListView` control. It's very common to list things out in an app. We're accustomed to seeing lists of friends, lists of stock prices, and lists of our email. These cases are covered well by the ListView, which is capable of laying out items as a grid with multiple rows and columns or as a vertical or horizontal list. The ListView has a few advantages over the more primitive flexboxes and grids, including but not limited to:

- Item selection
- Data binding to synchronous or asynchronous data sources
- Asymmetrical, cell-spanning layout
- Item grouping
- Custom render functions

Listing 7-15 shows the most basic ListView which is bound to the numbers one through eleven. Notice how a grid is used in the item template so that its contents can be centered horizontally and vertically.

Listing 7-15. The HTML, CSS, and JavaScript for implementing a ListView

```
<!-- HTML snippet -->
<div id="list" data-win-control="WinJS.UI.ListView"></div>
<div id="template" data-win-control="WinJS.Binding.Template">
    <div>
        <img data-win-bind="src:imageUrl" />
        <div data-win-bind="innerText:name"></div>
    </div>
</div>

/* CSS snippet */
.win-listview {
    height: 100%;
}

.win-listview .win-item .grid {
    display:-ms-grid;
    -ms-grid-rows:160px;
    -ms-grid-columns:160px;
```

```
    background-color:gray;
    color:white;
}

.win-listview .win-item .grid div {
    font-size: 36px;
    font-weight: bold;
    -ms-grid-column-align: center;
    -ms-grid-row-align: center;
}

// JavaScript snippet
var numbersList = new WinJS.Binding.List();

var list = document.getElementById("list").winControl;
list.itemTemplate = document.getElementById("template");
list.itemDataSource = numbersList.dataSource;

for (var i = 1; i <= 14; i++) {
    numbersList.push(i);
}
```

You may wonder if the ListView control itself uses a grid or a flexbox for its implementation, but actually it uses neither. The ListView is responsible for so many cases and combinations, that a bit more control was necessary, so it is implemented with custom positioning properties.

In Chapter 9, we will talk more about the ListView and learn how to target all of its individual components using CSS styling rules.

In Figure 7-19, you see a very basic ListView, but the ListView is capable of a lot of extended functionality including the grouping of items. In this case, headers are rendered above each group of items and the developer must provide a header template to define how that header should look.

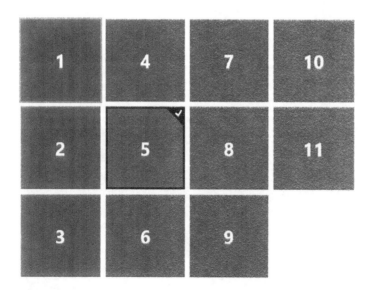

Figure 7-19. *The ListView is implemented and a single item is selected for effect*

Listing 7-16 starts with the same ListView from Listing 7-15, and then adds the header template and the JavaScript code necessary to do a simple grouping.

Listing 7-16. Add HTML and JavaScript to implement grouping on the ListView

```
<!-- HTML snippet -->
<div id="list" data-win-control="WinJS.UI.ListView"></div>
<div id="template" data-win-control="WinJS.Binding.Template">
    <div class="grid">
        <div data-win-bind="innerText:this"></div>
    </div>
</div>
<div id="headerTemplate" data-win-control="WinJS.Binding.Template">
    <h2 data-win-bind="innerText:this"></h2>
</div>

/* CSS snippet */
.win-listview {
    height: 100%;
}

.win-listview .win-item .grid {
    display:-ms-grid;
    -ms-grid-rows:160px;
    -ms-grid-columns:160px;
    background-color:gray;
    color:white;
}

.win-listview .win-item .grid div {
    font-size: 36px;
    font-weight: bold;
    -ms-grid-column-align: center;
    -ms-grid-row-align: center;
}

// JavaScript snippet
var numbersList = new WinJS.Binding.List().createGrouped(
    function(n) { return (n % 2 == 0 ? "even" : "odd"); },
    function(n) { return (n % 2 == 0 ? "even" : "odd"); }
);

var list = document.querySelector("#list").winControl;
list.itemTemplate = document.querySelector("#template");
list.itemDataSource = numbersList.dataSource;
list.itemHeaderTemplate = document.querySelector(".lst0714 #headerTemplate");
list.groupDataSource = numbersList.groups.dataSource;

for (var i = 1; i <= 11; i++) {
    numbersList.push(i);
}
```

As you can see in Figure 7-20, the even and odd numbered items are separated into different groups and the h2 element that we defined in our header template is announcing which is which. A couple of items have been selected for effect.

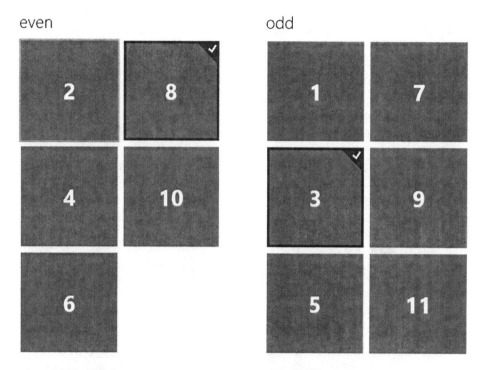

Figure 7-20. *The ListView items are grouped by even and odd values*

So far we've seen two ListViews that have symmetrically sized items, but it is possible to allow items to expand as long as they are even multiples of the smallest tile size in both width and height (plus the margin). The tiles in Listing 7-15 and Listing 7-16 are 160 pixels wide and high. A larger tile (expanded both in width and height) would be 330 pixels—160 times 2 plus the 10-pixel margin. We have to not only set some of our items to a new size, but we also must add a groupInfo function to our list's layout. Listing 7-17 implements an asymmetrical ListView completely.

Listing 7-17. The ListView is upgraded to allow cell spanning

```
<!-- HTML snippet -->
<div id="list" data-win-control="WinJS.UI.ListView"></div>
<div id="template" data-win-control="WinJS.Binding.Template">
    <div data-win-bind="className:size;">
        <div data-win-bind="innerText:number" class="number"></div>
    </div>
</div>

/* CSS snippet */
.win-listview {
    height: 100%;
}
```

```
.normal {
    display:-ms-grid;
    -ms-grid-rows:160px;
    -ms-grid-columns:160px;
    background-color:gray;
    color:white;
}

.oversized {
    display:-ms-grid;
    -ms-grid-rows:330px;
    -ms-grid-columns:330px;
    background-color:gray;
    color:white;
}

.number {
    font-size: 36px;
    font-weight: bold;
    -ms-grid-column-align: center;
    -ms-grid-row-align: center;
}

// JavaScript snippet
var numbersList = new WinJS.Binding.List();

var list = document.querySelector(".lst0715 #list").winControl;
list.itemTemplate = document.querySelector(".lst0715 #template");
list.itemDataSource = numbersList.dataSource;
list.layout.groupInfo = function () {
    return { enableCellSpanning: true, cellWidth: 160, cellHeight: 160 };
};

for (var i = 1; i <= 11; i++) {
    numbersList.push({ number: i, size: calculateSize(i) });
}

function calculateSize(n) { return (n == 1 ? "oversized" : "normal"); }
```

Notice in Figure 7-21 that the second and third tiles were displaced by the first, but all of the slots were filled. If varying sized items are added to the ListView in the wrong order, it is possible to get gaps in the layout. It may be necessary to add some logic that assures the order in which items are added according to their size.

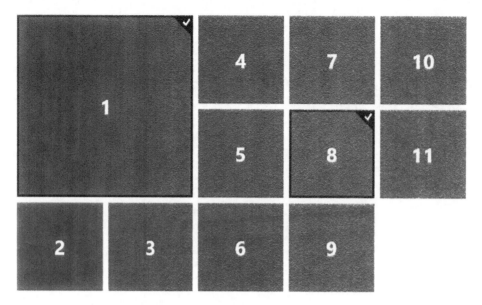

Figure 7-21. *The ListView items are assymetrical with the first item being larger than the others*

Scroll Control

When the contents of an element overflow the bounds of the element and the element's overflow property is set to auto or scroll, a scrollbar will be rendered and the user will be able to use the mouse or touch to scroll. It's an old solution to the problem of having more content than we have screen.

Most of the control over how a container scrolls has traditionally been left up to the user agent, but some Microsoft vendor-specific properties give the app author some say in the matter. We'll have say over the scrolling limits, rails, snap points, and over a behavior called *chaining*. We'll look at each of these now.

Limits

The distance that a container has been scrolled is controlled by the scrollLeft DOM property and it is possible to set minimum and maximum values for this property and thus constrain the scrolling of a container by setting the -ms-scroll-limit-* properties.

Limit Properties

Let's look at some limit properties.

-ms-scroll-limit-x-min and -ms-scroll-limit-y-min

Specify a length value for these properties to constrain a container's minimum scrolling distance in the horizontal and vertical directions respectively. An -ms-scroll-limit-x-min value of 100px, for example, will cause a container to start out already scrolled 100 pixels and make it impossible to scroll left from there.

-ms-scroll-limit-x-max and -ms-scroll-limit-y-max

The maximum value determines how far from the start of content a user can scroll within a container. An `-ms-scroll-limit-x-max` value of 500px would make it impossible to scroll beyond 500 pixels from the start of the container's content.

-ms-scroll-limit

This shorthand property is available to set the `-ms-scroll-limit-x-min`, `-ms-scroll-limit-y-min`, `-ms-scroll-limit-x-max`, `-ms-scroll-limit-y-max` all at once.

I generally recommend using shorthand properties where you can because CSS can get awfully long sometimes and using a shorthand property is an opportunity to be a bit more concise.

Rails

The scroll properties also facilitate control over a behavior of scrolling known in Microsoft terminology as *rails*. When scrolling is in rails mode, the direction that content scrolls is locked to the first axis the user started scrolling in. If the user started scrolling down, then rails mode will allow scrolling along the vertical axis, but disallow it along the horizontal. When rails mode is off, a user can freely scroll in either direction.

The reason rails mode exists at all is because it is a common for a user browsing a web page to read a long vertical column of text and want to keep the horizontal scrolling position constant to maintain orientation. The rails behavior attempts to predict based on the user's initial scroll direction whether this constraint should take effect. If a user scrolls vertically then scrolling will be locked to the y-axis. If the user scrolls horizontally then scrolling will be locked to the x-axis. If the user scrolls in any diagonal direction then scrolling will be free-form and the user will be allowed to scroll on either axis.

The sole property for giving your content rails is `-ms-scroll-rails`. The values are either `none` or `railed` and the default is `railed`.

Snap Points

Sometimes the content is entirely linear and should scroll smoothly from beginning to end stopping wherever the user stops it, but other times the content is arranged in digital units or sections and it makes more sense to help the user land so that the beginning of the next section snaps to the start of the container. These points are called snap points.

Microsoft has implemented snap points in its browser engine, though they do not exist in the CSS standard. This is why the related properties have the vendor-specific prefix.

You can define snap points in one of two ways: mandatory or proximity.

Defining a container to use mandatory snap points means that it will always stop at the nearest snap point. It will never stop somewhere in between. Defining it to use proximity snap points, however, means that if it ends up close enough to a snap point then it will find its way there, but if it's not close enough then it will concede to coming to rest between points.

Snap Point Properties

Let's look at some snap point properties.

-ms-scroll-snap-points-x and -ms-scroll-snap-points-y

The snap points are defined using one of two functions: `snapInterval()` or `snapList()`.

The `snapInterval()` function takes a start length and a snap length. Passing in `0px` and `100px` will create snap points every 100 pixels starting at 0. Use `snapInterval` when your content is repeating and regular and you can predict the width.

The `snapList()` function is a better choice when content is not regular. You define snap points manually as parameters. So `snapList(0px,200px,500px)` will set snap points at 0, 200, and 500 pixels even though those obviously are not regular intervals.

-ms-scroll-snap-type

The -ms-scroll-snap-type property gives the developer a chance to choose between *proximity* snap points and *mandatory* snap points. A value of `proximity` will snap to a snap point if the users panning action is going to come to a rest near that point, whereas a value of `mandatory` will never stop between two snap points.

-ms-scroll-snap-x and -ms-scroll-snap-y

The `-ms-scroll-snap-x` and `-ms-scroll-snap-y` properties are shorthand properties that encapsulate both the snap points and the type.

Look back at Listing 7-9 and notice that it is the -ms-scroll-snap-x snap point that is being used to set the points and the type at the same time. That property was `-ms-scroll-snap-x:mandatory snapInterval(0%,80%)`, and it would require that the panning come to rest only at some increment of 80% of the flexbox's width.

Chaining

Scroll chaining is the behavior of passing the user's scroll gesture from a child container up to its parent container when the child has reached the end of its content. If you have, for instance a horizontally panning list view placed on a page that is capable of panning horizontally and the user touches the ListView and slides horizontally, the gesture will be recognized at the ListView level and it will pan its contents. Once the ListView runs out of content and reaches its limit, however, the same slide gesture will continue panning the overall page. The `-ms-scroll-chaining` property is the one responsible for this behavior. The default value of none will not pass the scrolling gesture to the parent, but will instead simply show a bounce animation to indicate the edge of the content. The value must instead be set to `chained` to get the chaining behavior.

Summary

We've covered a lot of content on the subject of layout. We looked at a couple of legacy methods for laying out content on the web, and then we looked at some exciting, modern alternatives.

The first legacy method we looked at was layout via tables. Tables are great for showing tabular data, but not a good idea for laying out your app. They're unsuitable because being defined in your HTML markup makes them rigid and difficult to manipulate at run time. We also looked at using display and positioning properties on standard `div` elements for layout. This is a decent and rather popular strategy, but it has its pain points and easier and more expressive modern options exist now.

The modern layout techniques we've discussed are the CSS flexbox and grid, but we also looked at some controls available in a Windows 8 app by way of the WinJS JavaScript library called the ViewBox and the ListView that do some very helpful layout work for us.

I like to generalize that the flexbox *flows* its children and the grid *places* its children. The flexbox lets you easily lay out a few elements to create horizontal or vertical lists of content. Within the list, individual items can be packed, aligned, and sized to handle their space as the design dictates. The grid lets you create a framework within which it's very easy to place children. Items can be place anywhere within the grid relative to any of the cells formed by the grid's structure.

The ViewBox and ListView—the two WinJS layout implements that we explored—are native Windows 8 controls and not available (as they exist anyway) to the development of public websites. The ViewBox responds to changes in the users' view state such as when the user rotates their tablet to a portrait orientation. It then applies CSS transforms to its contents to translate and scale them to fit. The ListView is the ultimate tool for laying out lists of data items. It facilitates item selection, sorting, grouping, and a whole lot more.

An app's layout is the foundation of its design and its function, but web developers have traditionally had a relatively difficult time performing such a simple task as placing visual elements where they want. The Windows 8 implementation of the very latest CSS standards, however, provide some awesome functionality that will certainly ease this pain.

In Chapters 8, 9, and 10, we'll look at a higher level view of the collections of style rules in the built-in WinJS library and our own homemade style sheets. We'll also look at applying these rules to our app as well overriding and extending them to make them our own.

So shift gears with me and let's keep cruising!

CHAPTER 8

Global Styles

Note The WinJS library provides a ton of CSS that has already been written for you-almost 4,000 lines of it actually. This big collection of style rules makes your app look right at home in Windows 8.

In this chapter on what I'm dubbing the *global styles*, we're going to look at the styles from the WinJS library that affect the general environment and typography of your Windows 8 app. We'll also look at the styling of the app bar, the settings pane, flyouts, and menus. There are a lot of rules that go in to styling the WinJS controls, and Chapter 9 is dedicated to just that.

I highly recommend two methods for quickly and fully learning CSS for Windows 8. First, spend time scrolling all the way through the `ui-light.css` file that you'll find in the References section of any Windows 8 JavaScript project in Visual Studio. You can find some very helpful references on this file at `http://msdn.microsoft.com/en-us/library/windows/apps/hh465498.aspx`. Second, learn the class names that inherently exist on the various controls and structures in this chapter. Once you know, for instance, that the element that contains the settings flyout contains a class value of `win-settingsflyout`, you can scope styles to that element and add styling of your own, using a simple class selector.

Typography

Typography plays a very important role in Windows 8 apps. The font face and size is chosen purposefully to convey information about the relative significance of the various bits of content on the screen. A large title positioned consistently is quickly and subconsciously identified by the user and progressively smaller type is easy to locate and easy to relate.

Fonts

The primary Windows typeface is Segoe UI (pronounced SEE-go). It is a clean, modern, sans serif font that supports the Latin, Cyrillic, Greek, Arabic, Hebrew, Armenian, and Georgian alphabets, so it's super versatile. The Windows 8 design guidelines do not strictly require the use of the Segoe UI font for your app. It is a good choice though because it gives your app that familiar feel that helps users to feel like it's part of a cohesive platform. If your brand has a standard font, however, that people might identify as a characteristic of your brand, then it might be a better choice.

The Calibri typeface is also a recommended font for Windows 8 apps. It acts as more of a reading or writing font than Segoe UI and it supports Latin, Greek, and Cyrillic alphabets. Calibri is good for things like email and chat apps. Finally, the Cambria typeface is used for bigger blocks of reading text that you would find in a book reader or the like. More extensive coverage of the typographic guidelines in Windows 8 can be found at `http://msdn.microsoft.com/en-us/library/windows/apps/hh700394.aspx`.

One of the first things that the WinJS style sheets does is define (using @font-face like we learned in Chapter 4) a number of font-family values around Segoe UI. They are all the same font, but they use different values for the font weight. The font weights are:

- Segoe UI Light - 200 weight

- Segoe UI Semilight - 300 weight

- Segoe UI - 400 (normal) weight

- Segoe UI Semibold - 600 weight

- Segoe UI Bold - 700 weight

To use these, you only have to specify a CSS `font-family` property with the defined font family name (i.e., Segoe UI Light, Segoe UI, etc.).

Type Styles

Type styles are the style rules defined by WinJS that affect text in your app. We learned in Chapter 1 that the type ramp is that standard set of font sizes that gives a Windows 8 app its characteristic and identifiable look. The type ramp from largest to smallest is 42 points, 20 points, 11 points, and 9 points. This is a rather broad font size spectrum and the reason for it is to provide a quick visual hierarchy of text content on the screen. Seeing a header in 42 point and a sub-header in 20 point will cause the content to speak for itself about its structure and relative significance.

You can see a typical example of this type ramp in effect in Figure 8-1. Notice how easy it is to discern the title of the app, to differentiate the parts from one another, and to read the headings and content of the body text. Also notice that this was accomplished with the type ramp and some strategic use of space. Our layout did not require any lines or boxes to separate out the various parts of the app.

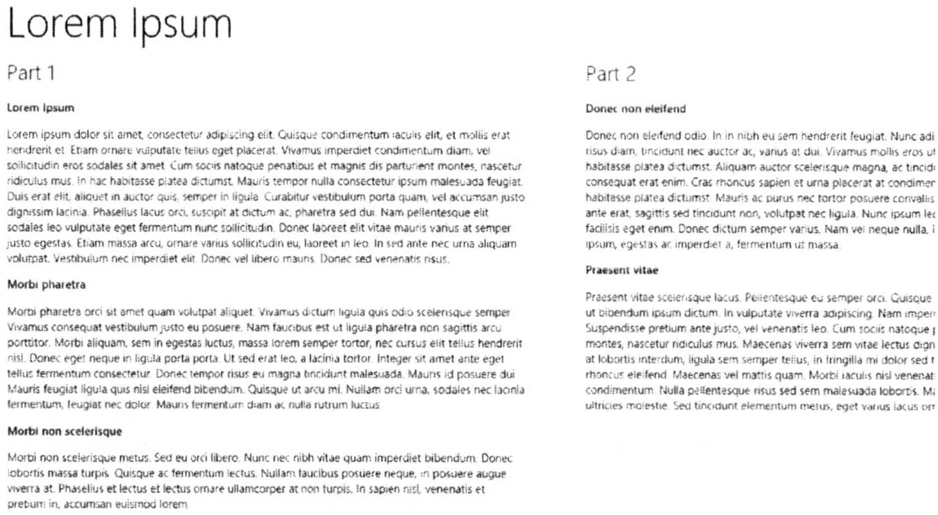

Figure 8-1. *Windows 8's type ramp makes it easy to discern the relative significance of content*

The sample app screen in Figure 8-1 is using the standard Windows 8 light theme (`ui-light.css`). This theme is the cause for the white background and the black text. In stark contrast, a dark theme (`ui-dark.css`) is also available. Figure 8-2 shows the same view using the dark theme this time. The app developer gets to choose which of the themes to use, and it's an app-by-app decision. It is not controlled by an operating system level setting. The type ramp in the dark theme is obviously still just as effective in communicating structure.

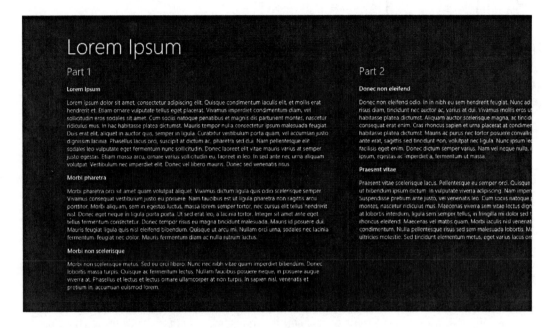

Figure 8-2. *The same view as Figure 8-1, this time using the ui-dark theme*

The 42-point page title is relatively large and makes it quick and easy for a user to become oriented with the current page. This may not seem important, but it very much is. When a user is switching from one app to another, snapping apps beside, and launching new apps, an unconscious glance at the top of the screen provides a remedy to application vertigo.

The 20-point section headers will quickly become a familiar organization indicator to users who will look for them to see how the app is categorized or sub-divided. A user will see the sections spilling off the right side of the screen and naturally swipe to see more content.

The 11- and 9-point subheader and body text is certainly readable, but it's also obviously less significant than the page title and section headers.

Listing 8-1 defines header text at all six levels and also paragraph text, and Figure 8-3 shows the rendered results. Notice that heading 3, heading 4, heading 5, and the standard paragraph text are all the same point size (11) and differ only in their weight.

Listing 8-1. The six header levels and a paragraph

```
<!-- HTML snippet -->
<h1>Heading 1</h1>
<h2>Heading 2</h2>
<h3>Heading 3</h3>
<h4>Heading 4</h4>
```

```
<h5>Heading 5</h5>
<h6>Heading 6</h6>
<p>Paragraph text</p>
```

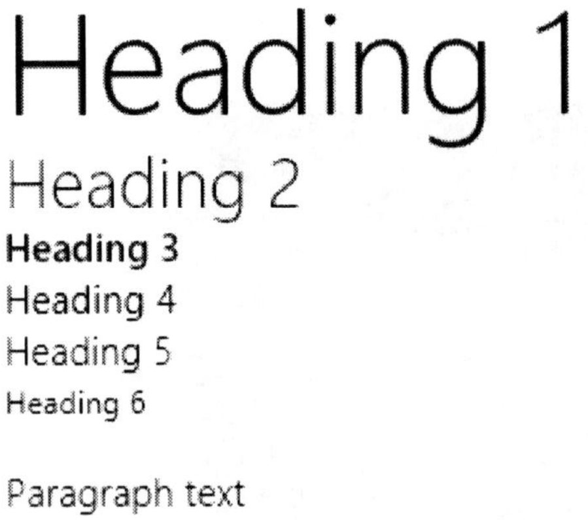

Heading 1
Heading 2
Heading 3
Heading 4

Heading 5

Heading 6

Paragraph text

Figure 8-3. *The rendered result according to the WinJS style sheet*

Each of these heading styles applies only when you define a heading tag (h1, h2, h3, h4, h5, and h6) in the HTML, but for each there is also a corresponding class that can be added to any element you wish.

The class equivalent of h1 is win-type-xx-large, of h2 is win-type-x-large, of h3 is win-type-large, of h4 is win-type-medium, of h5 is win-type-small, and of h6 is win-type-xx-small. There is also a style for win-type-x-small, though it does not map to a heading level. To use one of these styles, you have only to add the right class to whatever element you're attempting to affect.

You would choose to use a style when you want to match the type ramp but without explicitly using a heading tag. Heading tags have certain behaviors that you may not always want, the biggest is that it is a block level element. Listing 8-2 provides a standard button (for comparison) followed by a button that has been given a class of win-type-x-large to effectively give it the look of an h2. The larger text in the second button in Figure 8-4 is obvious. You should think twice before changing the styling of any default element, and move forward only if it is an intentional change to support your apps overall design.

Listing 8-2. The win-type-x-large class is defined on a standard HTML button

```
<!-- HTML snippet -->
<div><button>Button 1</button></div>
<div><button class="win-type-x-large">Button 2</button></div>

/* CSS snippet */
.lst0802 button {
    margin: 5px;
}
```

Button 1

Button 2

Figure 8-4. *The result is a button that is styled like an h2 element*

There are two more win-type style rules, which are `win-type-ellipsis` and `win-type-interactive`.

The `win-type-ellipsis` definition contains the text-overflow property with a value of ellipsis ("..."), which renders an ellipsis character when text does not fit in its container.

The `win-type-interactive` style rule is very helpful for causing text to render like a link even when it is not actually a link as is common in Windows 8 apps that follow the standard single-page app navigation pattern.

WinJS gives us a standard style for text that has been selected by the user, too. Selected text is identified using the `::selection` pseudo-element. In the light theme, for instance, selected text is given a background color that is a variation of blue with a text color of white.

Keep in mind that class-based style rules can be applied in combination with an element, because multiple classes can be specified on a single element. In Listing 8-3, a span of text in the middle of a paragraph is given multiple classes to render it like an h3 and to make it interactive. In Figure 8-5, you can see the effect of simply adding this class to a span.

Listing 8-3. Two classes are applied to a span that surrounds some paragraph text

```
<!-- HTML snippet -->
<p>Lorem ipsum dolor sit amet, <span class="win-type-x-large win-type-interactive">consectetur
adipiscing elit</span>. Maecenas hendrerit posuere nulla...</p>
```

Lorem ipsum dolor sit amet, consectetur adipiscing elit. Maecenas hendrerit posuere nulla, non scelerisque leo imperdiet eget. Nulla id massa orci. Praesent ut ultricies nunc. Praesent purus ipsum, lacinia tempus imperdiet eu, ultrices semper velit. Nulla eget nibh non neque egestas volutpat. Nulla id leo tortor, ut facilisis tortor. Etiam id elit id velit facilisis mollis quis in diam. Etiam mattis, odio ut consectetur egestas, urna sem hendrerit magna, hendrerit sollicitudin odio tellus sit amet velit. Nunc sodales pellentesque placerat. Phasellus sed arcu id arcu fringilla iaculis et imperdiet felis. Pellentesque habitant morbi tristique senectus et netus et malesuada fames ac turpis egestas. Quisque turpis massa, feugiat a gravida sed, euismod sit amet diam. Etiam scelerisque lacus lectus. Donec eget quam vel nisl vestibulum mattis. Nulla convallis vulputate turpis ut rutrum. Etiam mollis molestie ipsum in congue.

Figure 8-5. *The span of text is rendered larger than the rest and will provide hover feedback because of the win-type-interactive class*

Snapped View

An app is snapped by a user when he wishes to keep it available (though in a smaller format) while working on another app. It's a great feature for the user to get a terse, vertical view of a secondary task while using Windows 8. For the developer it's a design consideration, and a necessary one because there is no way to configure your app to disallow snapping. A lot changes when your app is snapped; most notably, your available horizontal pixels go from at least 1024 down to only 320. Absolutely every app can be snapped, so you must account for the case even if it's only to inform the user that the app is not capable of functioning normally until it's unsnapped.

At least some of the work of transforming your app for snapped view is done for you by WinJS. The CSS files in WinJS define a media query to detect that your app is in snapped view and sets various style properties to maintain your app's usability and design.

Figures 8-6 and 8-7 show a sample app in the fullscreen state and then in the snapped state. In this case, no provisions have been made to adjust the app when snapped, so it's essentially just showing the left 320 pixels of the full screen app. First, this is definitely a behavior you should avoid delivering to the Windows Store.

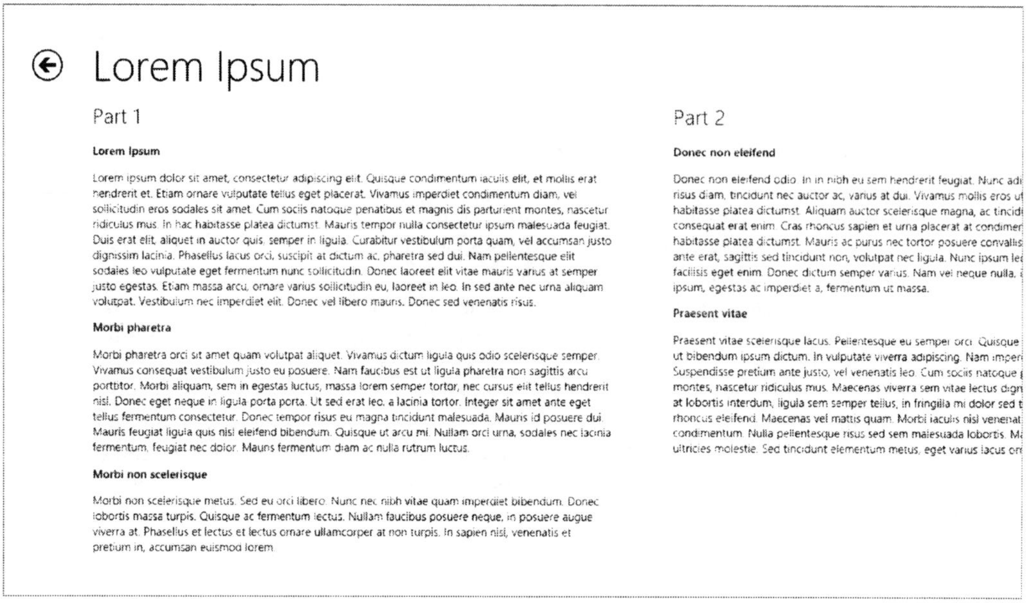

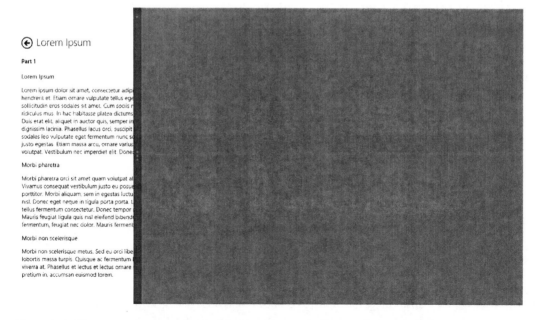

Figure 8-6. *A sample app displayed in fullscreen landscape*

Figure 8-7. *The same app snapped to the left side of the screen illustrating the inherent differences in style between the fullscreen view state and the snapped view state*

You can see, however, that there are a few differences between the full-view view and the left-most 320 pixels in the snapped view. The app title is smaller, because the h1 element and the win-type-xx-large class are changed to use a 20-point font instead of the normal 42-point. The section titles (Part 1 and Part 2) are smaller too, because the style rules for the h2 element and the win-type-x-large class are changed to use an 11-point font instead of the normal 20. The back button is smaller too. All of this is built-in functionality in WinJS.

Obviously this app is not entirely in support of snapped view, but with a few more media queries and style properties it could be.

App bar

Windows 8 apps have app bars that are optional. A developer can choose to define a lower app bar that can slide up from the bottom of the screen or an upper app bar that can slide down from the top. Both app bars can obviously be defined as well. A simple swipe, right mouse click, or keyboard shortcut (Win + Z) is all it takes for the user to access either.

Remember how I mentioned in Chapter 1 that a core principle of good Windows 8 design is to immerse the user and remove the distractions. This is why app bars are a great place for commands, because they don't distract the user from their content and they don't demand valuable design surface until the user elects.

Figure 8-8 shows the Bing Maps app with the lower app bar revealed. This lower app bar should be used for commanding. Commands are a means for the app user to interact with the app or issue commands. Most often commands will be buttons and should conform to the recommended design—a round button with a simple icon. If the command can be represented using one of the default Windows 8 icons, then it should be. Only create a custom icon if it cannot be represented using one from the built-in collection.

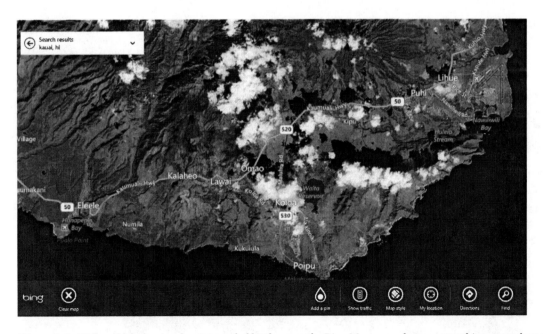

Figure 8-8. *Unless the lower app bar is revealed by the user, the Bing Maps app shows you nothing more than a map. This is what it means for a user to be immersed in content*

Besides a lower app bar for commanding, an upper app bar is available to developers and should primarily be used for navigation of some form. In Figure 8-9, you can see the Internet Explorer 10 app (Windows Store version), and you can see that the upper app bar is used to display thumbnails for browser tabs.

Figure 8-9. *Internet Explorer implements both an upper and a lower app bar*

Figure 8-10 illustrates the Sports app that is built by the Bing team and is pre-installed in Windows 8. In this app, the lower and upper app bars are both in use. The upper is used for navigating to the various available sports while the lower app bar avails an option to refresh sports data.

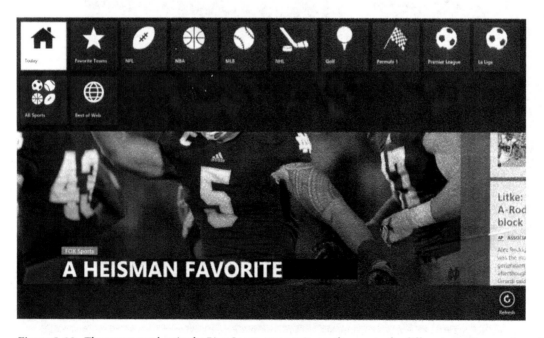

Figure 8-10. *The upper app bar in the Bing Sports app navigates the user to the different sporting events available*

It is important for app bars to have uniform appearance and functionality across apps, so you'll find that you don't usually need to add style rules to your app bar. More often than not, their default styling is sufficient.

What we really want to do in a book about using CSS to style your app, is understand the general structure of an app bar and what classes it is decorated with so that we have some hope of customizing it by adding or overriding styles. To do this, we'll look at the complete code for implementing an app bar and then we'll see what the resulting DOM looks like and highlight the significant parts (see Figure 8-11).

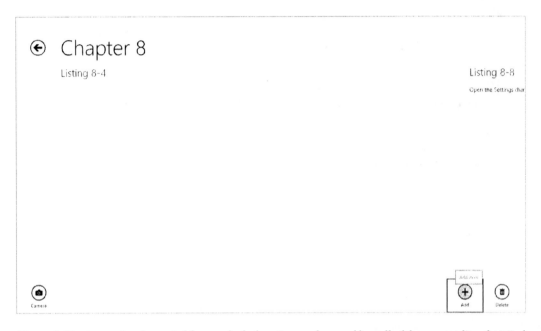

Figure 8-11. *An app bar is created from only declarative markup and has all of the personality of a Windows 8 app bar*

In Listing 8-4, we have declared an app bar (in bold) complete with command buttons. The declaration of these elements is simple, yet it results in a robust control composed of many native HTML elements being built out in the DOM.

Listing 8-4. Full implementation of an app bar in a Windows 8 app

```
<!-- lst0804.html -->
<!DOCTYPE html>
<html>
<head>
<meta charset="utf-8" />
<title>Listing 8-4</title>

<!-- WinJS references -->
<link href="//Microsoft.WinJS.1.0/css/ui-light.css" rel="stylesheet" />
<script src="//Microsoft.WinJS.1.0/js/base.js"></script>
<script src="//Microsoft.WinJS.1.0/js/ui.js"></script>

<link href="lst0804.css" rel="stylesheet" />
<script src="lst0804.js"></script>
</head>
```

```
<body>
<div class="lst0804 fragment">
<section aria-label="Main content" role="main">

</section>
<div id="myAppBar" data-win-control="WinJS.UI.AppBar">
<button
            data-win-control="WinJS.UI.AppBarCommand"
            data-win-options="{ id:'cmdAdd', label:'Add', icon:'add', section:'global',
                tooltip:'Add item' }"></button>
<button
            data-win-control="WinJS.UI.AppBarCommand"
            data-win-options="{ id:'cmdDelete', label:'Delete', icon:'delete',
                section:'global', tooltip:'Delete item' }"></button>
<button
            data-win-control="WinJS.UI.AppBarCommand"
            data-win-options="{ id:'cmdCamera', label:'Camera', icon:'camera',
                section:'selection', tooltip:'Take a picture' }"></button>
</div>
</div>
</body>
</html>


/* lst0804.css */
(empty)


// lst0804.js
(function () {
    "use strict";

    WinJS.UI.Pages.define("/pages/chapter8/lst0804/lst0804.html", {
        ready: function (element, options) {
            //empty
        }
    });
})();
```

Notice that the CSS and JavaScript files are essentially empty. An app bar and its buttons can be created entirely declaratively. I've included the .css and .js files just so you know there's no magic happening.

The lst0804.html file in Listing 8-4 will define our app bar, but it does not represent the actual HTML that ends up in the DOM while the app is actively running. This is because of the way that WinJS handles controls. You create a control by adding a data-win-control attribute to a standard HTML element. Then, when the WinJS.UI.processAll function is executed, all of these declared controls get transformed into the real deal. In this process the class names are added to each element as are some inline styles in many cases.

To get a good idea of what's going on in this process, let's look at the DOM Explorer while our app is running and see the real live DOM. The app bar in the previous example resulted in the code in Listing 8-5.

Listing 8-5. The DOM that results from the app bar we have created

```
<!-- HTML snippet from DOM Explorer -->
<div class="win-overlay win-appbar win-commandlayout win-bottom" id="myAppBar" role="menubar"
style="visibility: hidden; opacity: 0;" aria-label="App Bar"
    data-win-control="WinJS.UI.AppBar" unselectable="on">
<button class="win-command win-global" id="cmdAdd" role="menuitem" aria-label="Add"
        type="button" data-win-options="{ id:'cmdAdd', label:'Add', icon:'add',
        section:'global',&#10; tooltip:'Add item' }"
        data-win-control="WinJS.UI.AppBarCommand">
<span tabindex="-1" class="win-commandicon win-commandring" aria-hidden="true">
<span tabindex="-1" class="win-commandimage" aria-hidden="true"> </span>
</span>
<span tabindex="-1" class="win-label" aria-hidden="true">Add</span>
</button>
<button class="win-command win-global" id="cmdDelete" role="menuitem" aria-label="Delete"
        type="button" data-win-options="{ id:'cmdDelete', label:'Delete', icon:'delete',&#10;
        section:'global', tooltip:'Delete item' }"
        data-win-control="WinJS.UI.AppBarCommand">
<span tabindex="-1" class="win-commandicon win-commandring" aria-hidden="true">
<span tabindex="-1" class="win-commandimage" aria-hidden="true"></span>
</span>
<span tabindex="-1" class="win-label" aria-hidden="true">Delete</span>
</button>
<button class="win-command win-selection" id="cmdCamera" role="menuitem" aria-label="Camera"
        type="button" data-win-options="{ id:'cmdCamera', label:'Camera', icon:'camera',&#10;
        section:'selection', tooltip:'Take a picture' }"
        data-win-control="WinJS.UI.AppBarCommand">
<span tabindex="-1" class="win-commandicon win-commandring" aria-hidden="true">
<span tabindex="-1" class="win-commandimage" aria-hidden="true"> </span>
</span>
<span tabindex="-1" class="win-label" aria-hidden="true">Camera</span>
</button>
</div>
```

The bolded content in Listing 8-5 is the class attributes that have been added into the DOM elements. These class names act as handles for us to select the different parts of the control and add or override style rules for them.

The app bar itself (the highest level div in Listing 8-5) has been given four class names: win-overlay, win-appbar, win-commandlayout, and win-bottom. Each of these classes applies to the app bar a style rule that is defined in the WinJS CSS, and each of the classes serves a distinct purpose; that's why there are four classes instead of just one. A developer may elect, for instance, to set the app bar's placement option to top to render it at the top of the screen, in which case the win-bottom class would be omitted and replaced with win-top.

The goal, once again, is to understand the structure of our HTML so we can add or override styles that affect it. Let's take one example and follow it through. The buttons that we declared on our app bar have each been given content that makes them look like a proper app bar button—a circle with an icon and a label below. This is achieved using span elements with classes defined. The ring is given the classes of win-commandicon and win-commandring, and the label below is a span with the class of win-label. Imagine that our project requirements state that our app bar buttons should have a border of gray instead of the standard white when the user hovers their mouse over them.

First, let's look at how the buttons get their white border by looking into ui-light.css at lines 2511–2599 (Listing 8-6). Pay special attention to the bolded section. This style rule affects the element with a class of win-commandring that is a child of a button that is currently being hovered over. That's exactly what we're looking to override.

Listing 8-6. From ui-light.css (lines 2511–2599), we can see the styles that the circle around our command buttons gets when the user hovers over one

```
/*
Command ring colors.
*/
...
.win-commandring, button:active .win-commandring {
    background-color: transparent;
    border-color: rgb(0, 0, 0);
}
button:hover .win-commandring {
    background-color: rgba(0, 0, 0, 0.13);
    border-color: rgb(0, 0, 0);
}
button:hover:active .win-commandring {
    background-color: rgb(0, 0, 0);
    border-color: rgb(0, 0, 0);
}
button:-ms-keyboard-active .win-commandring {
    background-color: rgb(0, 0, 0);
    border-color: rgb(0, 0, 0);
}
button:disabled .win-commandring,
button:disabled:active .win-commandring {
    background-color: transparent;
    border-color: rgba(0, 0, 0, 0.4);
}
button[aria-checked=true] .win-commandring,
button[aria-checked=true]:active .win-commandring {
    background-color: rgb(0, 0, 0);
    border-color: rgb(0, 0, 0);
}
button[aria-checked=true]:hover .win-commandring {
    background-color: rgb(33, 33, 33);
    border-color: rgb(33, 33, 33);
}
button[aria-checked=true]:hover:active .win-commandring {
    background-color: transparent;
    border-color: rgb(0, 0, 0);
}
button[aria-checked=true]:-ms-keyboard-active .win-commandring {
    background-color: transparent;
    border-color: rgb(0, 0, 0);
}
button[aria-checked=true]:disabled .win-commandring,
button[aria-checked=true]:disabled:active .win-commandring {
    background-color: rgba(0, 0, 0, 0.4);
    border-color: rgba(0, 0, 0, 0.4);
}
```

Although it's not related to our current requirement of modifying the border color, notice that the background color is getting an opacity value of 0.13 when it's being hovered. This makes the button somewhat less than entirely transparent only when the user hovers over it.

The border color is what we're trying to affect, and the border color in this case is exactly the same in a hover state as it is in its normal state. We cannot modify the ui-light.css file, but we can override the style rule in question. If we add the style rule from Listing 8-7 to our own page's CSS file, then we will get the effect we are looking for. Figure 8-12 shows that effect with a gray border around it.

Listing 8-7. A slight overriding style change to the border-color for the hover state

```
button:hover .win-commandring {
    background-color: rgba(0, 0, 0, 0.13);
    border-color: gray;
}
```

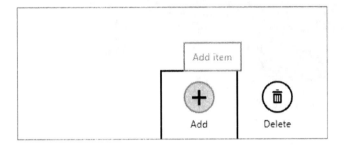

Figure 8-12. Hovering over a command button now changes the circular border around it to be gray

The thing to note here is that nothing is hidden from the developer. All of the style properties used to create Windows 8 apps are available to browse, append, and override.

Settings Pane

Like the app bar, the settings pane in Windows 8 apps is predictable for the user. It's always accessible by swiping the Charms out from the right side of the screen and selecting the Settings charm (see Figure 8-13). Choosing a settings category from the main settings pane flies a specific settings pane out from the right side of the screen. This specific settings pane is the one we're going to customize using a WinJS.UI.SettingsFlyout control.

Figure 8-13. *The Settings charm is always visible as the gear icon on the bottom of the charms bar*

Unlike the app bar, the settings pane is a blank slate that the developer is expected to design and implement, so you have a lot of freedom, but you're not without help. There are many styles that affect the settings pane and give it a standard Windows 8 design. I'll highlight those here.

Consider the snippet of HTML in Listing 8-8 and the resulting settings pane in Figure 8-14.

Listing 8-8. Complete definition of a settings flyout

```html
<!-- lst0808.html -->
<!DOCTYPE html>
<html>
<head>
<meta charset="utf-8" />
<title>Listing 8-8</title>

<!-- WinJS references -->
<link href="//Microsoft.WinJS.1.0/css/ui-light.css" rel="stylesheet" />
<script src="//Microsoft.WinJS.1.0/js/base.js"></script>
<script src="//Microsoft.WinJS.1.0/js/ui.js"></script>

<link href="lst0808.css" rel="stylesheet" />
<script src="lst0808.js"></script>
</head>
<body>
<div class="lst0808 fragment">
<section aria-label="Main content" role="main">

<p>Open the Settings charm and choose Listing 8-8 to see the resulting settings pane</p>
```

```html
<!-- BEGINSETTINGSFLYOUT -->
<div id="sampleSettings" data-win-control="WinJS.UI.SettingsFlyout"
          aria-label="App Settings Flyout">
<div class="win-ui-dark win-header">
<button type="button" onclick="WinJS.UI.SettingsFlyout.show()"
                  class="win-backbutton"></button>
<div class="win-label">Preferences</div>
</div>
<div class="win-content">
<div class="win-settings-section">
<h3>Toggle switch</h3>
<p>Use toggle switches to let users set Boolean values.</p>
<div id="Toggle1" data-win-control="WinJS.UI.ToggleSwitch"
                      data-win-options="{title:'Download updates automatically',
                          checked:true}">
</div>
<div id="Toggle2" data-win-control="WinJS.UI.ToggleSwitch"
                      data-win-options="{title:'Install updates automatically'}">
</div>
</div>
</div>
</div>
<!-- ENDSETTINGSFLYOUT -->

</section>
</div>
</body>
</html>
```

```css
/* lst0808.css */
```

```javascript
// lst0808.js
(function () {
    "use strict";

    WinJS.UI.Pages.define("/pages/chapter8/lst0808/lst0808.html", {
        ready: function (element, options) {
            addSettingsContract()
        }
    });

    function addSettingsContract() {
        app.onsettings = function (e) {
            e.detail.applicationcommands = {
                "sampleSettings": {
                    title: "Listing 8-8",
                    href: "/pages/chapter8/lst0808/lst0808.html"
                }
            };
            WinJS.UI.SettingsFlyout.populateSettings(e);
        };
    }
})();
```

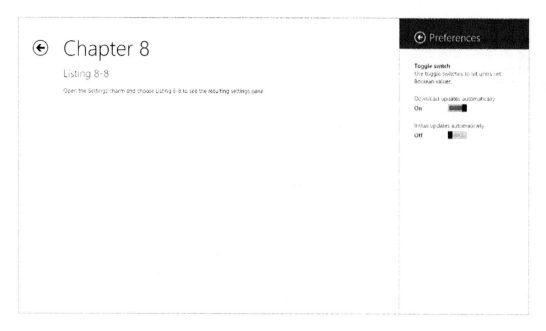

Figure 8-14. *The settings flyout is available from the settings pane*

The styles rules for this settings pane already exist, and we simply apply them by writing the structure and then decorating the elements with the right CSS class values.

Once again we'll use DOM explorer to look at the resulting DOM in Listing 8-9. The classes and styles added by WinJS are shown in bold. Also in bold are two div elements (win-firstdiv and win-finaldiv) that are added, though those don't concern us too much now since they don't have much to do with the styling of the control

Listing 8-9. Here's how the settings flyout looks once it's rendered into the live DOM

```
<!-- HTML snippet from DOM Explorer -->
<div class="win-overlay win-settingsflyout" id="Div1" role="dialog" aria-hidden="true"
style="left: auto; right: -346px; display: none; visibility: hidden; opacity: 1;"
    aria-label="App Settings Flyout" data-win-control="WinJS.UI.SettingsFlyout"
    unselectable="on">
<div tabindex="0" class="win-firstdiv" role="menuitem"
        aria-hidden="true" style="display: inline;"></div>
<div class="win-ui-dark win-header">
<button class="win-backbutton" aria-label="Back"
            onclick="WinJS.UI.SettingsFlyout.show()" type="button"></button>
<div class="win-label">Preferences</div>
</div>
<div class="win-content win-ui-light" style="opacity: 1;">
<div class="win-settings-section">
<h3>Toggle switch</h3>
<p>Use toggle switches to let users set Boolean values.</p>


        ...
```

```
</div>
</div>
<div tabindex="0" class="win-finaldiv" role="menuitem" aria-hidden="true"
        style="display: inline;"></div>
</div>
```

The div element that contains the back button and the settings title is decorated with win-ui-dark and win-header class values, and the background-color is set using the only style rule we had to write in the CSS snippet. The back button is a standard HTML button with the win-backbutton class, which is identical to the way the back button is declared for pages. The two back buttons are not the same, however, and the way the CSS discerns is with the use (again in the ui-light.css document) of a style rule with a selector of .win-settingsflyout .win-backbutton. As you can likely tell by the presence of .win-settingsflyout, this style rule will be limited to back buttons that are within a settings flyout.

Flyouts and Menus

Flyouts and menus are offered by the WinJS library and are more global, app-level controls, so I'll cover the styling of them now.

Flyouts and menus are closely related since they both have similar behavior. Both flyouts and menus appear as on overlay over the existing design surface (much like dialog boxes in most any programming framework). They are also light dismiss, which means the user can dismiss them by simply touching or clicking anywhere outside.

Flyouts give you free reign in formatting the contents, whereas menus are more structured and make it easier to create consistent menu systems. You can find much more information about flyouts and menus at http://msdn.microsoft.com/en-us/library/windows/apps/hh465325.aspx.

Flyouts

The flyout is just an HTML container, so you're free to create anything inside it that you want. Flyouts are an excellent way to prompt the user for input by displaying a small input panel very near where the user initiated the action. You could, for instance, prompt the user to add a new item by providing them an *Add user* button, and then when the user touches it, show a flyout near the button prompting them for a name. Listing 8-10 and Figure 8-15 show an *Add user* button that shows a flyout (positioned to the right of the button). When the user touches it, an event is executed which shows the flyout. Again, we'll see the full example for implementing the button and the flyout as well as the resulting DOM created by WinJS.

Listing 8-10. A complete example of a flyout implementation

```
<!-- lst0810.html -->
<!DOCTYPE html>
<html>
<head>
<meta charset="utf-8" />
<title>Listing 8-10</title>

<!-- WinJS references -->
<link href="//Microsoft.WinJS.1.0/css/ui-light.css" rel="stylesheet" />
<script src="//Microsoft.WinJS.1.0/js/base.js"></script>
<script src="//Microsoft.WinJS.1.0/js/ui.js"></script>
```

```html
<link href="lst0810.css" rel="stylesheet" />
<script src="lst0810.js"></script>
</head>
<body>
<div class="lst0810 fragment">
<section aria-label="Main content" role="main">
<button id="showFlyoutButton">Add user</button>

<div id="flyout1" data-win-control="WinJS.UI.Flyout"
                data-win-options="{placement: 'right'}">
<label for="input">Name</label>
<input type="text" />
</div>
</section>
</div>
</body>
</html>
```

```css
/* lst0810.css */
(empty)
```

```javascript
// lst0810.js
(function () {
    "use strict";

    WinJS.UI.Pages.define("/pages/chapter8/lst0810/lst0810.html", {
        ready: function (element, options) {
            var showFlyoutButton = element.querySelector("#showFlyoutButton");
            var flyout = element.querySelector("#flyout1");
            showFlyoutButton.onclick = function(e) {
                flyout.winControl.show(showFlyoutButton);
            }
        }
    });
})();
```

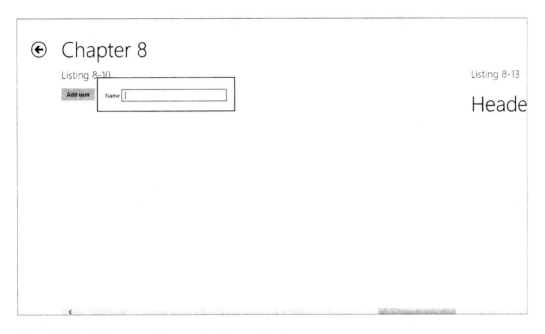

Figure 8-15. *A Flyout control prompting the user to enter a username*

Listing 8-11 is the resulting DOM with added classes and inline styles added by WinJS shown in bold

Listing 8-11. The resulting DOM for a flyout control

```
<div class="win-overlay win-flyout win-ui-light" id="Div1" role="dialog"
    aria-hidden="true" style="left: 210px; top: 146.5px; right: auto;
        bottom: auto; display: none; visibility: hidden; opacity: 0;"
        aria-label="Flyout" data-win-options="{placement: 'right'}"
    data-win-control="WinJS.UI.Flyout" unselectable="on">
<div tabindex="0" class="win-firstdiv" role="menuitem" aria-hidden="true"
        style="display: inline;"></div>
<label for="input">Name</label>
<input class="win-hidefocus" type="text">
<div tabindex="0" class="win-finaldiv" role="menuitem" aria-hidden="true"
        style="display: inline;"></div>
</div>
```

Like all other controls, a flyout control is instantiated using a standard HTML element—most often a div element. You can refer to any flyout you create using the ID that you gave it, of course, but what if you want to reference every flyout in your application? If you know that every flyout control is given a win-flyout class in the resulting DOM, then you know that you can refer to all of the flyouts in your app (or in any given scope you choose) by using a class selector (.win-flyout). The CSS in Listing 8-12, then, would set the flyout controls in your app to have a gray background and a thin, dark blue border.

Listing 8-12. Affects all flyouts with a gray background and a dark blue border

```
/* CSS snippet */
.win-flyout {
    background-color: gray;
    border: 1px solid darkblue;
}
```

Menus

Menus are made up of one or more MenuCommand objects. Listing 8-13 and Figure 8-16 include a complete example of a Windows 8 page with a header menu. A header menu is a recommended design for navigating the user from one part of the app to another quickly. A small chevron symbol is rendered next to the page title and gives the user the clue that the title is a menu and can be touched to invoke the header menu.

Listing 8-13. A WinJS.UI.Menu is declared in HTML and JavaScript is added to show it when the user clicks

```
<!-- lst0813.html -->
<!DOCTYPE html>
<html>
<head>
<meta charset="utf-8" />
<title>Listing 8-13</title>

<!-- WinJS references -->
<link href="//Microsoft.WinJS.1.0/css/ui-light.css" rel="stylesheet" />
<script src="//Microsoft.WinJS.1.0/js/base.js"></script>
<script src="//Microsoft.WinJS.1.0/js/ui.js"></script>

<link href="lst0813.css" rel="stylesheet" />
<script src="lst0813.js"></script>
</head>
<body>
<div class="lst0813 fragment">
<section aria-label="Main content" role="main">
<h1 class="menu win-type-ellipsis">
<span class="title">Header Menu</span>
<span class="chevron win-type-x-large">&#xe099</span>
</h1>

<div id="headerMenu" data-win-control="WinJS.UI.Menu">
<button data-win-control="WinJS.UI.MenuCommand"
                data-win-options="{id:'s1',label:'Section One'}"></button>
<button data-win-control="WinJS.UI.MenuCommand"
                data-win-options="{id:'s2',label:'Section Two'}"></button>
<button data-win-control="WinJS.UI.MenuCommand"
                data-win-options="{id:'s3',label:'Section Three'}"></button>
<hr data-win-control="WinJS.UI.MenuCommand"
                data-win-options="{id:'separator',type:'separator'}" />
<button data-win-control="WinJS.UI.MenuCommand"
                data-win-options="{id:'sHome',label:'Home'}"></button>
</div>
```

```
</section>
</div>
</body>
</html>

/* lst0813.css */
. lst0813 .chevron {
    vertical-align:8px;
}

// lst0813.js
(function () {
    "use strict";

    WinJS.UI.Pages.define("/pages/chapter8/lst0813/lst0813.html", {
        ready: function (element, options) {
            element.querySelector(".menu").onclick = function () { showHeaderMenu(element); };
        }
    });

    function showHeaderMenu(element) {
        var title = element.querySelector(".menu");
        var menu = element.querySelector("#headerMenu").winControl;
        menu.anchor = title;
        menu.placement = "bottom";
        menu.alignment = "left";

        menu.show();
    }
})();
```

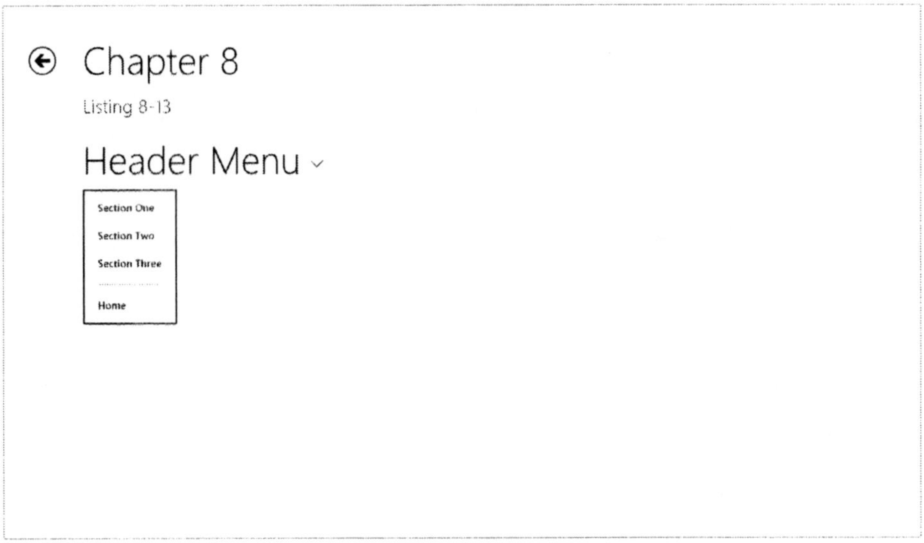

Figure 8-16. *The title has been transformed into an operational menu*

209

Now that you've seen how to create this simple menu, let's have a look at the HTML that is actually rendered for the app. This can be found using the DOM Explorer.

As you can see from the bolded text in Listing 8-14, each of the buttons has been given a class of win-command. This is very convenient for us as consumers of the WinJS.UI.Menu control because it means that it's going to be easy enough to apply a style to all menu items.

Listing 8-14. The resulting DOM for the menu created in Listing 8-13

```
<!-- HTML snippet from DOM Explorer -->
<div class="win-overlay win-flyout win-ui-light win-menu" id="headerMenu" role="menu"
style="display: none; visibility: hidden; opacity: 0;" aria-label="Menu"
    data-win-control="WinJS.UI.Menu" unselectable="on">
<button class="win-command" id="s1" role="menuitem" aria-label="Section One"
        type="button" data-win-options="{id:'s1',label:'Section One'}"
        data-win-control="WinJS.UI.MenuCommand">Section One</button>
<button class="win-command" id="s2" role="menuitem" aria-label="Section Two"
        type="button" data-win-options="{id:'s2',label:'Section Two'}"
        data-win-control="WinJS.UI.MenuCommand">Section Two</button>
<button class="win-command" id="s3" role="menuitem" aria-label="Section Three"
        type="button" data-win-options="{id:'s3',label:'Section Three'}"
        data-win-control="WinJS.UI.MenuCommand">Section Three</button>
<hr class="win-command" id="separator" data-win-options="{id:'separator',type:'separator'}"
        data-win-control="WinJS.UI.MenuCommand">
<button class="win-command" id="sHome" role="menuitem" aria-label="Home" type="button"
        data-win-options="{id:'sHome',label:'Home'}"
        data-win-control="WinJS.UI.MenuCommand">Home</button>
</div>
```

Let's modify the CSS with the bolded style rule in Listing 8-15.

Listing 8-15. The CSS from Listing 8-13 with an override to the menu buttons to italicize them

```
/* menus.css */
.lst0813 .chevron {
    vertical-align:8px;
}
.lst0813 .win-command {
    font-style: italic;
}
```

As you might expect and can see in Figure 8-17, each of the menu commands has been italicized.

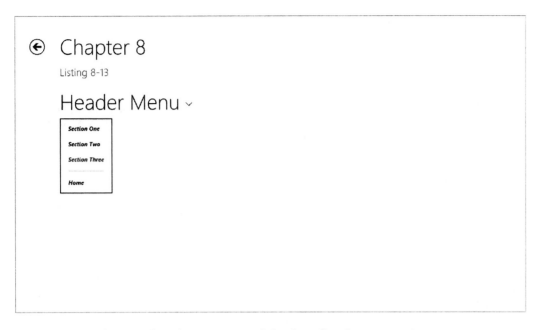

Figure 8-17. *Applying a style to the win-command class has affected every menu item*

High Contrast Mode

Windows 8 accommodates users with low vision by providing a high-contrast mode that the user can choose from PC settings | Easy of Access and expect that the choice will apply to all apps on their system.

For the most part, if you use the standard styles and methods for creating the visual elements in your app, you won't have to do anything to implement high-contrast support in your app. You may have custom considerations, however, regarding visibility in high-contrast mode, and you should be familiar with the styles you'll need to override to make that happen.

High-contrast styles are applied by way of a media query. A vendor-specific value of -ms-high-contrast is available as an expression to media queries and will be true when the user has chosen high-contrast mode on his device.

There are high-contrast style rules to control virtually every visual aspect of your app.

I'll draw just one example of a style property that affects your app in high-contrast mode and show you how to override it. Line 2848 in `ui-light.css` begins the main media query for high-contrast mode, and lines 3068–3074 (Listing 8-16) define the styles for the `win-appbar` class.

Listing 8-16. Just one of the many style rules defined in the -ms-high-contrast media query

```
@media (-ms-high-contrast)
{
    ...

    /*
    AppBar high contrast colors.
    */
    .win-appbar {
```

```
        background-color: ButtonFace;
        border-color: Highlight;


    ...
}
```

Let's pretend that the customer we're developing for has determined that a pure white app bar background is just as visible and matches their branding better and has asked us to override the default value. To do so, we need only clone this style rule (including the media query) in our page's CSS file, as you see in Listing 8-17.

Listing 8-17. *An override to the background color of the app bar in high contrast mode*

```
@media (-ms-high-contrast)
{
    .win-appbar {
        background-color: white;
}
```

If you do need to override the built-in high-contrast styles, be careful to maintain good visibility at all times. An app that does not do a good job of providing a high-contrast mode will likely be caught in the app certification process and, worse still, will exclude low-vision users from enjoying your app.

Summary

In this chapter, we've seen the many ways that WinJS affects the style of our app and extends it to us as developers so that we can not only take on the personality of the Windows 8 ecosystem, but can also display our own personality.

We've seen how to style our app's typography, the app bar, settings pane flyouts, and menus, and we've learned how high-contrast mode is implemented and how to extend it where necessary.

In the next chapter, we're going to remain in the same vein, but look more at the styling of the many controls provided to us by WinJS.

CHAPTER 9

WinJS Control Styles

■ **Note**   HTML gives us standard elements and WinJS extends them with custom controls. All we need to style them well.

We've learned how to select and style elements with style rules. We've learned that we author these rules in style sheets. And we've learned that the WinJS library that is available in your Windows 8 app provides us with two themed versions of a style sheet that give our app that Windows 8 personality. The style sheets affect things like the background color, the font face, and the text size.

The style sheets in the WinJS library also affect all of the standard HTML controls. When you declare a button control in your HTML, it comes out looking like a Windows 8 button because of the WinJS style sheet. When you add a select box, text box, checkbox, or any of the other built-in HTML controls, they will look like Windows 8 controls, and again because of the WinJS style sheet.

But WinJS also gives you some more controls (and a framework to write your own controls), and has defined them to render in such a way that you can affect their styling to give them the personality of your own app.

The styling of these built-in HTML controls and of the WinJS extended controls are what we're going to cover in this chapter. We'll look at the default styling of each and we'll look at the custom classes that are added and the pseudo-elements that are defined that will give us good control with our style rules.

Remember that WinJS provides us with two different CSS style sheets: ui-dark.css and ui-light.css. Their names do reveal their purpose. The ui-dark.css style sheet provides us with a black background and a white foreground and ui-light.css gives us the inverse. We'll be looking at the ui-light.css file only for simplicity's sake, since both are identical in structure.

Besides the two themed style sheets, we discuss two themed classes that can apply the dark or light themes not to the entire app, but to certain subsections of it. Don't be confused between the style sheets (ui-dark.css and ui-light.css) and the classes (win-ui-dark and win-ui-light).

We saw some classes in the previous chapter that were prefixed with win-, and we'll see more here. It's convenient to have this naming convention in place to remind us of what is there because of WinJS versus what's baked in. Most of the classes that we'll cover belong to or apply to a certain control, but the win-scrollview class can be tacked on to most any element. It applies just four style properties that give the target element the ability for the user to swipe (with touch) or scroll (with the mouse) to see more from off-screen.

HTML Controls

The HTML standard defines a number of controls. Actually, there are a fair number of them that were recently introduced in the latest version of HTML—in HTML5. The HTML controls cover a lot of common user interactions tasks and the Windows 8 app developer is encouraged to use HTML controls when they exist and fit the job.

For each of the HTML controls I will discuss the default styling that the WinJS style sheet assigns to them, the pseudo-classes and pseudo-elements that are available for them, and any classes that can be added to the element to affect the way it is rendered. I will discuss the following HTML controls:

- Button
- File upload
- Text input
- Radio buttons
- Checkboxes
- Range
- Select box
- Progress indicator

Unlike WinJS controls, HTML controls don't get "messed with". When you put something like `<img src="mypicture.png"/>` in your markup, it goes all the way to the client unchanged. WinJS controls work much differently. You put a WinJS control in your markup, but it gets processed by some JavaScript before it's rendered for the user. We'll talk about this in a later section.

For our HTML controls (elements), we'll just look at how the style sheets in the WinJS library style these controls by default. Do keep in mind that you'll be able to completely override these styles and we'll research that endeavor exhaustively in Chapter 10.

Button

A button issues a command. Users know buttons, and have been pushing them since long before computers came about. And buttons have long been a part of HTML too.

There are multiple ways to declare a button in HTML. You can declare a button using the input element and determine its behavior using one of the *type* attributes in the three following snippets: `<input type="button"/>`, `<input type="reset"/>`, and `<input type="submit"/>`. The buttons will look the same, but their functionality will vary.

- A type of `button` declares a button without any functionality at all. It would require that some JavaScript be written to assign it some actual functionality.
- A type of `reset` declares a button that when pressed will reset all other controls in the form to their initial values.
- A type of `submit` creates a button that, when pressed, will issue a POST HTTP request that includes all of the form values.

HTML5 introduces a new and slightly simpler way to define a button—with the `button` element. The `button` element is equivalent to `<input type="button"/>` in that it declares a button but does not assign any functionality. The `button` element is more semantic than the input element. By that I mean that it is more readily apparent to the human reader. I recommend using the `button` element exclusively.

Listing 9-1. A super simple button

```
<!-- HTML snippet -->
<button>click me!</button>
```

214

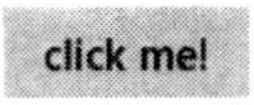

click me!

Figure 9-1. *A simple button*

For this first control, let's discuss discovering the applied style properties on an element. To discover applied properties for a button element, follow these steps:

1. Create a new Windows 8 project (or a new page in an existing project) in Visual Studio 2012

2. Add a simple HTML button to your HTML

   - `<button>My Button</button>`

3. Start your app with debugging by pressing F5

4. Switch back to Visual Studio and go to the DOM Explorer tab. If you don't have a DOM Explorer tab then go to the Debug menu, to Windows, and then choose DOM Explorer.

5. Press the Select Element button at the top-left corner of the DOM Explorer. You should be switched automatically to your running app.

6. Hover over your button and notice the blue outline, and then click the button. You should be switched automatically back to Visual Studio still in debug mode.

7. Click the Trace Styles tab in the right pane of the DOM Explorer.

The Trace Styles panel lists all of the style properties affecting the selected element and tells you where those properties were defined and will even render the properties with a strikethrough if they've been overridden by another rule elsewhere. In the Trace Styles panel for the button you made in the above steps, you should see a rule that has a heading of `:::-ms-browse background-color`. Under that property there is a rule for `button:hover` (as well as other chained selectors) and it defines the `background-color` to be `rgba(205,205,205,0.82)`. This method can be used to determine all applied style properties affecting any of the elements in your document.

Regardless of which method is used to declare a button, WinJS determines that the button should have a minimum width of 90 pixels and a minimum height of 32 pixels. One of the primary reasons for this minimum button size is to preserve *touchability*. Even large fingers should be able to consistently land on a button and anything smaller than 90 x 32 may be too small.

Buttons are also given a little padding, a 2-pixel border, and an 11-point font. The background color of a button is gray and slightly transparent with an actual color value of rgba (182,182,182,0.7), and as we saw in the previous exercise, its hover color is slightly lighter. This difference in background color creates a subtle but important visual cue that the button is being hovered over.

There are many other properties that are in effect for a button too, and you can find all of them in the Trace Styles panel of the DOM Explorer.

All of these properties together make a button look at home in Windows 8. You can see the simplicity of the Microsoft design style coming through strong in Figure 9-2.

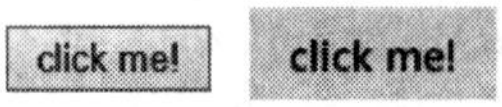

click me!   click me!

Figure 9-2. *The default rendering of a button in IE10 compared with the version that appears in a Windows 8 app after the WinJS style sheets are applied*

The following pseudo-classes are pertinent to a button element:

- **:hover.** As mentioned before, the background-color of a button being hovered is slightly lighter than normal.

- **:disabled.** Disabled buttons have by default a transparent background and white text and borders with low (40%) opacity.

If you declare a button and include a class of `win-backbutton`, the WinJS style sheet will turn that button into a back button. Back buttons are round with an arrow glyph rendered inside. This characteristic Windows 8 feature can be added to your app with the following very simple HTML markup:

```
<button class="win-backbutton"/>
```

File Upload Control

The file upload control is not new to HTML5, but it has received some significant improvements. It looks mostly the same in the browser—simply displaying a text box and a browse button. The control allows the user to upload one file or multiple files at once.

Listing 9-2. An input with a type of "file" will render a file upload control.

```
<input type="file"/>
```

Figure 9-3. The default file upload control

Since the file upload control renders multiple visual elements (namely the text box and the browse button), it has been difficult in the past to target for styling. The composite element could easily be targeted, but it was not possible to target the text box and the browse button separately. In Internet Explorer, however, the `::-ms-value` and `::-ms-browse` pseudo-elements are recognized and allow this finer level of control.

WinJS styles the file upload control to by 340 pixels wide by 32 pixels high with a custom margin around it. The `::-ms-value` (which represents the text box) and the `::-ms-browse` (which represents the browse button) both have 2-pixel borders.

Text Input Controls

Some of the HTML controls amount to a single control with a single behavior, but the `input` element is not one of them. The `input` element's behavior depends on the value of its `type` attribute. However, many of the values result in a control that looks to the user like a text box and accepts (as one would expect) alphanumeric keyboard input. Any of the following values in the `type` attribute will result in an alphanumeric text box: `text`, `password`, `email`, `number`, `tel`, `url`, or `search`. Additionally, a `textarea` element will also result in a text box that accepts alphanumeric input. The styling for all of these resulting controls will work mostly the same, so we'll look at them all together in Listing 9-3.

Listing 9-3. Seven ways to declare a text box

```
<!-- HTML snippet -->
<input type="text"/> text<br />
<input type="password" /> password<br />
```

```
<input type="email" /> email<br />
<input type="number" /> number<br />
<input type="tel" /> tel<br />
<input type="url" /> url<br />
<input type="search" /> search<br />
<textarea></textarea> textarea
```

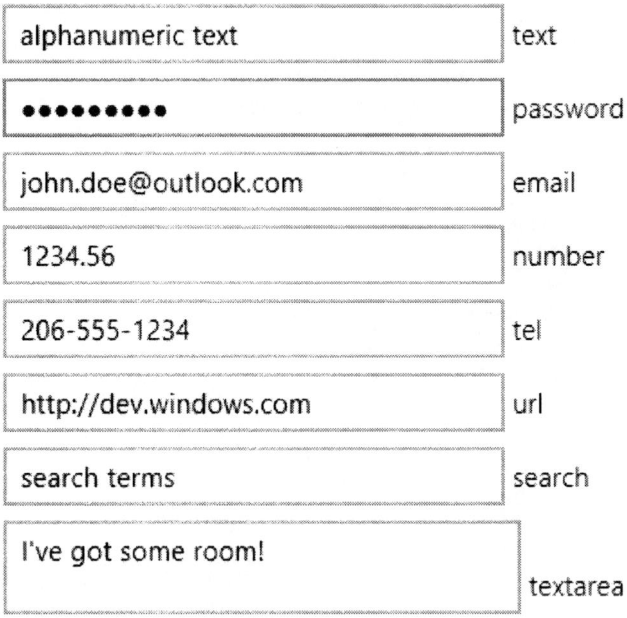

alphanumeric text	text
●●●●●●●●	password
john.doe@outlook.com	email
1234.56	number
206-555-1234	tel
http://dev.windows.com	url
search terms	search
I've got some room!	textarea

Figure 9-4. *Several different text box types*

As of HTML5, Internet Explorer and Windows 8 apps render most of the text box types with a small *X* on the right that allows a user to clear the text box value more easily. In Internet Explorer 10 and Windows 8 apps, you can target this small glyph for styling by using the `::-ms-clear` pseudo-element. That's very helpful for people that want very fine control over their styling.

Figure 9-5. *A small "x" glyph is rendered in text boxes to make it simple to clear out the box*

Likewise, for password text boxes, Internet Explorer and Windows 8 apps render a small eyeball glyph that will reveal the password that's been typed into the field only as long as the user presses the glyph. When a user knows that nobody is lurking over their shoulder or watching via screen share, it is helpful to be able to see the password that was typed to be sure there are no mistakes.

Figure 9-6. *A glyph is also rendered for a password field to temporarily unmask and reveal the contents*

Text boxes are at least 28 pixels high and 64 pixels wide with 2-pixel, solid borders.

The textarea element is a minimum of 39 pixels high by 260 pixels wide and has the same 2-pixel, solid border. For textarea elements, the vertical overflow is set to scroll by default, so if a user enters too much text, a scroll bar will be rendered and still enable the user to access and edit all of their text.

You can add a win-textarea class to any element to give it the style characteristics of a textarea regardless of what the actual element is.

Radio Buttons

Radio buttons are for choices—either or choices. You give your users radio buttons when you want them to decide on a single value only. Most people will recognize the familiar small round radio buttons. Listing 9-4 shows how they look in Windows 8.

Listing 9-4. Three radio type inputs are specified with labels. All three elements have the name "fruit" so that they will function mutually exclusive (selecting one will deselect the others)

```
<!-- HTML snippet -->
<label><input type="radio" name="fruit" value="Apple"/> Apple</label><br />
<label><input type="radio" name="fruit" value="Orange"/> Orange</label><br />
<label><input type="radio" name="fruit" value="Banana"/> Banana</label>
```

Figure 9-7. Three radio buttons ready for interaction

Radio buttons (and their closely related siblings, the checkboxes) are filled with a glyph when they are selected, and the developer can target that glyph itself using the ::-ms-check pseudo-element. If you want a more colorful dot in your radio button, this pseudo-element is going to be your only hope.

Like a lot of Windows 8 controls, radio buttons have a 2-pixel, solid border. They are also given a default size of 23 pixels square.

Checkboxes

Checkboxes and radio buttons have a lot in common behind the scenes, but for the user they are entirely different. Checkboxes are for options; they're for binary flags. If this is what you're shooting for, however, you should consider the ToggleSwitch control that WinJS offers. It is a bit friendlier and more touchable control with a lot of Windows 8 personality. More importantly, the ToggleSwitch implies to the user that the change is going to take effect immediately, whereas checkboxes imply that a change will take effect only after a form is submitted. Listing 9-5 shows a basic sample of checkboxes being laid out in a vertical list.

Listing 9-5. The type is now "checkbox".

```
<!-- HTML snippet -->
<label><input type="checkbox" value="Apple"/> Apple</label><br />
<label><input type="checkbox" value="Orange"/> Orange</label><br />
<label><input type="checkbox" value="Banana"/> Banana</label>
```

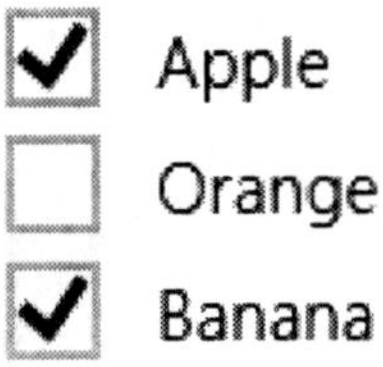

☑ Apple

☐ Orange

☑ Banana

Figure 9-8. *Checkboxes are rendered allowing multiple items to be selected*

By default, a checkbox will be 21 pixels square and have the typical 2-pixel, solid border.

Range

A range (or slider control) is a new control for HTML5. The range control gives the user a user interface (UI) for easily selecting from a range of values such as an integer range of values.

Listing 9-6. A simple input of type "range" is declared

```
<!-- HTML snippet -->
<input type="range" />
```

A number of the parts that make up a range control can be targeted with pseudo-elements.

- **::-ms-track.** - the track the slider follows that represents the range of possible values

- **::-ms-thumb.** - the part the user drags that represents the current value on the control

- **::-ms-ticks-before.** - applies to the tick marks that appear on top (in left-to-right layout) or on the left (in top-to-bottom layout) of the track

- **::-ms-ticks-after.** - applies to the tick marks that appear on the bottom (in left-to-right layout) or on the bottom (in top-to-bottom layout) of the track

- **::-ms-fill-lower.** - applies to the portion of the track from the smallest value to the current value

- **::-ms-fill-upper.** - applies to the portion of the track from the current value to the largest value

As you can see in the example in Figure 9-9, range indicators render as a simple rectangle with a small thumb slider and with the *lower* portion of the range filled in with color. As you can also see, the range control shows up horizontally by default. You can add the win-vertical class value to it, however, and it will appear vertically instead. Decide whether your range indicators will be horizontal or vertical based on your own unique UI.

Figure 9-9. *A Windows 8-style range control is rendered*

Select Box

A select box is practically an antique in the HTML world. This control has one or more options in a list. It can be configured to either show the entire list of options or to show only a single option, in which case the rest will be listed when the user expands the list. It can also be configured to allow a single selected value or multiple values.

Listing 9-7. Three fruit are declared as options to a select list, but only one of them is selected

```
<!-- HTML snippet -->
<select>
    <option selected>Apple</option>
    <option>Orange</option>
    <option>Banana</option>
</select>
```

Figure 9-10. *A select list is rendered with the selected value showing*

Select lists, by default, adopt the same flat, basic, unadorned look as other controls with a 2px rectangular border. The expansion glyph that is rendered on the right side of the select list appears as a simple chevron, but it can be targeted with the `::-ms-expand` pseudo-element, so you can change that glyph very easily. You can also use the `::-ms-value` pseudo-element to target the individual elements in the list.

Progress Indicator

Progress indicators are ubiquitous and, frankly, very helpful. You saw them on the web before HTML5 introduced its semantic-tag version, but they were custom and they were a bit difficult. Now declaring a progress indicator is extremely simple; as is styling it. Listing 9-8 actually declares three progress indicators in the same number of lines of code.

Listing 9-8. Progress indicators set to render as the 3 basic types

```
<!-- HTML snippet -->
<progress value="1"></progress>
<progress></progress>
<progress class="win-ring"></progress>
```

Figure 9-11. *The 3 basic types of progress indicator*

You can target the bar that fills the progress indicator by using the `::-ms-fill` pseudo-element.

If you don't override and specify otherwise and you don't add any classes to your progress indicator, it will be 180 pixels wide and 6 pixels tall with no border. Like all of the other controls, the default styling for the progress element amounts to a clean and simple UI element.

If you don't provide a value for the value attribute of your progress control then it will be considered an *indeterminate* progress indicator. That means that it will not render as a bar that fills up to full, but instead will just be fancy, flying dots that indicate that a task is running but will not commit to when that task might be done. You can select indeterminate progress elements using the :indeterminate pseudo-class.

There are a few classes that are recognized by the WinJS style sheets, so you can add them to your progress element to affect its appearance. They are:

- **win-medium.** Progress indicators with a class of win-medium will be 280 pixels wide instead of the default 180 pixels.

- **win-large.** Progress indicators with a class of win-large will snap to 100% width in their parent container.

- **win-paused.** The moment a determinate progress indicator is assigned a class of win-paused, it will animate from full opacity down to 50%. So in plain terms, when you pause a progress indicator, it fades out.

- **win-error.** When a progress indicator is in error (when it has a win-error class) the ::-ms-fill of the indicator will be hidden entirely.

- **win-ring.** Add a class of win-ring to your progress indicator to completely transform it into a spinning circle of dots. This compact format may fit better in your design.

WinJS Controls

Like HTML elements, WinJS controls result in UI that allows the user to interact with an app. That's about where the similarities end however. HTML elements are indicated once in your markup and then rendered on the user agent. A WinJS control, on the other hand, starts out as a div element with a special data-win-control attribute, is then processed by the JavaScript in the WinJS library, and finally results in the rendering of HTML elements that the user agent knows what to do with.

Consequently, in this section, we're going to look not only at the default styling of the controls, but we'll look extensively at what exactly gets rendered by the JavaScript processing. We'll actually use the very valuable DOM Explorer to take the exact HTML rendered and see everything it includes.

You'll see that the rendered HTML elements are painted with class values that act as handles for you to add styling to the various aspects of each possible complex control. Let me give you an example of what I'm talking about.

A DatePicker control results in multiple elements that represent the components of a data. If you need to add some styling to the month component alone, you're in luck, because the month component will be rendered in an HTML element that WinJS has decorated with win-datepicker-month.

All of these classes begin with win-datepicker-, so they should be easy to spot and easy to differentiate.

Let's go ahead and detail the many WinJS controls, what they render by default, and how they allow you to control their styles with class values. We'll look at the following WinJS controls:

- Binding Template

- DataPicker

- TimePicker

- Rating

- ToggleSwitch

- ListView

- SemanticZoom

- FlipView
- ViewBox
- HtmlControl
- Page

Binding Template

Most of the WinJS controls are found in the WinJS.UI namespace, but the Template control is in the WinJS.Binding namespace because of its close relationship to the features of that namespace.

Templates are used to create a boilerplate into which objects may be rendered. Renders are intended to allow a developer to write terse HTML that represents an object, but allows for the display of any object that might eventually be rendered into it.

Not a lot needs to be said about the styling of templates because most of the styling is left up to the developer. A single value—win-template—is added to the class of a template, however, and that allows you to target them effectively.

DatePicker

DatePicker and the rest of the WinJS controls that we'll discuss are found in the WinJS.UI namespace. Just like its name states, DatePicker allows the user to pick a calendar date. It's a very simple control that really just renders three HTML select lists to the markup—the month, the date, and the year. A default DatePicker looks like the one in Figure 9-12.

Listing 9-9. A DatePicker control from WinJS, declared using a standard div with a data-win-control attribute

```
<!-- HTML snippet -->
<div data-win-control="WinJS.UI.DatePicker"></div>
```

Figure 9-12. *A DatePicker is rendered as three select boxes*

It should be apparent when you look at the output in Figure 9-12 that the one line of HTML markup has been processed. The result contains three separate select boxes. Let's look at Listing 9-10 at the HTML that has actually been created in the processing.

Listing 9-10. The DatePicker in Listing 9-9 and Figure 9-12 results in three select lists for month, date, and year (shortened for brevity)

```
<!-- DOM Explorer snippet -->
<div class="win-datepicker" role="group" lang="en-US" dir="ltr"
    data-win-control="WinJS.UI.DatePicker">
    <select tabindex="0" class="win-datepicker-month win-order0"
        aria-label="Select Month">
        <option value="January">January</option>
        <option value="February">February</option>
```

```
        <option value="March">March</option>
        ...
        <option value="October">October</option>
        <option value="November">November</option>
        <option value="December">December</option>
    </select>
    <select tabindex="0" class="win-datepicker-date win-order1"
        aria-label="Select Day"><option value="1">1</option>
        <option value="2">2</option>
        <option value="3">3</option>
        ...
        <option value="28">28</option>
        <option value="29">29</option>
        <option value="30">30</option>
    </select>
    <select tabindex="0" class="win-datepicker-year win-order2"
        aria-label="Select Year">
        <option value="1912">1912</option>
        <option value="1913">1913</option>
        <option value="1914">1914</option>
        ...
        <option value="2110">2110</option>
        <option value="2111">2111</option>
        <option value="2112">2112</option>
    </select>
</div>
```

TimePicker

If you understood how the DatePicker works, you'll have no trouble with TimePicker. They're almost identical. Instead of rendering select lists for month, date, and year, the TimePicker control provides hour, minute, and period.

Listing 9-11. All WinJS controls use this same syntax for declaration

```
<!-- HTML snippet -->
<div data-win-control="WinJS.UI.TimePicker"></div>
```

Figure 9-13. *The TimePicker control also uses three select boxes*

Again, we've added a single line of HTML markup and yet our output contains three distinct select boxes. Listing 9-12 shows the resulting HTML from the DOM Explorer.

Listing 9-12. The TimePicker from Listing 9-11 and Figure 9-13 results in three select lists for hour, minute, and period (shortened for brevity)

```
<!-- DOM Explorer snippet -->
<div class="win-timepicker" role="group" lang="en-US" dir="ltr"
    data-win-control="WinJS.UI.TimePicker">
    <select tabindex="0" class="win-timepicker-hour win-order0"
        aria-label="Select Hour">
        <option value="12">12</option>
        <option value="1">1</option>
        <option value="2">2</option>
        ...
        <option value="9">9</option>
        <option value="10">10</option>
        <option value="11">11</option>
    </select>
    <select tabindex="0" class="win-timepicker-minute win-order1"
        aria-label="Select Minute">
        <option value="00">00</option>
        <option value="01">01</option>
        <option value="02">02</option>
        ...
        <option value="57">57</option>
        <option value="58">58</option>
        <option value="59">59</option>
    </select>
    <select tabindex="0" class="win-timepicker-period win-order2"
        aria-label="Select A.M P.M">
        <option value="AM">AM</option>
        <option value="PM">PM</option>
    </select>
</div>
```

Rating

Many apps include functionality for allowing users to rate goods and services for the good and service of other users. The 5-star rating system is a popular one, and that's exactly what the Rating control provides you by default, though it's not limited to 5 and it's not even limited to stars. Figure 9-14 shows you what you'll get with a typical Rating control.

Listing 9-13. A WinJS Rating control

```
<!-- HTML snippet -->
<div data-win-control="WinJS.UI.Rating"></div>
```

Figure 9-14. A Rating control is be default rendered using the popular 5-star system

A quick look at the DOM explorer to see how a Rating control is composed reveals the code in Listing 9-14.

Listing 9-14. The resulting DOM markup for a default rating control

```
<!-- DOM Explorer snippet -->
<div tabindex="0" class="win-rating" role="slider" aria-readonly="false" aria-valuenow="Unrated"
    aria-valuemin="0" aria-valuemax="5" aria-label="User Rating" aria-valuetext="Unrated"
    data-win-control="WinJS.UI.Rating">
    <div class="win-star win-empty win-user"></div>
    <div class="win-star win-empty win-user"></div>
    <div class="win-star win-empty win-user"></div>
    <div class="win-star win-empty win-user"></div>
    <div class="win-star win-empty win-user"></div>
    <div class="win-star win-average win-full win-user" style="-ms-flex: 0 0 auto;
        padding-right: 0px; padding-left: 0px; border-right-color: currentColor;
        border-left-color: currentColor; border-right-width: 0px; border-left-width: 0px;
        border-right-style: none; border-left-style: none; display: none;"></div>
</div>
```

Adding a class of win-small to your Rating control will result in a rating control that's half the size of a standard Rating control. The stars will be 14 pixels instead of the normal 28. Don't think that normal and small are your only options for sizing the Rating control. As with all of these controls, the power is in your hands as the developer. You could, for instance, use huge stars for your rating control by using a style rule like the one in Listing 9-15. We'll see many more of these overrides and extended styles in Chapter 10, but here's a taste of what I'm talking about.

In Listing 9-15, we see the style rule (included in WinJS) to make the starts smaller, and in the same listing we see a custom rule called win-huge that does the opposite and makes the stars bigger.

Listing 9-15. A custom style rule to increase the size of the stars

```
/* .win-small (from WinJS) */
.win-rating.win-small .win-star {
    width: 14px;
    height: 14px;
    font-size: 14px;
    padding: 0 3px;
}

/* custom .win-huge style */
.win-rating.win-huge .win-star {
    width: 56px;
    height: 56px;
    font-size: 56px;
    padding: 0 12px;
}
```

ToggleSwitch

As I mentioned previously, the ToggleSwitch control is a great alternative to the traditional checkbox. The ToggleSwitch is a larger and touch-friendlier target for binary decisions. Use it, for example, to give your users the option to turn their in-game music on or off.

Listing 9-16 shows the control and Figure 9-15 shows what a typical ToggleSwitch looks like.

Listing 9-16. A WinJS ToggleSwitch control

```
<!-- HTML snippet -->
<div data-win-control="WinJS.UI.ToggleSwitch"></div>
```

On

Figure 9-15. The ToggleSwitch is a more user-friendly way of answering a binary question such as Yes/No

The HTML that is generated for the ToggleSwitch control might surprise you. HTML doesn't have a native element that looks like a toggle control. It simply doesn't exist. Yet, WinJS controls do not render new graphic elements. The Windows team got creative in this case and used a progress indicator, but changed the dimensions of the bar itself and the slider to look like a toggle. You can see the progress indicator in resulting HTML in Listing 9-17.

Listing 9-17. The resulting DOM output for a default ToggleSwitch control

```
<!-- DOM Explorer snippet -->
<div class="win-toggleswitch win-off" data-win-control="WinJS.UI.ToggleSwitch">
    <div class="win-title" id="ms__id32" role="note"></div>
    <div style="display: -ms-grid;">
        <div class="win-label ">On</div>
        <div class="win-label win-hidden">Off</div>
        <input class="win-switch" role="checkbox" aria-checked="false"
            aria-disabled="false" aria-labelledby="ms__id32" type="range"
            max="1" step="1"></div>
</div>
```

Notice that the ToggleSwitch control is actually implemented using an `<input type="range"/>` element. A max value of 1 and a `step` value of 1 make the range control act like a binary switch. It's a very clever way to reuse something that already exists.

Because the ToggleSwitch uses a range control, all of the same pseudo-elements that apply to the range element can apply to the ToggleSwitch as well. The range element within the toggle is given a class of win-switch, so a CSS selector of `#myToggle .win-switch::-ms-thumb` would select the slider of a ToggleSwitch with an `id` of `myToggle`. Here is that list of pseudo-elements once again: `::-ms-thumb`, `::-ms-tooltip`, `::-ms-ticks-before`, `::-ms-ticks-after`, `::-ms-track`, `::-ms-fill-upper`, and `::-ms-fill-lower`.

ListView

The ListView is an important control in a Windows 8 app. I introduced you to its functionality in Chapter 7, but now it's time to dissect the control for its classes and figure out how we can style it the way we want. Figure 9-16 shows you again what that ListView from Chapter 7 looked like.

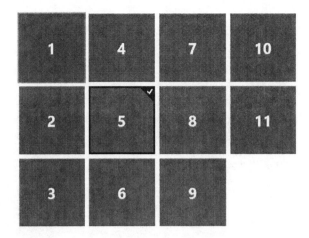

Figure 9-16. *A typical ListView borrowed from Figure 7-19 in Chapter 7*

The syntax for declaring a ListView is the same as every other WinJS control as you can see in Listing 9-18, but that declaration alone results in an empty ListView that you can't even see when you execute your app. Consulting the DOM Explorer assures us that it's there, however, and you can see the result in Listing 9-19.

Listing 9-18. Declaration for a simple (and empty) ListView control

```
<!-- HTML snippet -->
<div data-win-control="WinJS.UI.ListView"></div>
```

In Listing 9-19, the DOM Explorer shows us the HTML generated by a simple ListView control with no data bound to it at all.

Listing 9-19. The markup for an empty ListView

```
<!-- DOM Explorer snippet -->
<div tabindex="-1" class="win-listview win-swipeable" role="listbox"
    style="position: relative;" data-win-control="WinJS.UI.ListView">
    <div tabindex="-1" class="win-viewport win-horizontal" role="group"
        aria-label="Scrolling Container">
        <div id="ms__id31" aria-flowto="ms__id32"></div>
        <div class="win-surface">
            <div class="win-backdrop" aria-hidden="true" style="width: 0px; height: 0px;"></div>
            <div class="win-backdrop" aria-hidden="true" style="width: 0px; height: 0px;"></div>
            <div class="_win-proxy"></div>
            <div tabindex="0" aria-hidden="true"></div>
            <div style="left: 0px; top: 0px; width: 100%; height: 100%; position: absolute;">
            </div>
            <div tabindex="0" aria-hidden="true"></div>
        </div>
        <div id="ms__id32" x-ms-aria-flowfrom="ms__id31"></div>
    </div>
    <div tabindex="0" aria-hidden="true"></div>
    <div aria-hidden="true" style="left: 50%; top: 50%; position: absolute;">
```

```
        <div tabindex="0" aria-hidden="true"></div>
        <div aria-hidden="true" style="width: 0px; height: 0px;"></div>
        <div tabindex="0" aria-hidden="true"></div>
    </div>
    <div tabindex="0" aria-hidden="true"></div>
</div>
```

As you can tell, there's a lot going on with this one (and keep in mind this is an empty list!) Let's take a look now at a ListView with just a little bit of data populating it.

Listing 9-20. HTML and JavaScript for not only declaring a ListView, but populating it too

```
<!-- HTML snippet -->
<div data-win-control="WinJS.UI.ListView"></div>
<div data-win-control="WinJS.Binding.Template">
    <span data-win-bind="innerText:this"></span>
</div>


// JavaScript snippet
var list = new WinJS.Binding.List(["one", "two", "three"]);
var listViewElement = element.querySelector("[data-win-control='WinJS.UI.ListView']");
var templateElement = element.querySelector("[data-win-control='WinJS.Binding.Template']");
listViewElement.winControl.itemDataSource = list.dataSource;
listViewElement.itemTemplate = templateElement;
```

Listing 9-21. The resulting DOM markup for a ListView with some data bound to it

```
<!-- DOM Explorer snippet -->
<div tabindex="-1" class="win-listview win-swipeable" role="listbox" style="position: relative;"
    data-win-control="WinJS.UI.ListView">
    <div tabindex="-1" class="win-viewport win-horizontal" role="group"
        style="opacity: 1; -ms-scroll-limit-x-min: 0px;" aria-label="Scrolling Container">
        <div id="ms__id42" aria-flowto="ms__id35"></div>
        <div class="win-surface" style="width: 35px; opacity: 1;">
            <div class="win-backdrop" aria-hidden="true"
                style='left: 35px; top: 0px; width: 0px; height: 390px;
                background-image: url("data:image/png;base64,…");'></div>
            <div class="win-backdrop" aria-hidden="true"
                style='left: 0px; top: 0px; width: 0px; height: 390px;
                background-image: url("data:image/png;base64,…");'></div>
            <div class="_win-proxy"></div>
            <div tabindex="0" aria-hidden="true"></div>
            <div style="left: 0px; top: 0px; width: 100%; height: 100%;
                position: absolute; clip: auto;">
                <div class="win-container" style="left: 0px; top: 0px;
                    width: 25px; height: 20px;">
                    <div tabindex="0" aria-hidden="true"></div>
                    <span class="win-item" id="ms__id35" role="option" aria-posinset="1"
                        aria-setsize="3" aria-flowto="ms__id37" x-ms-aria-flowfrom="ms__id42">
                        one
                    </span>
```

```
                <div tabindex="0" aria-hidden="true"></div>
            </div>
            <div class="win-container" style="left: 0px; top: 30px;
                width: 25px; height: 20px;">
                <span class="win-item" id="ms__id37" role="option" aria-posinset="2"
                    aria-setsize="3" aria-flowto="ms__id39" x-ms-aria-flowfrom="ms__id35">
                    two
                </span>
            </div>
            <div class="win-container" style="left: 0px; top: 60px;
                width: 25px; height: 20px;">
                <span class="win-item" id="ms__id39" role="option" aria-posinset="3"
                    aria-setsize="3" aria-flowto="ms__id43" x-ms-aria-flowfrom="ms__id37">
                    three
                </span>
            </div>
        </div>
        <div tabindex="0" aria-hidden="true"></div>
    </div>
    <div id="ms__id43" x-ms-aria-flowfrom="ms__id39"></div>
</div>
<div tabindex="0" aria-hidden="true"></div>
<div aria-hidden="true" style="left: 50%; top: 50%; position: absolute;">
    <div aria-hidden="true" style="width: 0px; height: 0px;"></div>
</div>
<div tabindex="0" aria-hidden="true"></div>
</div>
```

There's obviously even more going on in this data-bound ListView, including a few things that I want to bring to your attention:

- Notice that the entire ListView is in an element that has a class of win-listview. This becomes a convenient handle for the entire control.

- Notice the use of the class win-swipeable. If you look up the styling on win-swipeable in the default style sheet, you'll see that it's responsible for the scrolling behavior.

- Notice the use of the win-horizontal class. ListView controls can be set to vertical as well, and this is the class that ends up determining the orientation and behavior.

- Notice the win-container and win-item elements around each individual item in the list. When you need to style the items in your list, one of these two classes is a great way to narrow down your selection to just list containers or list items.

- Notice the absolute positioning. The first item is set with a top value of 0px, the second with 30px, and the third with 60px.

- Notice the use of the win-viewport and win-surface classes. The distinction between these two components is important as you'll see in a second.

The article at http://msdn.microsoft.com/en-us/library/windows/apps/hh850406.aspx on the Windows Dev Center is extremely helpful in visualizing the visual (and functional) components that make up a ListView. Have a look at Figure 9-17, which comes from that article. It's absolutely essential to understand the win-listview, win-surface, and win-viewport classes.

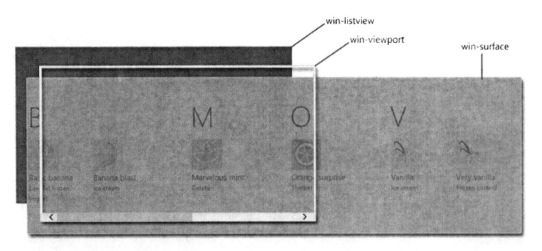

Figure 9-17. A diagram showing the various components that make up a ListView, which is very helpful when trying to add or override styles that affect this relatively complex WinJS control

Think of the `win-viewport` as a frame behind which the `win-surface` can slide as the user is scrolling. Add or manipulate style properties on the `win-listview` if it should affect the entire control. The `win-viewport` contains the scrolling behavior (`overflow-x` and `overflow-y`). Style `win-surface` if you want to affect the background that actually appears behind your list items.

SemanticZoom

Related to the ListView is the SemanticZoom control. A SemanticZoom control is meant to contain two ListView controls—the standard ListView (the *near* view) and another that represents a logically zoomed out view of the same data (the *far* view). Typically, the far view shows groups representing the data in the near view. A list of groups is terser than the complete set of data, and an additional feature is the ability for the user to select a group from the far view and be navigated directly to that group in the near view.

Figure 9-18 shows a simplified model of a semantic zoom control. In the first image, multiple groups are displayed with their associated items. After the user does a pinch zoom gesture on the list, they are animated and converted to the second image where the groups are displayed, but not their items.

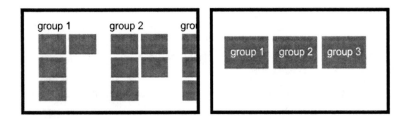

Figure 9-18. Semantic zoom orients the user and facilitates navigation as well

Notice that the third group is not entirely visible in the zoomed in list (the first image in Figure 9-18) but it is in the zoomed out list. Semantically zooming out of a list of data becomes a way to not only orient and digest a large list but also becomes an easier way to navigate one.

Semantic zoom is a feature unique to Windows 8 and is intended to help a user more easily orient to and navigate large lists of data.

You may need to target your SemanticZoom control either to style it or to otherwise manipulate it. The rendered version of a SemanticZoom control is a little on the complex side, but to reference one it suffices to know the class that WinJS assigns it. You can see in Listing 9-23 that that class name is win-semanticzoom. You can also see the complexity I was referring to. The near and far view lists have been collapsed and dimmed in the listing and still quite a bit of markup exists. This markup styles and positions the control as well as adding transformations and transitions to it to give it the unique personality and behavior that is a Windows 8 SemanticZoom control.

Listing 9-22. The HTML, CSS, and JavaScript for creating a SemanticZoom control

```
<!-- HTML snippet -->
<div data-win-control="WinJS.UI.SemanticZoom">
    <div id="list1" data-win-control="WinJS.UI.ListView"></div>
    <div id="list2" data-win-control="WinJS.UI.ListView"></div>
</div>
<div id="itemtemplate" data-win-control="WinJS.Binding.Template">
    <span data-win-bind="innerText:this"></span>
</div>
<div id="grouptemplate" data-win-control="WinJS.Binding.Template">
    <h2 data-win-bind="innerText:this"></h2>
</div>
<div id="semantictemplate" data-win-control="WinJS.Binding.Template">
    <div data-win-bind="innerText:this"></div>
</div>

/* CSS snippet */
.lst0922  #list1 .win-item { width:80px; }

// JavaScript snippet
var numbersList = new WinJS.Binding.List([1,2,3,4,5,6,7,8,9,10]).createGrouped(
    function(item) { return (item <= 5 ? "1-5" : "6-10"); },
    function (item) { return (item <= 5 ? "1-5" : "6-10"); }
);
var list1 = element.querySelector("#list1").winControl;
list1.itemDataSource = numbersList.dataSource;
list1.itemTemplate = element.querySelector("#itemtemplate");
list1.groupDataSource = numbersList.groups.dataSource;
list1.groupHeaderTemplate = element.querySelector("#grouptemplate");

var list2 = element.querySelector("#list2").winControl;
list2.itemDataSource = numbersList.groups.dataSource;
list2.itemTemplate = element.querySelector("#semantictemplate");
```

Listing 9-23. The resulting DOM markup for a SemanticZoom control (with lists dimmed and collapsed for brevity)

```
<!-- DOM Explorer snippet -->
<div class="win-semanticzoom" role="ms-semanticzoomcontainer" aria-checked="false"
    style="overflow: hidden; position: relative;" aria-label=""
    data-win-control="WinJS.UI.SemanticZoom">
    <div style="left: 0px; top: 0px; width: 1264px; height: 400px; overflow: hidden;
        position: absolute;">
```

```
    <div style="left: 0px; top: 0px; width: 1264px; height: 400px; overflow: hidden;
        visibility: visible; position: absolute; transition-property: transform;
        transition-duration: 0s; transition-timing-function: linear;">
        <div style="transform-origin: 695.615px 200px; transition: transform 0.33s
            ease-in-out 34ms, opacity 0.33s ease-in-out 34ms; left: -680.61px; top: 0px;
            width: 2625.23px; height: 400px;overflow: hidden; position: absolute;
            opacity: 1; transform: scale(1);">

            <div class="win-listview win-swipeable win-groups" id="list1" ...>...</div>

        </div>
    </div>
    <div style="left: 0px; top: 0px; width: 1264px; height: 400px; overflow: hidden;
        visibility: hidden; position: absolute; transition-property: transform;
        transition-duration: 0s;transition-timing-function: linear;">
        <div style="transform-origin: 78.2px 200px; transition: transform 0.33s
            ease-in-out 34ms, opacity 0.33s ease-in-out 34ms; left: -63.2px; top: 0px;
            width: 1390.4px; height: 400px; overflow: hidden; position: absolute;
            opacity: 0; transform: scale(1.53846);">

            <div class="win-listview win-swipeable" id="list2" ...>...</div>

        </div>
    </div>
  </div>
  <button tabindex="-1" class="win-semanticzoom-button win-semanticzoom-button-location ltr"
      style="visibility: hidden; opacity: 0;"></button>
  <div tabindex="-1" aria-hidden="true"></div>
</div>
```

FlipView

The FlipView control is an excellent choice for many cases. It can be used to provide browsing for images, articles, or entire sections of your application. A simple swipe gesture from side to side is all it takes to command the FlipView to switch to its next item, complete with animation, easing, and snapping.

A FlipView is another one of those controls that takes a bit of code to demonstrate and the reason is that it is a data-bound control. This means that, just like the ListView, we're going to bind our FlipView to a WinJS.Binding.List object and whenever anything in that List changes, our FlipView will automatically respond without us having to manually catch that event and update the items in our FlipView.

Also, like the ListView, the FlipView gives us the opportunity to specify a template which is used to render each item.

Listing 9-24. A FlipView with some simple images bound to it

```
<!-- HTML snippet -->
<div id="flipview" data-win-control="WinJS.UI.FlipView"></div>
<div id="template" data-win-control="WinJS.Binding.Template">
    <img data-win-bind="src:this"/>
</div>
```

```
/* CSS snippet */
.lst0924 .win-flipview {
    width: 480px;
    height: 320px;
}

//JavaScript
var flipview = element.querySelector("#flipview").winControl;
var template = element.querySelector("#template");

var fruitList = new WinJS.Binding.List([
    "/pages/chapter9/lst0924/peaches.png",
    "/pages/chapter9/lst0924/grapes.png",
    "/pages/chapter9/lst0924/orange.png
"]);
flipview.itemDataSource = fruitList.dataSource;
flipview.itemTemplate = template;
```

Figure 9-19 appears to be a single image, but you can see that arrows are rendered on each edge. The arrows are visible so a mouse user has something to click, but a touch user can simply swipe the list to change to a new image.

Figure 9-19. *When you're using a mouse to interact with Windows 8, next and previous arrows are rendered onto each side of the FlipView. You can always use a swipe gesture to switch too*

The entire FlipView itself gets a `win-flipview` class, which makes it easy to refer to the FlipView control(s) in your running app. The items that populate your FlipView, however are rendered onto an embedded div that is given the win-surface class. Like the ListView, you can think of this element as a long strip that contains all of the items and that slides to reveal one frame at a time.

Finally, the FlipView has the two navigation buttons that appear only if the user is using a mouse. There's no need for the navigation buttons to appear if the user has been using touch to interact, because a simple swipe gesture is all it takes to navigate forward or backward. You can see the markup for these buttons in Listing 9-25. They are HTML buttons and they have been granted class values of `win-navbutton` and `win-navleft` or `win-navright`. You certainly don't have to be content with the left and right arrows that render for a FlipView by default. You can override this by referencing those class values. We're going to learn much more about that in Chapter 10.

Listing 9-25. The markup that results from WinJS FlipView declaration

```
<div tabindex="-1" class="win-flipview" id="flipview" role="listbox" style="overflow: hidden;"
    aria-label="" data-win-control="WinJS.UI.FlipView">
    <div style="width: 100%; height: 100%; position: relative; z-index: 0;">
        <div tabindex="0" aria-hidden="true"></div>
        <div class="win-surface" role="group" style="-ms-scroll-snap-x: mandatory
            snapInterval(0px, 480px); width: 100%; height: 100%; position: relative;
            -ms-overflow-x: scroll; -ms-overflow-y: hidden; -ms-scroll-limit-x-min: 240000px;
            -ms-scroll-limit-x-max: 240960px; -ms-overflow-style: none;"
            aria-label="Scrolling Container">
            <div style="width: 100%; height: 100%; position: relative;">
                <div id="ms__id5" aria-flowto="ms__id36"></div>
                <div style="left: 240000px; width: 480px; height: 320px; overflow: hidden;
                    position: absolute;">
                    <div class="win-item" style="-ms-overflow-style: auto;">
                        <div tabindex="0" aria-hidden="true"></div>
                        <div tabindex="0" class="win-template" id="ms__id36" role="option"
                            aria-selected="true" aria-posinset="1" aria-setsize="3"
                            aria-flowto="ms__id37" x-ms-aria-flowfrom="ms__id5">
                            <img src="/pages/chapter9/lst0924/peaches.png"
                                data-win-bind="src:this">
                        </div>
                        <div tabindex="0" aria-hidden="true"></div>
                    </div>
                </div>
                <div style="left: 240480px; width: 480px; height: 320px; overflow: hidden;
                    position: absolute;">
                    <div class="win-item" style="-ms-overflow-style: auto;">
                        <div tabindex="0" class="win-template" id="ms__id37" role="option"
                            aria-selected="false" aria-flowto="ms__id38"
                            x-ms-aria-flowfrom="ms__id36">
                            <img src="/pages/chapter9/lst0924/grapes.png"
                                data-win-bind="src:this">
                        </div>
                    </div>
                </div>
                <div style="left: 240960px; width: 480px; height: 320px; overflow: hidden;
                    position: absolute;">
                    <div class="win-item" style="-ms-overflow-style: auto;">
                        <div tabindex="0" class="win-template" id="ms__id38" role="option"
                            aria-selected="false" aria-flowto="ms__id6"
                            x-ms-aria-flowfrom="ms__id37">
                            <img src="/pages/chapter9/lst0924/orange.png"
                                data-win-bind="src:this">
                        </div>
                    </div>
                </div>
                <div style="left: 239040px; width: 480px; height: 320px; overflow: hidden;
                    position: absolute;">
                    <div class="win-item" style="-ms-overflow-style: auto;"></div>
                </div>
```

```
                    <div style="left: 239520px; width: 480px; height: 320px; overflow: hidden;
                        position: absolute;">
                        <div class="win-item" style="-ms-overflow-style: auto;"></div>
                    </div>
                    <div id="ms__id6" x-ms-aria-flowfrom="ms__id38"></div>
                </div>
            </div>
            <div tabindex="0" aria-hidden="true"></div>
            <button tabindex="-1" class="win-navbutton win-navleft" aria-hidden="true"
                style="visibility: hidden; z-index: 1000; opacity: 0;" aria-label="Previous"
                type="button">·</button>
            <button tabindex="-1" class="win-navbutton win-navright" aria-hidden="false"
                style="visibility: hidden; z-index: 1000; opacity: 0;" aria-label="Next"
                type="button">·</button>
        </div>
</div>
```

ViewBox

The function of a ViewBox was covered in Chapter 7, but let's review it quickly. A ViewBox snaps to the size of its parent container and then scales a single child item (it can have only one) without affecting its aspect ratio to fit the size of the ViewBox. It responds to changes in view state as well, so when the user rotates their tablet, the ViewBox handles the scaling of its contents accordingly.

We didn't take the time in Chapter 7 to see how a ViewBox is actually implemented. So let's see that now complete with the entire DOM Explorer output of a rendered ViewBox.

In Listing 9-26, we have a *parent* div which contains a ViewBox which contains a *child* div. Notice in the CSS that the parent is oriented vertically with a width of 100 pixels and a height of 300 pixels. Notice too that the child is oriented horizontally with a width of 300 pixels and a height of 100 pixels. Instead of clipping the child, stretching the parent, or rendering scroll bars to reveal hidden content, the ViewBox has preserved the child element and simply scaled it to fit in the parent div.

Listing 9-26. A parent div that contains a ViewBox that contains a child div

```
<!-- HTML snippet -->
<div class="parent">
    <div data-win-control="WinJS.UI.ViewBox">
        <div class="child"></div>
    </div>
</div>

/* CSS snippet */
.lst0926 .parent {
    width: 100px;
    height: 300px;
    border: solid 2px gray;
}

.lst0926 .child {
    width: 300px;
    height: 100px;
    border: solid 2px;
}
```

Listing 9-27. The ViewBox has scaled the child div to fit right in its parent

```
<div class="parent">
    <div class="win-viewbox" data-win-control="WinJS.UI.ViewBox">
        <div class="horizontal" style="transform-origin: left top;
            transform: translate(0px, 133.333px) scale(0.333333);"></div>
    </div>
</div>
```

One huge advantage of the behavior of the ViewBox is that the child div can contain any manner of content and yet it will be scaled and positioned the same. It's an excellent way to take, for instance, an entire game board and scale it to fit either in landscape mode or portrait mode.

HtmlControl

The HtmlControl makes it really simple to bring HTML in from another document and render it into any area of another. You might use HtmlControls to build up a page out of smaller page components that might be easier to maintain or collaborate on.

Listing 9-28. An HTML snippet that uses a WinJS HtmlControl to "import" the HTML in a separate file

```
<!-- HTML snippet -->
<div class="parent">
    <div data-win-control="WinJS.UI.HtmlControl"
        data-win-options="{uri:'/pages/chapter9/lst0928/page.html'}">
    </div>
</div>

/* CSS snippet */
.parent {
    border: solid 2px gray;
    width: 200px;
    padding: 5px;
}

<!-- page.html -->
<!DOCTYPE html>
<html>
    <head>
        <title></title>
    </head>
    <body>
        Hello, I came from page.html
    </body>
</html>
```

Hello, I came from page.html

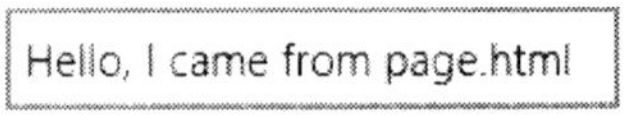

Figure 9-20. *The result of importing external HTML into a div*

You can see that the "Hello, I came from page.html" is in a separate HTML file, but we have used an HtmlControl to declaratively (there is no JavaScript in Listing 9-28) import it into the HTML in the snippet.

Listing 9-29. The resulting DOM markup for an HtmlControl includes a pagecontrol class

```
<!-- DOM Explorer snippet -->
<div class="parent">
    <div class="pagecontrol" data-win-options="{uri:'/pages/chapter9/lst0929/page.html'}"
        data-win-control="WinJS.UI.HtmlControl">
        Hello, I came from page.html
    </div>
</div>
```

The div that we originally gave the `data-win-control` and `data-win-options` attributes is also given a class name of pagecontrol which will again make it easy for us to identify and target.

Page

A *page* in WinJS is a complete set of HTML, CSS, and JavaScript that represents a single view. In traditional web development, pages were most often navigated between using hyperlinks. That style of navigation is certainly still supported in Windows 8, but it's usually a better idea to use the built-in framework for doing single page navigation. When implementing this navigation model, a logical page is still an actual HTML page (and usually a CSS and a JavaScript file as well), but you won't typically hyperlink to it. Instead, you'll use the navigation framework to *navigate* to it, which will result in the final rendering of the page being appended to the DOM of the starting page (default.html).

Understanding the way these pages are identified becomes rather important for a few reasons. Fortunately, it's a very elegant and easy to understand convention.

Just inside the body element of each page's HTML file, you'll find a div element with two class names. The first is the name of the page and the second is fragment. The helloworld page would then look something like what you see in Listing 9-30.

Listing 9-30. A page using WinJS's navigation model contains a fragment—a simple div with two class names that make it easy for WinJS and for us to target

```
<!-- helloworld.html -->
<!DOCTYPE html>
<html>
<head>
    <meta charset="utf-8" />
    <title>Orders Page</title>

    <!-- WinJS references -->
    <link href="//Microsoft.WinJS.1.0/css/ui-light.css" rel="stylesheet" />
    <script src="//Microsoft.WinJS.1.0/js/base.js"></script>
    <script src="//Microsoft.WinJS.1.0/js/ui.js"></script>

    <link href="helloworld.css" rel="stylesheet" />
    <script src="helloworld.js"></script>
</head>
```

```
<body>
    <div class="helloworld fragment">
        <section aria-label="Main content" role="main">
            <p>Hello, World!</p>
        </section>
    </div>
</body>
</html>
```

Notice the bolded class names. The first matches the name of the page and the second is `fragment`. It is this entire fragment that is going to be injected into the `default.html` page.

You can use these classes as handles of your own, though, too. If you want to create a style that affects pages, you can prefix it with `.fragment`. If you want to apply a style that affects only the `helloworld` page, you can prefix it with `.helloworld`.

This glimpse into the styling of the basic HTML controls and the extra controls given to us by WinJS is not enough to thoroughly understand this robust library for creating Windows 8 apps, so I suggest that you spend some quality time in the `ui-light.css` document to understand what it's doing to the various controls and thus what you can extend or override.

The next chapter is all about extending and overriding. If WinJS has determined that a button's border is gray and you'd rather it be dark green, then that would be an override. If WinJS doesn't say anything at all about that button's background color, but you need one, then that's an extension to the button's styles.

Summary

In this chapter, we've learned that WinJS helps us out a lot in a Windows 8 app. WinJS provides a number of controls that are composed of nothing more than native HTML elements. They provide richer user interaction and a more consistent Windows 8 experience.

WinJS also gives us a massive collection of CSS style rules that apply to the native HTML elements and the WinJS controls alike. These style rules make it simple to get the visual elements in your app laid out and styled to look like a Windows 8 app and also to give it its own unique flavor.

The WinJS library makes its controls easy for us to declare while it handles the processing of our simple declaration to turn it into native HTML elements. While it's creating the HTML that ends up being rendered, it adds helpful class names to the various parts so that we have "hooks" that we can use to style the control at large or target individual components.

It's all an effort to provide the user a balance of great control and great ease of development, and it's quite effective.

CHAPTER 10

Overriding and Defining Styles

Note You've learned all about CSS and how it's implemented in Windows 8 apps. Now it's high time to start creating your own styles and overriding and extending those provided by WinJS to give your app its own personality while conforming to Microsoft design principles.

The objective of this chapter is to learn how to style our app like we want. Good design is not entirely objective, but there are a lot of principles that apply and there are certainly a lot of principles around *good Windows 8 design* that can contribute significantly to your app's success.

To get some control over the UI in our app, we will first find the style rules defined in the WinJS style sheet that apply to the elements in our app, and then we will either override the style properties defined in those rules or we will add our own properties to extend them. Furthermore, we will create our own style rules to apply to elements on the page or perhaps to custom controls that we write.

Locating Style Selectors

Before we can override and extend the style rules defined in WinJS, we have to find the one or more rules that are affecting the visual elements in question. With so many rules, this is not a trivial task.

We've already seen that WinJS provides a wealth of styles for us and that's why without any styling code at all, we start out with an app that looks like a Windows 8 app. The styles in the WinJS library are not only numerous, but some are rather lengthy as well. Listing 10-1 displays two of the many style rule selectors you'll find in the `ui-light.css` style sheet. The first simply selects *a button*, but the second shows how specific they can get and selects *the selection border for selected, hovered containers in ListViews that are not "selectionstylefilled"*.

Listing 10-1. One very simple and one very complicated style selector

```
button {
    ...
}

.win-listview:not(.win-selectionstylefilled)
    .win-container.win-selected:hover .win-selectionborder {
    ...
}
```

Discovering where and how style rules are being applied would be a daunting task full of guesswork if you didn't have the Trace Style pane in the DOM Explorer to assist. It turns an otherwise painful task into a painless one.

Let's walk through an exercise to uncover relevant style rules. First, we'll look for a rule that's affecting the ListView control.

EXERCISE 10-1: LOCATING THE SELECTION BORDER IN A LISTVIEW

When you select an item in a ListView, you get some visual indicators that let you know you have an item selected. You can set properties on the ListView to determine whether the user can select zero, one, or many items. In this exercise, we're going to dig into the live DOM and locate the style rules that determine the selection border and checkmark for a ListView. After all, we have to find them if we're going to change them.

Listing 10-2 resurrects one of the ListView examples from Chapter 7. In Figure 10-1 notice the border, corner fill, and checkmark on list item number 5.

Listing 10-2. Here's some code you've seen before in Chapter 7. It's a ListView bound to a series of numbers.

```
<!-- HTML snippet -->
<div id="list" data-win-control="WinJS.UI.ListView"></div>
<div id="template" data-win-control="WinJS.Binding.Template">
    <div class="grid">
        <div data-win-bind="innerText:this"></div>
    </div>
</div>

/* CSS snippet */
.win-listview {
    height: 100%;
}

.win-listview .win-item .grid {
    display:-ms-grid;
    -ms-grid-rows:160px;
    -ms-grid-columns:160px;
    background-color:gray;
    color:white;
}

.win-listview .win-item .grid div {
    font-size: 36px;
    font-weight: bold;
    -ms-grid-column-align: center;
    -ms-grid-row-align: center;
}

//JavaScript snippet
var numbersList = new WinJS.Binding.List();
```

```
var list = document.querySelector("#list").winControl;
list.itemTemplate = document.querySelector("#template");
list.itemDataSource = numbersList.dataSource;

for (var i = 1; i <= 11; i++) {
    numbersList.push(i);
}
```

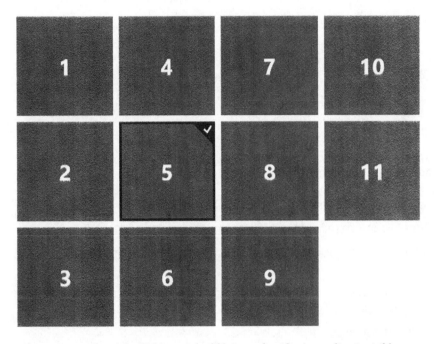

Figure 10-1. *After right clicking on the fifth item, the selection styling is visible*

These extra features of that tile are there because that item is selected. We know that the styles for that selected item are going to be in the WinJS library, and since we've elected to use the ui-light.css file on this page, we know that it's going to be in that file. Let's discover where in that style sheet this border and checkmark are defined so that we have some hope of modifying them.

In this exercise you can use the sample project that accompanies this book and is available at www.apress.com/9781430249832 and http://codefoster.com/cssbookcode.

1.   Run the app in debug mode by pressing F5.

When you press F5 or choose Debug | Start Debugging, your app is launched and Visual Studio associates its debugging tools to it and gives you the DOM Explorer. You should see something like Figure 10-2 in Visual Studio.

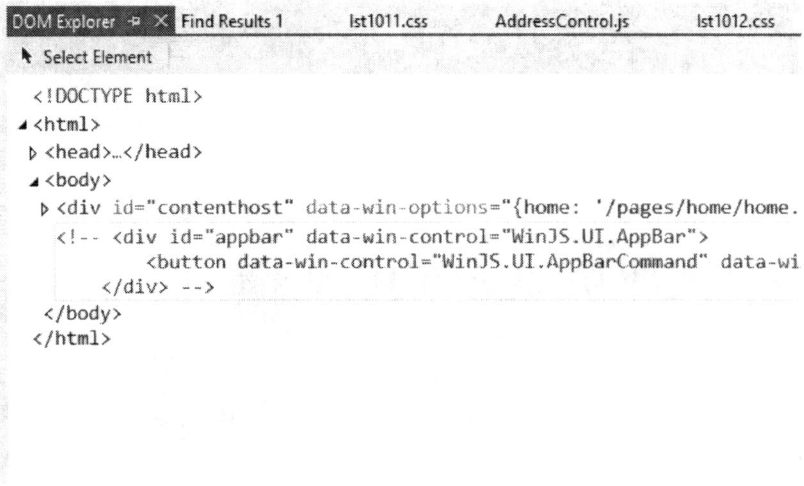

```
DOM Explorer  ⊷ ✕  Find Results 1        lst1011.css        AddressControl.js        lst1012.css
  ▶ Select Element

   <!DOCTYPE html>
 ◢ <html>
   ▷ <head>…</head>
   ◢ <body>
     ▷ <div id="contenthost" data-win-options="{home: '/pages/home/home.
       <!-- <div id="appbar" data-win-control="WinJS.UI.AppBar">
               <button data-win-control="WinJS.UI.AppBarCommand" data-wi
          </div> -->
     </body>
   </html>
```

Figure 10-2. The extremely helpful DOM Explorer is always available when Visual Studio 2012 is running in debug mode (but only for HTML/JS apps)

2. In the running app, navigate to the Chapter 10 section and then to Listing 10-2.

3. Select item number 5 by right clicking on it.

4. Switch to Visual Studio and press the Select Element button (CTRL + B) at the top of the DOM Explorer.

Visual Studio should switch you to the running app, and you should notice that hovering over elements highlights them in blue to make it easier to select the target you want.

5. Click on the selected ListView item.

Selecting your target element should take you back to the DOM Explorer in Visual Studio with the element you selected highlighted in the DOM and allowing you to see the HTML markup that defines your element. It's the *live* DOM so it's not restricted to the HTML that you authored in the .html file in development, but rather includes even the DOM elements that may have been programmatically appended at runtime. That's a relief because pretty much the entire ListView was created at runtime by WinJS. Remember, all we did to declare the ListView in our markup was <div data-win-control="WinJS.UI.ListView"></div>.

By the way, if you aren't able to click directly on the element you're interested in, you can try to just click near it and then finish locating the exact element by manually navigating the DOM in DOM Explorer.

6. Locate the div with a class value of win-selectionbordercontainer, expand it, and select one of its child elements.

When you selected the ListView item, you were taken back to Visual Studio and likely the element in the DOM that was highlighted was the <div class="grid">, and a little further down you should see some more div elements that have been added (when you selected item number 5), one of which has a class of win-selectionbordercontainer.

If you expand this div, you'll find that it has four individual div elements that make up the border of the selected item. Select one of them. Figure 10-3 should make it clear which element to select.

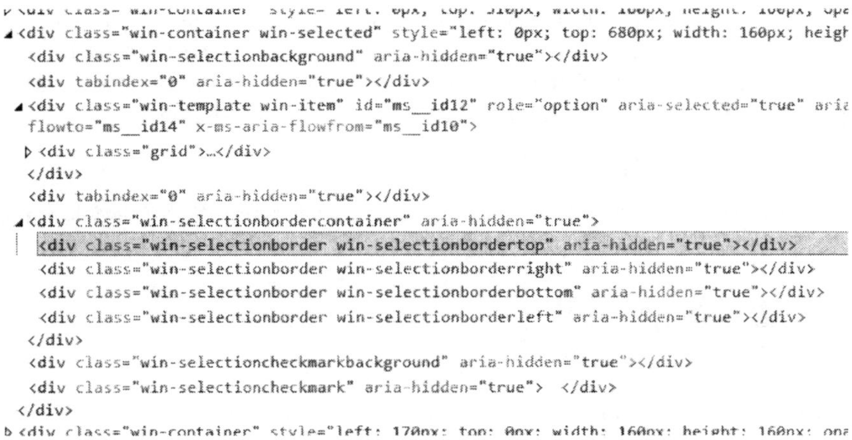

```
▷ \uiv class="win-container" style="left: 0px, top. 510px, width. 160px, height. 160px, op
▲<div class="win-container win-selected" style="left: 0px; top: 680px; width: 160px; heigh
  <div class="win-selectionbackground" aria-hidden="true"></div>
  <div tabindex="0" aria-hidden="true"></div>
  ▲<div class="win-template win-item" id="ms__id12" role="option" aria-selected="true" aria
    flowto="ms__id14" x-ms-aria-flowfrom="ms__id10">
   ▷ <div class="grid">…</div>
   </div>
   <div tabindex="0" aria-hidden="true"></div>
  ▲<div class="win-selectionbordercontainer" aria-hidden="true">
    <div class="win-selectionborder win-selectionbordertop" aria-hidden="true"></div>
    <div class="win-selectionborder win-selectionborderright" aria-hidden="true"></div>
    <div class="win-selectionborder win-selectionborderbottom" aria-hidden="true"></div>
    <div class="win-selectionborder win-selectionborderleft" aria-hidden="true"></div>
   </div>
   <div class="win-selectioncheckmarkbackground" aria-hidden="true"></div>
   <div class="win-selectioncheckmark" aria-hidden="true"> </div>
  </div>
 ▷ <div class="win-container" style="left: 170px; top: 0px; width: 160px; height: 160px; one
```

Figure 10-3. *The win-selectionbordercontainer is only present in the DOM when an item is selected*

7. Select the Trace Styles tab in the right pane of the DOM Explorer.

You should see a list of all of the style properties that are affecting the selected element, and that list should look like Figure 10-4.

Figure 10-4. *All of the styles that apply to the selected object along with their value and tracing information are displayed in the Trace Styles pane of the DOM Explorer*

One thing that Visual Studio does that helps a lot when looking for the origin of a color is render a small, square sample of the color next to the value in the Trace Styles pane. I realize that Figure 10-4 might be rendered in grayscale as you read this, but trust me when I say that it's showing us the same color that we saw around the selected item back in Figure 10-1. So, it appears that we've located the source of that style property.

8. Expand one of the border color properties to see the origin.

When you expand the `border-left-color` property, for instance (by clicking small triangular glyph next to it) you see something like Figure 10-5.

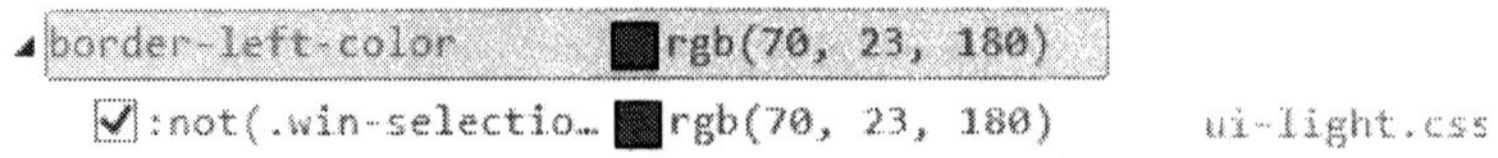

Figure 10-5. The Trace Styles pane shows you not only what the value of a style rule is, but where it is defined

The rightmost column tells us that this style rule has been defined in the `ui-light.css` file. We probably could have guessed that since most of our rules are in there. Clicking on the file name launches that file in Visual Studio. If you have not installed Visual Studio 2012 Update 1 you'll be taken to the file, but unfortunately you won't be navigated directly to the style rule. With Update 1 installed, however, you'll be taken directly to the rule in question. One thing you can't rely on is the style rule being verbatim between the Trace Styles pane and the actual CSS file. Sometimes the order of the class and pseudo-class selectors gets rearranged. I found the style rule in Figure 10-5 to originate from lines 2250–2252 of `ui-light.css`:

```
win-listview:not(.win-selectionstylefilled) .win-container.win-selected .win-selectionborder
{
    border-color: rgb(70, 23, 180);
}
```

Having found the source and the reason that selected ListView items have a border color of `rgb(70, 23, 180)` (a deep purple color), we are armed with what we need to override the color of this border or add other properties to it.

Before we start overriding and adding properties, however, let's look at one more exercise in style rule location.

EXERCISE 10-2: LOCATING A PROGRESS ELEMENT'S FILL COLOR

In this exercise, we're going to locate the style rule that gives a `progress` element its fill color. Listing 10-3 and the resulting Figure 10-6 show one of these simple progress elements. You can see that the area left of the progress value is filled by default with the same color we found the selection rectangle in a ListView to be: a deep purple.

Listing 10-3. A simple progress tag filled to 60%

```
<!-- HTML snippet -->
<progress value="60" max="100"></progress>
```

Figure 10-6. The filled area is indicated with a color, while the unfilled area is a light shade of gray

In this exercise, follow the same steps that you used in Exercise 10-1, and you should end up with a Trace Styles pane that looks like Figure 10-7.

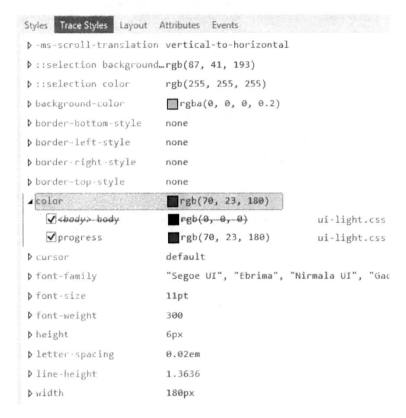

Figure 10-7. *The Trace Styles pane also gives you an indication of what styles have been overridden. This can be very helpful if you're expecting a style to apply and can't figure which other rule is overriding it*

As shown in Figure 10-7, expanding the color property reveals something a bit different from the last exercise. There are two rules and the first is struck through. This indicates that the first style rule took effect on this element, but was later (later in the style sheet that is) overridden by another more specific or subsequent rule. Recall from Chapter 3 that this intentional cascading of styles is a normal function of CSS, and the Trace Styles pane is very helpful in informing us which rules are being applied, which are not, and why.

Clicking on the style sheet link next to the rule in question brings us to lines 2172–2175 in the ui-light.css file, which are:

```
progress {
    background-color: rgba(0, 0, 0, 0.2);
    color: rgb(70, 23, 180);
}
```

Once again, we've found the culprit. This style rule is not only determining the fill color to be the same, deep purple, but it's determining the background color (the color of the unfilled portion) to be black at 20% opacity.

Overriding and Extending Styles

The style sheets that come with WinJS are baked. They are read only and it's neither recommended nor necessary for you to consider changing them. Instead, you should override and extend the built-in styles.

Overriding Styles

In the previous exercises, we learned how to search out the style rules that are affecting a certain element in our UI, and that's important. It's important to know why some elements look the way they do or are placed where they are. It may seem irrelevant to locate the style rule in the ui-light.css style sheet, since that file is read only and offers us no hope of changing it.

It's true we can't (or at least *shouldn't!*) change the style in the WinJS style sheet, but we are able to change the appearance of that certain element and we do that by overriding the style properties in the rule.

Remember that the WinJS style sheet is defined *before* all other style sheets. Listing 10-4 shows what the <head> of a typical HTML file looks like in a Windows 8 app.

Listing 10-4. A typical <head> section from a Windows 8 HTML page showing the order in which the style sheets are referenced

```
<head>
    <meta charset="utf-8" />
    <title>Lorem Ipsum</title>

    <!-- WinJS references -->
    <link href="//Microsoft.WinJS.1.0/css/ui-light.css" rel="stylesheet" />
    <script src="//Microsoft.WinJS.1.0/js/base.js"></script>
    <script src="//Microsoft.WinJS.1.0/js/ui.js"></script>

    <link href="lorem.css" rel="stylesheet" />
    <script src="lorem.js"></script>
</head>
```

The ui-light.css style sheet is the first to be declared, and is followed later by the lorem.css style sheet that applies only to this page. This means that assuming the specificity is the same or greater, properties in a style rule that we define in lorem.css will override properties in a style rule from ui-light.css.

You may want to review the topic of *specificity* from Chapter 3 if it's not clear in your mind, because this is where it rears its head. If ui-light.css sets a property using a style rule that is more specific than a rule in lorem.css, then former will win and there will be no override.

This means that we can simply write a style rule in our local CSS file (lorem.css in the previous example), match the selector of a style rule that already exists, and expect the properties in our style rule to override those in ui-light.css. You can see an example of this in Listing 10-5.

Listing 10-5. The progress rule below matches the selector of a rule that already exists in the WinJS style sheet. The properties defined come after the WinJS style sheet though, so we can expect them to override.

```
<!-- HTML snippet -->
<progress value="60" max="100"></progress>

/* CSS snippet */
progress {
    background-color: gray;
    color: lightgray;
}
```

As you can see in Figure 10-8, our override has amounted to a reversal of the colors that make up the progress bar. The filled area is now lighter (lightgray) and the unfilled area is now darker (gray).

Figure 10-8. *As expected, the fill color is light gray and the background (unfilled) is darker now*

It is possible to add the term important! (including the exclamation point) to a style property to force the override to happen even when the specificity values would have determined otherwise.

Listing 10-6 shows an HTML paragraph with two style rules that both appear to apply. The ID selector wins, though, in specificity, so even though the .error style rule comes after the #footerText rule, it would not have an effect.

Listing 10-6. Two style rules competing to set the text color of an element

```
<!-- HTML snippet -->
<p id="footerText" class="error">
    There was an error loading the file.
</p>

/* CSS snippet */
#footerText {
    color: black;
}

.error {
    color: red;
}
```

We could force the override, however, with Listing 10-7.

Listing 10-7. Two style rules competing to set the same element

```
<!-- HTML snippet -->
<p id="footerText" class="error">
    There was an error loading the file.
</p>
```

```
/* CSS snippet */
#footerText {
    color: black;
}

.error {
    color: red important!;
}
```

I recommend against using the important! keyword. It may produce the desired result today, but you'll run into trouble tomorrow. It's a definite code smell and usually leads to poor CSS architecture that will be difficult to read and difficult to maintain.

Extending Styles

Locating style rules in the WinJS (or any other) library is helpful not only so that we can override the properties they define, but also so we can add properties they don't define. Using the same selector assures that our added property will always apply to the exact same element(s) and saves us time trying to compose the selector from scratch.

Let's look at the progress control again to illustrate how to extend a style. In Listing 10-5, we *overrode* a style property by defining a style rule in our local style sheet with the same selector as that of the WinJS style sheet and then redefining a property that already existed. To *extend* the style we do the same except we add style properties that were not originally defined.

The progress style rule that we redefined in Listing 10-5 already contained a color property. In Listing 10-8, we have changed the overriding properties to give the progress control a gray fill color and a white unfilled color, and we have added a new property (border) that was not defined in WinJS.

Listing 10-8. Besides overriding style properties that existed, we can specify new ones that did not

```
<!-- HTML snippet -->
<progress value="60" max="100"></progress>

/* CSS snippet */
progress {
    background-color: white;
    color: gray;
    border: 1px solid gray;
}
```

Adding the solid, gray border gives our progress element a containing box as you can see in Figure 10-9.

Figure 10-9. *A border gives this progress indicator a whole new look*

Some examples are helpful for learning what sort of style overrides and extensions are useful in a Windows 8 app. We've already seen the progress control example. Next we'll look at two more. We'll look at:

- Formatting the slider on a range input element
- Changing the default icon in the Rating control

Formatting the slider on a range input element

Let's aim to change the default range input element (`<input type="range"/>`) so that the slider the user grabs with a touch is round with an outline color that matches the element's lower fill color. Figure 10-10 shows the default look of a range input element.

Figure 10-10. *The default look of a range input element*

The Trace Styles pane gives us some good information about the styles that make the range input element look the way it does and help us to know what selectors to use in our own style selectors to override and extend the properties and affect the changes we're after. Listing 10-9 shows the CSS that we should put in our local style sheet to accomplish this.

Listing 10-9. The HTML and CSS to get a round thumb slider on the range input

```
<!-- HTML snippet -->
<input type="range" />

/* CSS snippet */
input[type=range]::-ms-track {
    height:16px;
}
input[type=range]::-ms-fill-lower {
    background-color:gray;
}

input[type=range]::-ms-thumb {
    background-color:white;
    border:1px solid gray;
    height:14px;
    width:14px;
    border-radius:14px;
}
```

Figure 10-11. *A round slider might be a better design choice for your app's personality*

Changing the default icon in a rating control

Next, we'll take a look at the Rating control. Unlike the range input element, the Rating control is a custom control that is provided by WinJS. In general, the WinJS controls are going to be more complex than base HTML elements because they are often composed of a large number of base HTML elements. The Trace Styles pane is all the more our friend when sleuthing into WinJS controls to find out how to override and extend styles.

I'm going to change the number of stars from the default of 5 and then I'm going to change the icon to get away from the boring, old star system. Normally, rating systems use five stars and ask the users to rate something from one to five. It's a common system, but let's say we're working on an app for a chicken restaurant. We might want to give customers a one through ten system using chickens instead of stars to rate their meals. Now that's an app with personality!

Figure 10-12 shows the default look of a rating control where three stars have been selected.

Figure 10-12. *The default Rating control uses a star icon and a max rating value of five*

I found a chicken icon in the free Microsoft Office image library at http://office.microsoft.com. I then used my favorite vector editing tool—CorelDRAW—and made four variations of it for all of the possible states the image might be in. The results are in Figure 10-13.

enabled filled   *disabled filled*

enabled empty   *disabled empty*

Figure 10-13. *Four variations of a chicken icon to cover every state a Rating control element might be in*

In Listing 10-10, I've declared a Rating control and given it an arbitrary averageRating value of 6.4 to illustrate how partial values are displayed by the control. Usually the value for averageRating won't be hard coded but rather calculated from a table of data.

The Rating control styles are easy to locate in the ui-light.css file with a simple search. Notice the style rule that looks like this:

```
.win-rating .win-star:before {
    content: "\E082";
}
```

If you remember back to Chapter 3, the content property is an interesting one that actually adds content in through styling. So, this is how the default Rating control gets its stars. You can change the character that is referenced there if you can find one that suits, but you can also forego the character and use an image instead. That's what we're doing in Listing 10-10. Look at the style rule that overrides.win-rating .win-star:before. It is clearing out the content value and thus omitting the star glyph.

Once the star is gone, we're free to add the image of our own and you can see how we do that in the remaining style rules in Listing 10-10.

Listing 10-10. The code for turning five stars into ten chickens

```
<!-- HTML snippet -->
<div class="chicken" data-win-control="WinJS.UI.Rating"
    data-win-options="{averageRating: 6.4, maxRating: 10}"></div>

/* CSS snippet */
.win-rating.chicken .win-star:before
{
    content: ""; /*hide the default star glyph*/
}

.win-rating.chicken .win-star
{
    background-repeat: no-repeat;
    background-origin: content-box; /*to allow putting padding between chickens*/
    background-position: left;
    height: 30px;
    background-size: 100% 100%;
}

.win-rating.chicken .win-star.win-empty, .win-rating.chicken .win-star.win-tentative.win-empty
{
    background-image: url("/images/chicken_empty.svg");
}

.win-rating.chicken .win-star.win-full, .win-rating.chicken .win-star.win-tentative.win-full
{
    background-image: url("/images/chicken_full.svg");
}

.win-rating.chicken .win-star.win-disabled.win-empty
{
    background-image: url("/images/chicken_disabled_empty.svg");
}

.win-rating.chicken .win-star.win-disabled.win-full
{
    background-image: url("/images/chicken_disabled_full.svg");
}
```

Figure 10-14 shows the resulting chicken icons. I designed the `chicken_empty.svg` image to appear like a placeholder so it's clear to the user how many possible chicken ratings he is able to select.

Figure 10-14. We're seeing an average of 6.4 out of 10 chickens

It is also possible (though the code in Listing 10-10 does not go so far) to differentiate between the images the user has chosen and those which represent an average of all user choices. We could have done that by adding a class of `.win-user` to some rules and `.win-average` to others.

It's extremely common to override and extend style rules that have already been defined, but the WinJS style sheet is really just a starting point and you're going to find plenty of reason to create your own style rules in your app. In the next section we'll look at some technique as well as some strategy for defining our own styles in our app.

Defining Styles

There will be plenty of cases where you will override existing styles and plenty more where you will define your own. For your own style definitions, you may be creating simple class rules or you may be creating your own entire custom control complete with its own classes, its own default styles, and a capability for any developers that use it to override its styles just like we have been to the WinJS library.

In each of the following examples, I am going to include the entire code listing. The objective is to learn the CSS styling, and the entire context of the solution should help with that. You will see prefixes such as `.lst1011` in the CSS styles which scope that CSS to that particular code listing.

Featured items in a ListView

As an example, let's say we're working on the hub page of a point of sale app that has two ListView controls on it. The first is a list of product offerings and the second is a list of possible discounts that might apply. The items in the discounts list are all the same, but it's possible for items in the product list to be "featured" to draw attention. The concept of featured items should only apply to the first list. Featured items should have a solid gray background, while all other non-featured items should have a simple white background. Use an ID selector to scope styles to the appropriate list and class selectors to handle the featured items.

The solution in this example is going to be rather simple, but it involves targeting the products list (and not the discounts list) and within the products list it involves differentiating between the featured products and the rest. There obviously may be more than one featured item, so we should employ a class selector. Class selectors are made for just that.

The entire solution is represented in Listing 10-11, and an explanation of the code will follow.

Listing 10-11. Complete solution code for featuring items in a ListView

```
<!-- lst1011.html -->
<!DOCTYPE html>
<html>
<head>
    <meta charset="utf-8" />
    <title>Listing 10-11</title>

    <!-- WinJS references -->
    <link href="//Microsoft.WinJS.1.0/css/ui-light.css" rel="stylesheet" />
    <script src="//Microsoft.WinJS.1.0/js/base.js"></script>
    <script src="//Microsoft.WinJS.1.0/js/ui.js"></script>

    <link href="lst1011.css" rel="stylesheet" />
    <script src="lst1011.js"></script>
</head>
```

```html
<body>
    <div class="lst1011 fragment">
        <section aria-label="Main content" role="main">

            <div id="productsList" data-win-control="WinJS.UI.ListView"></div>
            <div id="discountsList" data-win-control="WinJS.UI.ListView"></div>

            <div id="productItemTemplate" data-win-control="WinJS.Binding.Template">
                <div data-win-bind="className:isFeatured
                    lst1011.Converters.isFeaturedToString;">
                    <h3 data-win-bind="innerText:name"></h3>
                    <div data-win-bind="innerText:price" class="win-type-xx-small"></div>
                </div>
            </div>
            <div id="discountItemTemplate" data-win-control="WinJS.Binding.Template">
                ...
            </div>
        </section>
    </div>
</body>
</html>
```

```css
/* lst1011.css */
.lst1011 #productsList .widget {
    width:200px;
    height:100px;
    border: 1px solid gray;
    padding:10px;
}
.lst1011 #productsList .widget.featured {
    background-color: lightgray;
}
```

```javascript
// lst1011.js
(function () {
    "use strict";

    var products = [
        {name: "Widget 1", isFeatured: true, price: 72.99},
        {name: "Widget 2", isFeatured: false, price: 149.99},
        {name: "Widget 3", isFeatured: true, price: 14.99},
        {name: "Widget 4", isFeatured: true, price: 50.99},
        {name: "Widget 5", isFeatured: false, price: 71.99},
        {name: "Widget 6", isFeatured: false, price: 65.99},
        {name: "Widget 7", isFeatured: false, price: 66},
        {name: "Widget 8", isFeatured: false, price: 165.99},
        {name: "Widget 9", isFeatured: true, price: 60.99},
        {name: "Widget 10", isFeatured: false, price: 6.99}
    ];
```

```
WinJS.Namespace.define("lst1011.Converters", {
    isFeaturedToString: WinJS.Binding.converter(function(value) {
        return (value ? "widget featured" : "widget");
    })
});

WinJS.UI.Pages.define("/pages/chapter10/lst1011/lst1011.html", {
    ready: function (element, options) {
        var productsList = element.querySelector("#productsList").winControl;
        productsList.itemDataSource = new WinJS.Binding.List(products).dataSource;
        productsList.itemTemplate = element.querySelector("#productItemTemplate");


    }
});
})();
```

Figure 10-15. *The featured items have been highlighted with a gray background*

lst1011.html

The lst1011.html file declares the products and discounts ListViews with their unique ID attributes. That ID attribute is important because it allows us to scope the styles that we will create to affect only the products list.

The first div in the products item template contains an attribute called data-win-bind in which we define (in bold) a property of the data bound item (isFeatured) and a property of the element (className). We are also implementing something called a converter which is certainly out of the scope of our subject. I wanted to bring it to your attention, however, so you don't wonder how a property value of isFeatured turns into a class name such as widget featured.

lst1011.js

The list binding that the lst1011.js file takes care of is also out of scope, but you've seen it a few times now, so perhaps you'll pick up the syntax anyway. Nevertheless, the code is defining an array of widgets each of which has a property called isFeatured, where a Boolean value of true should indicate a featured product. That simple array is turned into a Binding.List so it can be bound to the ListView.

lst1011.css

Finally, our lst1011.css file makes featured items actually stand out. It defines two style rules: one for items with the widget class and another for items with both the widget and the featured classes.

All widgets get the first rule applied, but only the featured ones get the extra background-color property that sets the background of the item to lightgray.

Custom WinJS controls

In the following example, let's imagine that we find ourselves repeating some markup more than we'd like and so we decide to create a custom WinJS control to encapsulate it. The markup we've found to be repetitious is the fields of the address: address, city, state, and zip code. In our application we need to collect both the billing and shipping addresses.

WinJS not only provides a number of custom, composite controls for us to use, but allows us to create our own as well. We create the controls entirely in JavaScript and then declare them in our HTML identical to the way the built-in WinJS controls are declared. In my opinion, it's a very elegant and powerful pattern.

From the consuming page (where we actually *use* this custom control), we need to still have access to the individual elements of the address control so that we could, for instance, add some CSS properties to the address field. And that's exactly what we'll do in this example. We'll add a double border around the address in both controls to show that we have that capability. Listing 10-12 puts it all together and is followed by an explanation of each file.

Listing 10-12. The code for creating a custom WinJS control and declaring two of them very easily in the markup

```
<!-- lst1012.html -->
<!DOCTYPE html>
<html>
<head>
    <meta charset="utf-8" />
    <title>Listing 10-12</title>

    <!-- WinJS references -->
    <link href="//Microsoft.WinJS.1.0/css/ui-light.css" rel="stylesheet" />
    <script src="//Microsoft.WinJS.1.0/js/base.js"></script>
    <script src="//Microsoft.WinJS.1.0/js/ui.js"></script>

    <link href="lst1012.css" rel="stylesheet" />
    <script src="AddressControl.js"></script>
    <script src="lst1012.js"></script>
</head>
<body>
    <div class="lst1012 fragment">
        <section aria-label="Main content" role="main">
            <h3>Billing Address</h3>
            <div data-win-control="lst1012.Controls.Address"></div>

            <h3>Shipping Address</h3>
            <div data-win-control="lst1012.Controls.Address"></div>
        </section>
    </div>
</body>
</html>
```

```css
/* lst1012.css */
.lst1012 .abc-address {
    background-color: lightgray;
}
```

```javascript
// lst1012.js
(function () {
    "use strict";

    WinJS.UI.Pages.define("/pages/chapter10/lst1012/lst1012.html", {
        ready: function (element, options) {


        }
    });
})();
```

```javascript
// AddressControl.js
WinJS.Namespace.define("lst1012.Controls", {
    Address: WinJS.Class.define(
        function (element) {
            element.innerHTML =
                "Address: <input class='abc-address' style='width:300px;'/><br/>" +
                "City/St/Zip: <input class='abc-city'/><select class='abc-state'>
                <option></option><option>Alabama</option><option>Alaska</option>
                <option>...</option></select><input class='abc-zip' style='width:80px;'/><br/>";
        }
    )
});
```

Billing Address

Address:

City/St/Zip:

Shipping Address

Address:

City/St/Zip:

Figure 10-16. *Both of the address fields have been styled as we determined, because the address fields were given a class name and the rules in our page's style sheet have targeted that class*

AddressControl.js

The AddressControl.js file does all the work of defining the custom address control, and we have complete control over the markup that it generates including the inclusion of class attributes (in bold) that can be used by the control consumer.

Those class attributes are the only thing you need to really pay attention to at this point, so if you're putting off your JavaScript studies for now, you can skim the rest of the file. Note that I've simplified a custom control creation severely. A well-implemented custom control would certainly have a bit more to it.

lst1012.html

In the lst1012.html file, you'll notice the reference to the AddressControl.js file and the markup that references the control (in bold). I've manually declared two instances of the custom control here, but they could just as easily have been declared within the template of a ListView or otherwise added to the page dynamically.

lst1012.css

Finally, a single and simple CSS rule in lst1012.css proves that we have access to the individual elements by adding a double border around the address field. If you are the author as well as the consumer of the custom control, then you'll have no problem matching up class definitions (in your control's JavaScript file) with the style definitions (in your CSS file). If you are using third-party controls, then discovering what elements and classes they define is a simple matter of using the DOM Explorer as I've already shown.

lst1012.js

The lst1012.js file is essentially empty, but I've left it in the listing so you know it's not doing anything behind your back.

Summary

We've seen how to dive into the DOM and view the structure of its elements whether those elements were explicitly written by us or written by including a custom WinJS control. We learned, then, how to find the style rules from the WinJS library that are already applying to those elements.

Locating those elements and the style rules that are already targeting them is an essential first step in understanding how to override and extend those styles to give the app our own brand and personality.

Beyond overriding what's there, we're enabled to create our own elements and classes explicitly or by creating a custom control and then defining our own styles to control their appearance.

The examples in this chapter are a very small sampling of the unlimited number of ways that you can style the elements in your app. Keep in mind that you can use the same techniques to locate and override styles in other CSS libraries as well (we will talk about CSS libraries other than WinJS in Appendix A).

APPENDIX A

CSS Libraries and Resources

We have covered CSS in general and focused on how it applies to creating Windows 8 apps, but I can guarantee you that there is a lot more to cover. To master CSS and master Windows 8 app creation you'll need to spend hundreds of hours actually writing apps, and you'll need an arsenal of information. I can't help you with the hundreds of hours, but luckily, I can help provide the arsenal of information.

In this Appendix, I'll attempt to distill for you the vast amount of information that is available down to just the essence of CSS. I'll introduce some CSS libraries, helpers, and some learning and reference websites that have been a big help to me.

Book Code

■ **Note**   www.apress.com/9781430249832 or http://codefoster.com/cssbookcode

---

The listings in this book amount to quite a bit of code and you may want the option of copying some of it to paste into your own project. You can access to all of this book's source code by visiting www.apress.com/9781430249832 or my website at http://codefoster.com/cssbookcode, where you'll be directed to the source code on CodePlex. The code compiles to a Windows 8 app that indexes all of this book's code listings by chapter and lets you see them in action.

codeSHOW

■ **Note**   codeshow.codeplex.com

---

codeSHOW is a Windows 8 app written in HTML, CSS, and JavaScript with the sole charter of helping you learn to make your own app in HTML, CSS, and JavaScript. You can access all of the codeSHOW project's source code by visiting codeshow.codeplex.com or if you have Windows 8 installed you can browse instead to aka.ms/codeshowapp and download the app.

The codeSHOW app shows off a number of demos and allows you to *see the code* to have a peek at the HTML, CSS, and JavaScript that it took to create it. It's an excellent way to learn how to implement a feature you know you need. It's not, however, a big lesson in app architecture. For that, you're welcome to download the full source code of the codeSHOW project itself from the CodePlex link and take a look at how codeSHOW is created.

The World Wide Web Consortium

■ **Note** w3.org/style/css

The World Wide Web Consortium—a.k.a. the W3C—is the international standards body that handles the technologies underlying the Internet (and there are a lot of them). The W3C started at the Massachusetts Institute of Technology (MIT) in the mid-90s. It was founded by a guy named Tim Berners-Lee, and he is the acting head even today.

As you might imagine, the W3C has its work cut out for it in facilitating discussions on so many proposed standards for the web and then deciding which standards will be recommended by the organization. Every proposed standard works its way through four stages: working draft, candidate recommendation, proposed recommendation, and finally W3C recommendation (REC).

If you're working in the web stack, you should frequent the w3.org website. All other discussions (including this book) and even the implementation of web standards are conjecture compared to w3.org, which is the standard by which it should all be measured.

You'd expect a pretty decent website from a web standards organization, and w3.org doesn't disappoint. To dig in to all of the W3 standards around CSS visit w3.org/Style/CSS/ and take some time to look around.

Microsoft Developer Network (MSDN)

■ **Note** http://msdn.microsoft.com/en-us/library/ie/ms531209(v=vs.85).aspx

---

The MSDN network is a vast library and tremendous source of documentation for every flavor of Microsoft development, including CSS. You'll certainly find corners of Microsoft's implementation of the CSS standard that I didn't find space to cover in this book.

When you've already referenced the W3C standard on some aspect of CSS and you're wondering about the nuances of behavior in Internet Explorer or Windows 8 apps, I recommend you look to MSDN.

CSS Tricks

■ **Note** css-tricks.com

I've benefited hugely from CSS Tricks by Chris Coyier. It's a beautiful site and has a wealth of information on the topic of CSS. The articles are first class and the sheer volume of information is staggering. I usually either search the site or scroll to the bottom and hit "More Blog Posts" to browse articles.

CSS Tricks not only has high-quality articles, but the community forum is good too. You can get some real help with CSS issues and hopefully you'll find some questions from others that you can answer. I tend to visit CSS Tricks when I'm looking for a little bit of design inspiration as well. The gallery section is particularly effective at this.

Web Platform Docs

■ **Note** webplatform.org

The Web Platform Docs site is an entirely community-driven web platform documentation website. It offers a lot of help on all of the significant web technologies such as HTML, CSS, JavaScript, SVG, and more.

The site is in alpha and the design is struggling a bit in my opinion, but it's a good, open platform for learning the web platform, helping to teach others, and cultivating community.

LESS

■ **Note** lesscss.org

This isn't just another link to a site with good CSS documentation. Oh no. LESS is more! LESS is a very simple but extremely helpful assistant to CSS. LESS allows us to describe our styles in a bit more intelligent and programmatic way.

We write LESS code and reference it on our HTML page just like we would with CSS, but before the page is requested, a processor transforms the LESS into CSS, and that's all our HTML file ever really sees. LESS creates CSS that you could have created yourself, but didn't want to.

Not all LESS code is valid CSS code until it gets processed. On the contrary, all CSS code *is* valid LESS code. This means that you can take your existing CSS files (whatever their size) and convert them to a LESS file simply by changing their file extension. You can then begin the process of introducing LESS features one at a time.

LESS also allows the definition of variables, mixins, nested rules, and functions and operations. Let's spend a bit of time of each of those and then how to set up LESS in Windows 8.

Variables

To introduce variables, let's use an example: your designer (even if you *are* your designer) informs you that your primary theme color is going to be R71 G82 B49, you can imagine that you're going to be sprinkling `rgb(71,82,49)` all over your CSS file. That specific color might end up being the border of the items on the main page, the color of the text in the header, and the background of the app bar.

Sprinkling a value like this all over a file should smell bad to you. It means that if your designer changes her mind, you're going to be changing colors in more than one place, and you're opening yourself up to a mistake.

If you're using LESS, however, you have the opportunity to define a variable to represent this primary color. You might even call the variable `primaryColor`. An example of the definition of that color and subsequent reference to it from a couple of places can be seen in Listing A-1.

Listing A-1. *A LESS variable used to store a color*

```
@primaryColor: rgb(71,82,49);

#myListView .win-item {
    border: 1px solid @primaryColor;
    color: @primaryColor;
}


.win-appbar { background-color: @primaryColor; }
```

Listing A-1 shows how the actual color—rgb(71,82,49)—is defined only one time. If at some point in the future our designer informs us that this hue should be adjusted a bit, it only has to be done in one place.

Mixins

Mixins allow us to *mix in* one class with another. That is, we can have one class inherit all of the style properties of another class. In Listing A-2 you'll see a reference class (.reference) that sets a border and a background color. Two subsequent classes (.styleA and .styleB) should both take the same border and background color properties, but also need to add some of their own.

Listing A-2. *An example of a LESS mixin*

```
.reference {
    border: 1px solid black;
    background-color: gray;
}

.styleA {
    .reference;
    font-size: large;
}

.styleB {
    .reference;
    font-weight: bold;
}
```

Mixins can save a good deal of typing in some cases.

Besides simply referencing another class, you'll have the opportunity to pass a parameter to the referenced style with a mixin. See what I mean in Listing A-3.

Listing A-3. *A mixin with a passed parameter*

```
.reference (@borderWidth: 1px) {
    border: @borderWidth solid black;
    background-color: gray;
}

.styleA {
    .reference;
    font-size: large;
}
```

```
.styleB {
    .reference(2px);
    font-weight: bold;
}
```

Can you see what's going on there? The .reference style now takes in a parameter called borderWidth with a default value of 1px. The .styleA property includes .reference but doesn't specify a value for the borderWidth parameter, thus it gets all of the properties of the .reference rule with a default value for the border width. The .styleB property, however, includes .reference but does specify a value of 2px for the borderWidth parameter and thus it gets the properties of the .reference rule with a 2-pixel border.

Mixins allow for some very elegantly defined CSS that is expressive and concise and centralized so it's easy to maintain.

Nested Rules

You've likely noticed that some CSS style selectors can get really lengthy. To access the list items in a list of class error in the div element called myDiv in the main section, you would end up with something like section[role=main] #myDiv .error li { ... }, and they can get much longer than that even.

To avoid this, you can use LESS's nested rules. Nested rules allow you to define rules inside of one another and the inference is that each rule's parent selector should apply to it. The two CSS sections in Listing A-4 have an identical effect.

Listing A-4. Comparison of class CSS to LESS using nested rules

```
/* using classic CSS */
section[role=main] {
    font-size: large;
}

section[role=main] #myDiv {
    font-weight: bold;
}

section[role=main] #myDiv .error li {
    color: red;
}

/* using LESS nested rules */
section[role=main] {
    font-size: large;
    #myDiv {
        font-weight: bold;
        .error {
            li {
                color: red;
            }
        }
    }
}
```

Notice the redundancy present in the classic CSS section of Listing A-4. That repetition turns in to difficult maintenance and error-prone code. The LESS version is not a lot shorter in this case, but the point is that it is more logically defined and makes for better readability and better maintainability.

Remember that even when LESS is employed in your app, the client ends up using the resulting CSS anyway. This isn't something that a browser engine has to decipher. It is still fed the CSS style rules in the format expected.

Functions and Operations

The final feature of LESS that we should look at is the functions and operations that it provides.

LESS gives us some intelligent ways to calculate values, and there are many times when calculated values are helpful. If a base length is 10 pixels, but some elements should be 2 pixels more or less than we should be able to calculate that difference, shouldn't we?

Functions and operations are very often used in conjunction with variables. Let's look at a few examples. First we'll look in Listing A-5 at some calculations of length.

Listing A-5. LESS calculations to determine border width

```
@borderWidth: 10px;

.styleA {
    border-width: (@borderWidth - 2);
    border-style: solid;
    border-color: black;
}

.styleB {
    border-width: (@borderWidth + 2);
    border-style: solid;
    border-color: black;
}
```

The .styleA rule in Listing A-5 would result in an 8-pixel border, and the .styleB rule would result in a 12-pixel border. The advantage over specifying those values explicitly comes when you decide to change the base border width. At that point all calculated borders are automatically adjusted.

These calculations can be done on colors too and there are some functions that give us some even fancier functionality. Adding colors may be counter-intuitive to you, but it's really just adding the individual red, green, and blue components of the colors. A hex color of #123456 added with another color of #111111 would result in a color of #234567. Colors can be multiplied, divided, or subtracted too.

Besides the basic mathematical operations, some color functions are available. If I have a base color of #77C121, and want a color that is 10% darker, I can avoid a design time round trip to my favorite graphics package, and instead just use LESS's darken() function. I'll show an example of this in Listing A-6.

Listing A-6. The darken() function used to calculate a darker color

```
@baseColor: #77C121;

.normal {
    background-color: @baseColor;
}

.disabled {
    background-color: darken(@baseColor, 10%);
}
```

In Listing A-6, a disabled item automatically gets a shade that's 10% darker than the base color. This is probably my favorite trick in LESS. Being able to create basic color pallets and then express derivative colors from it is a very elegant way to style your app. A simple change to the base color amounts to the automatic creation of an entirely new derived color scheme.

Setup

Setting up your Windows 8 app to use LESS is not difficult.

First, let's recall typical web architecture and where LESS fits into it. CSS normally lives in a web project and is served to the client from a static server file. For a web project using LESS, that CSS code is essentially dynamic, because a LESS processor has to generate it from the LESS code. This process can either happen on the server or on the client.

In Windows 8 apps, our architecture is a little bit different than a typical web application. A Windows 8 device is both the server and the client, so the division between server and client is effectively eliminated. For apps, therefore, I recommend following these steps to use the LESS JavaScript library for your processing:

1. Change the extension of your CSS files from .css to .less

2. Change your style sheet references to look like: `<link rel="stylesheet/less" type="text/css" href="myLessStylesheet.less">`. Pay attention to the `rel` (relationship) attribute value - `stylesheet/less`

3. Download the `less.js` library from lessjss.org and drop it into the `js` folder of your Windows 8 app. Remember, if you drop it directly into the folder structure of your app using Windows Explorer then you need to show the hidden files in Visual Studio and then right click on the `less.js` file and choose "Include in project".

4. Add a reference to the `less.js` library that you downloaded. I recommend you put this on the `default.html` page. It should look something like: `<script src="/js/less.js" type="text/javascript"></script>`

I think you're cruising with LESS now, and I think you'll like it.

Other Online Galleries

▪ **Note** cssflavor.com, csscollection.com, csselite.com, csstemplates.net

---

There are a number of galleries you'll find online that you can use as a learning tool, as a source of inspiration, and as a source of project templates. Sites like CSS Flavor, CSS Collection, CSS Elite, and CSS Templates contain good collections of sample sites created using CSS.

Spend some time browsing the galleries that these sites offer, and when you find a template you like or one that has a style or layout feature you're looking for just copy and study its CSS style sheets. Be sure to read the usage statements of the various sites to be sure you remain in compliance.

Reference sites like the ones I've outlined in this appendix are great when you need to target a piece of information to implement a new feature or overcome a challenging problem, but it's also very rewarding to simply spend time browsing the content. Try it and you'll find yourself learning things you never even knew you needed. Browsing online CSS galleries is another excellent way to learn how some of the theory you've acquired can be applied. So don't just find good code and use it. Write good code and share it! Being a part of the developer community at large is yet another way to accelerate your learning and have a good time while you're at it.

Styling SVG

> ▓ **Note** Too many modern developers are overlooking the power of vector graphics both for image generation and as a display solution.

Introduction to the SVG Format

Scalable Vector Graphics (SVG) is an XML format for defining vector-based graphics. Like HTML, CSS, and JavaScript, SVG is one of the many projects of the W3C. It's not a new project either—it's been underway since 1999.

SVG has had a difficult time gaining traction though, and I think there are a few different reasons for that. One reason is that vector graphics are not nearly as familiar to people as bitmaps. A lot of people know graphics packages like Adobe Photoshop, but far fewer have dug into Adobe Illustrator or any of the other excellent options for working with vector graphics. If you're new to vector image editing altogether, then let me clarify.

First, consider how bitmap images are stored as a two-dimensional matrix of color values. When the square color values (pixels) are small enough, the human eye is tricked into seeing an image. Vector images, on the other hand, are stored altogether differently. In a vector illustration, instead of a collection of pixels, we are working with a collection of objects that may be familiar shapes (like rectangles and ellipses) or may be complex lines defined by a number of points and curve values. In turn, these objects are made up of vertices (or other primitive shape descriptors). It is these vertices or shape descriptors that are stored instead of the matrix of pixels.

When you compare bitmap and vector graphics, SVG has some big advantages. Some of these advantages affect the *creation of graphics* (when you're starting from scratch or editing an existing graphic) and others affect the use of a vector image *in a running application.*

For graphics creation, some notable advantages of SVG are:

- Illustrations created and stored in vector format are **scalable**. That means that it doesn't matter what size you store a vector illustration because you will always be able to generate a bitmap from it as large as you like. You could use the same vector image to print a postage stamp or a road-side billboard.

- Vector illustrations are easier to **modify**. All of the component objects that make up the composite image exist individually and can be modified individually. You could open a vector image of a motorcycle, select just the headlight, and modify its shape. This feat would be much more difficult for a bitmap image.

- **Consuming** vector-based stock imagery is often much easier since modifications can be made to match your own project's color scheme.

Some other notable advantages of using vector images in your running app are:

- For just about every image, the vector version will be much **smaller**. It doesn't take nearly as much information to *describe* a circle's shape as it does to explicitly paint it with pixels.

- Vector illustrations, being composed of described object shapes, are much easier to **animate**. Software can calculate intermediate steps between two points, differences in color values, or even the mathematical model for morphing one shape into another. It's all but impossible to animate pixels in the same ways.

- Vector illustrations can resize to **adapt** to whatever size screen your user happens to be using. Windows 8 automatically scales all assets in your app. To keep your bitmap images looking good, you have to provide multiple versions of it. If an asset is a vector image, however, you don't need to do this and can be sure it will look great at any size.

I find too many developers (and even designers!) still trying to do *all* of their graphics work in bitmap editors like Photoshop. Bitmap editors are excellent for photographs, for painting, and for many other things, but in many graphics creation use cases, learning and switching to a vector package will dramatically boost your productivity.

My vector editor of choice is CorelDRAW. I've been using Corel's vector package for many years and find its interface very precise and intuitive. There are a few other professional vector design applications that you can research, but if you're looking for a free one that still offers a lot of bang, try InkScape at inkscape.org. This open-source vector graphics editor is very well done. InkScape doesn't have its own vector file format, but instead relies entirely on the SVG format.

Another major advantage of vector images is the possibility of animating them. Because vector images are described objects (instead of just pixels), they can be dynamically reshaped and because a vector image is made up of discreet elements, those elements can be moved rather easily. Think about the lower jaw of a vector-based dog moving to simulate speaking.

SVG Embedded in HTML

SVG is just XML and HTML is *almost* XML, so the two languages fit together quite well and SVG can be embedded into an HTML document with little trouble. The two languages being XML-like is also why CSS is naturally able to style and layout them both.

It used to be much more difficult to embed SVG in HTML, but HTML5 has made it much easier. HTML is not strictly XML, but SVG is, so embedded SVG needs to be clearly delimited and given a proper namespace. Listing B-1 shows what it looks like to put some SVG in your HTML.

Listing B-1. A simple circle in SVG with a fill attribute

```
<!-- HTML snippet -->
<!DOCTYPE html>
<head>
<title>SVG</title>
<meta charset="utf-8" />
</head>
<body>
<h2>SVG in HTML5</h2>
<svg id="mySvg" height="200" xmlns="http://www.w3.org/2000/svg">
    <circle id="graycircle" r="75" cx="75" cy="75" fill="gray" />
</svg>
</body>
</html>
```

The code in Listing B-1 describes the circle with a radius of 75 pixels that you see in Figure B-1. It does so inside of an svg tag that has a xmlns (XML namespace) attribute equal to http://www.w3.org/2000/svg. If namespaces are new to you, just know that this doesn't actually link out to the w3.org website. It just uses this URL as a namespace to uniquely identify the contents of this tag as being SVG.

Figure B-1. *A gray circle*

CSS Properties for SVG

In Listing B-1, we ended up with a gray circle because we used the fill attribute with a value of gray. You can use various attributes like this on SVG elements to style them, but I don't recommend this approach. It's better for all of your styling to be done in CSS so it can be modified later. Listing B-2 results in the same gray circle as Listing B-1 except the gray fill this time is provided using a CSS style property in a separate style sheet instead of using the fill attribute.

Listing B-2. The same gray circle except using a CSS property

```
<!-- HTML snippet -->
<!DOCTYPE html>
<head>
<title>SVG</title>
<meta charset="utf-8" />
</head>
<body>
<h2>SVG in HTML5</h2>
<svg id="mySvg" height="200" xmlns="http://www.w3.org/2000/svg">
    <circle id="graycircle" r="75" cx="75" cy="75" />
</svg>
</body>
</html>

/* CSS snippet */
#graycircle {
    fill: gray;
}
```

This is the foundation of everything I'll cover in this appendix. We will explore the various style properties that can be specified in CSS to affect our SVG graphics. Many of these properties you'll find to be in common with HTML, but others are unique to SVG. I will cover a few of the more common properties. For more information about all of the available properties visit `http://www.w3.org/TR/SVG11/propidx.html` where you'll find an exhaustive reference.

Fill

In HTML, you use the `color` property to specify the foreground color of things like text, and you use the background color to specify the color that should fill the background of an element. In SVG, you use the `fill` property to specify the color of a graphics element. You saw this already in Listing B-2 where our circle was *filled* with a gray color.

Beyond specifying the color that an element should be filled with, you can specify the opacity as well. In Listing B-3, I am using a CSS grid to stack an SVG element on top of a paragraph of text. The addition of a `fill-opacity` property set to `0.5` (50%) then makes the paragraph visible through the SVG as you can clearly see in Figure B-2.

Listing B-3. A gray circle with a partial opacity making it transparent over a paragraph of text

```
<!-- HTML snippet -->
<div id="parent">
    <p id="text">Lorem ipsum dolor sit amet...</p>
    <svg id="mySvg" height="200" xmlns="http://www.w3.org/2000/svg">
        <circle id="graycircle" r="75" cx="75" cy="75" />
    </svg>
</div>

/* CSS snippet */
.lstb03 #parent {
    display:-ms-grid;
}

.lstb03 #text {
    width:300px;

}
.lstb03 #graycircle {
    fill: gray;
    fill-opacity: 0.5;
}
```

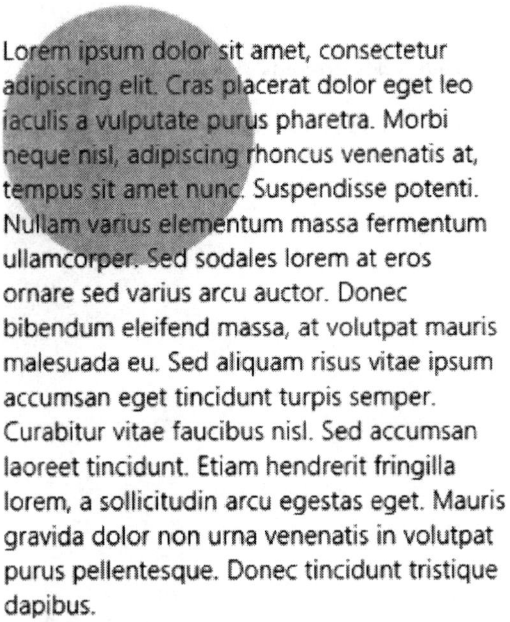

Lorem ipsum dolor sit amet, consectetur adipiscing elit. Cras placerat dolor eget leo iaculis a vulputate purus pharetra. Morbi neque nisl, adipiscing rhoncus venenatis at, tempus sit amet nunc. Suspendisse potenti. Nullam varius elementum massa fermentum ullamcorper. Sed sodales lorem at eros ornare sed varius arcu auctor. Donec bibendum eleifend massa, at volutpat mauris malesuada eu. Sed aliquam risus vitae ipsum accumsan eget tincidunt turpis semper. Curabitur vitae faucibus nisl. Sed accumsan laoreet tincidunt. Etiam hendrerit fringilla lorem, a sollicitudin arcu egestas eget. Mauris gravida dolor non urna venenatis in volutpat purus pellentesque. Donec tincidunt tristique dapibus.

Figure B-2. *A partially transparent circle reveals the paragraph text below it*

The fill-rule property determines the algorithm used when the styling engine is applying fill to determine what parts of the shape get filled. The two options are nonzero and evenodd. You shouldn't need to know the details of how these algorithms work. I always just try both and see which one gives me the result I'm looking for. The graphics in Figure B-3 are how the W3C illustrate some of the differences between the two algorithms.

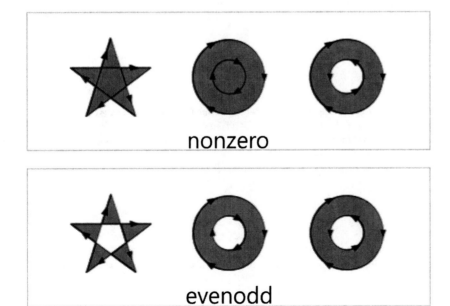

Figure B-3. *Two different ways that closed shapes can be filled*

Strokes

Strokes are the lines that either stand on their own (as straight or curved lines) or surround a shape. You'll use the stroke properties to set a stroke's color, width, opacity, and a lot more.

The first two stroke-related properties you might want to know are `stroke` and `stroke-width`. The `stroke` property controls the color of the stroke and the `stroke-width` controls the thickness. Listing B-4 sets both of these properties to add a black line around the gray circle we've been working with.

Listing B-4. Adding a thick, black outline to our gray circle

```
<!-- HTML snippet -->
<svg id="mySvg" height="200" xmlns="http://www.w3.org/2000/svg">
    <circle id="graycircle" r="75" cx="75" cy="75" />
</svg>
/* CSS snippet */
.lstb04 #graycircle {
    fill: gray;
    fill-opacity: 0.5;
    stroke:black;
    stroke-width: 4px;
}
```

The circle described in Listing B-4 will have a 4-pixel, black border as you see in Figure B-4.

Figure B-4. *The stroke property adds an outline around our element*

Besides these two simple properties, there are a lot more stroke-related properties. They are: `stroke-dasharray`, `stroke-dashoffset`, `stroke-linecap`, `stroke-linejoin`, `stroke-miterlimit`, and `stroke-opacity`. These properties allow you to control a lot of the other aspects of the lines on your SVG elements like the dashing/dotting of the line and the behavior of the line around corners and at the end of the line.

More in-depth information about these extended properties and all aspects of SVG element strokes can be found on W3.org at `http://www.w3.org/TR/SVG11/painting.html#StrokeProperties`.

Markers

Markers are the glyphs that appear at either end or in the middle of a line. Markers are most often used for creating an arrow head on the end of an element, but actually markers can be used to show any custom shape and have it appear at any vertex.

Creating a marker is a two-step process. First you define the shape of the marker and then you apply that marker definition to any of your SVG elements. You can find a detailed explanation of markers at `http://www.w3.org/TR/SVG11/painting.html#Markers`.

Filters

Filters are like lenses that can cause a lot of different effects to apply to some region of an SVG graphic. You could add a filter to the contents of an SVG circle for example that applied a Gaussian blur to the circle and its contents. Figure B-5 is a good example (again from W3C) of a filter in action.

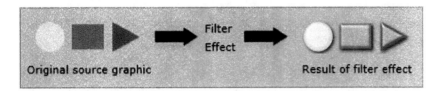

Figure B-5. *A W3C example of an applied filter*

Of course, the same effect that this filter provides could be achieved using your favorite graphics application, but there are huge advantages to having this filter applied at run time. Filters applied at run time can be targeted by your app's logic and so be applied conditionally. A filter could only take effect when a user hovers over an image, for instance. Again, this would be possible by conventional means by providing multiple bitmap images, but there's certainly a limit that applies to that technique. Image you wanted a filter's effect to be animated. There would be virtually no way to do that by conventional means.

Filter effects are added to an element in two phases. First you create a filter using the filter *element*, and then you apply that filter to an element using the filter *property*.

Filters are relatively involved, so for the sake of brevity I won't go in to more depth. I did want to mention their general function, however, and let you know that they are available. When you want to dive in to the topic of filters, start by visiting http://www.w3.org/TR/SVG11/filters.html#FilterProperty.

Masks

A mask is a way to apply a transparency layer (also called an alpha channel) to any SVG element(s) by providing an explicit mask and then applying it. Masks are potentially a very lengthy topic too, but once again you should know at least generally what they are.

A quick note about properties like masks, markers, and filters that are relatively verbose in application: you'd be crazy to attempt to define these properties manually because it's prohibitive to memorize the syntax and spend the time typing them in. Normally, these are applied automatically for you when you use vector editing graphics software like Adobe Illustrator, CorelDRAW, or InkScape.

You can find more information about masks at http://www.w3.org/TR/SVG/masking.html.

Pointer Events

As you've already seen, SVG shapes have an interior (the *fill*) and an exterior (the *stroke*). Either or both of the fill or stroke may have a value of none, and will thus render invisible. This implies an interesting choice that needs to be made regarding when the user clicks on your element. If you create a circle that has no fill and ends up over the top of another element, you may or may not want that circle to capture click events. The same is true for the stroke.

The pointer-events property is your chance to specify the behavior in this case. By default, the value is visiblePainted, which is a pretty intuitive choice, so you might not need to change this property very often.

The available values for the pointer-events property are: visiblePainted, visibleFill, visibleStroke, visible, painted, fill, stroke, all, and none. With visiblePainted (the default) set, the element will capture clicks (and other pointer events) on the fill only if your element is filled and visible and on the stroke only if the stroke is set and visible. With `visibleFill` set, the element will capture clicks on the fill if your element is visible (even if your element isn't filled!). With `visibleStroke` set, element will capture clicks on the stroke if it's visible (even if you didn't set a stroke) and it will not capture clicks on the fill. Using `painted`, `fill`, and `stroke` values have cause similar functionality except that they disregard whether or not the element is actually visible. The `all` value will cause a click always—even if you have no fill or stroke set and both are set to invisible! Finally, the `none` value will not pass on the pointer events.

If the idea of adding programming logic to a dynamic, vector-based graphics language like SVG excites you, then spend some time researching pointer events at `http://www.w3.org/TR/SVG/interact.html#PointerEventsProperty`.

Visibility

Just like HTML elements, the visibility of SVG elements can be manipulated to show or hide individual elements, and just like HTML the values for the `visible` property are `visible`, `hidden`, and `collapse`. The `collapse` value, however, acts just like `hidden` and hides the element. The `visible` value obviously allows the element to show.

That's all I'm going to include in this brief introduction to using CSS for SVG in your HTML apps, but I want to take a look at a few practical applications of these concepts in Windows 8.

Applying What You've Learned

Let's implement some of the SVG CSS concepts that we've learned so far in a few examples. We'll look first at using an SVG image as a watermarked image in the background of an app. Next we'll create some custom SVG images to appear behind the main item tiles for a ListView. Finally, we'll dynamically build a timeline graphic using JavaScript to generate SVG.

An SVG-Watermarked Background Image

The goal here is to find a good SVG image of a sailboat, and then place it in the background of our app light enough so that it doesn't obstruct the visual elements and text that appear on top of it.

When I'm looking for good vector images, I usually start at office.microsoft.com. If you do an image search you can specify that you're looking for *illustrations* and that you want their size to be *resizable*, and this will indicate that vector images should be returned. These images are usually in another vector image format—WMF (Windows Metafile). To get that image saved as SVG, you can simply copy the image from the website, paste it into your software package, and then save it out as an SVG file.

I found a sailboat image that I'd like to use (Figure B-6), saved it as SVG, and Listing B-5 shows the resulting SVG code. I've purposefully left the entire contents of the SVG file in the listing so you can get an idea how much SVG code it takes to describe this simple sailboat.

Figure B-6. *A simple sailboat image*

As a point of comparison, this sailboat in SVG format takes up 7,098 bytes of disk space uncompressed or 3,505 bytes compressed. That 7kb file could be used to create a sailboat 75 feet high if we wanted to. The same sailboat rendered as an uncompressed, full-color (though I realize it's not necessary) bitmap at 768 pixels high takes up 1,983,798 bytes. Compressing the bitmap in a lossless format (PNG) brings that down to 35,410 bytes, but you can certainly see the size advantage that vector format has over bitmaps.

Listing B-5. The entire SVG file that makes up a simple sailboat

```
<?xml version="1.0" encoding="UTF-8"?>
<!DOCTYPE svg PUBLIC "-//W3C//DTD SVG 1.1//EN" "http://www.w3.org/Graphics/SVG/1.1/DTD/svg11.dtd">
<!-- Creator: CorelDRAW X6 -->
<svg xmlns="http://www.w3.org/2000/svg" xml:space="preserve" width="509px" height="571px"
version="1.1" style="shape-rendering:geometricPrecision; text-rendering:geometricPrecision;
image-rendering:optimizeQuality; fill-rule:evenodd; clip-rule:evenodd"
viewBox="0 0 50900 57045"
 xmlns:xlink="http://www.w3.org/1999/xlink">
 <defs>
  <style type="text/css">
   <![CDATA[
    .fil0 {fill:black}
   ]]>
  </style>
 </defs>
```

```
<g id="Layer_x0020_1">
 <metadata id="CorelCorpID_0Corel-Layer"/>
 <g id="_695569408">
  <polygon class="fil0" points="22632,2398 22872,2368 23112,2308 23292,2188 23472,2038 23621,1859
23741,1679 23801,1439 23831,1199 23801,959 23741,719 23621,540 23472,360 23292,210 23112, 90
22872,30 22632,0 22392,30 22153,90 21973,210 21793,360 21643,540 21523,719 21463,959 21433,1199
21463,1439 21523,1679 21643,1859 21793,2038 21973,2188 22153,2308 22392,2368 "/>
  <polygon class="fil0" points="23741,5845 23681,6865 23561,9562 23352,13399 23142,17896
22932,22482 22782,26649 22722,29857 22752,31595 22932,32015 23382,32375 24011,32704 24850,33004
25840,33244 26919,33484 28118,33634 29347,33783 30606,33843 31865,33903 33094,33873 34263,33813
35312,33694 36212,33514 36961,33304 37531,33004 37890,32554 38100,31835 38160,30906 38070,29827
37890,28568 37590,27189 37201,25720 36781,24191 36271,22662 35762,21163 35192,19665 34653,18286
34113,16997 33604,15858 33154,14898 32734,14149 32315,13399 31775,12500 31146,11481 30456,10342
29707,9203 28957,8034 28178,6895 27398,5875 26649,4976 25960,4227 25300,3717 24761,3447 24311,3507
23981,3867 23771,4646 "/>
  <polygon class="fil0" points="8843,28178 9652,28687 10522,29167 11451,29587 12440,29946
13429,30246 14419,30516 15378,30726 16307,30936 17206,31086 18046,31205 18795,31295 19425,31385
19964,31415 20384,31445 20624,31475 20714,31475 20504,8933 20324,9113 19844,9652 19065,10462
18106,11511 16967,12800 15738,14239 14449,15798 13160,17446 11901,19125 10732,20774 9742,22392
8933,23921 8393,25300 8184,26499 8303,27458 "/>
  <polygon class="fil0" points="29017,35372 27968,35312 26949,35282 25960,35192 24970,35132
24041,35042 23112,34953 22213,34833 21313,34743 20414,34623 19515,34503 18615,34383 17686,34233
16757,34113 15828,33963 14838,33843 13849,33694 12860,33544 11811,33304 10702,33034 9562,32704
8393,32345 7254,31985 6115,31595 5036,31205 3987,30816 3058,30456 2188,30126 1439,29827 839,29587
390,29377 90,29257 0,29227 570,30186 989,31265 1319,32375 1589,33544 1829,34743 2068,35912
2338,37051 2668,38130 3088,39149 3627,40079 4347,40858 5216,41517 6325,41997 7674,42267 9323,42357
11271,42177 12740,41997 14149,41847 15468,41727 16727,41667 17896,41637 19035,41637 20084,41667
21073,41727 22033,41817 22932,41937 23771,42057 24581,42177 25330,42327 26050,42477 26739,42627
27398,42776 28028,42926 28628,43076 29197,43226 29767,43346 30306,43466 30846,43556 31385,43646
31895,43676 32435,43706 32944,43706 33484,43676 34023,43586 34563,43466 35132,43316 35702,43106
36301,42866 36931,42567 37560,42237 38190,41877 38819,41517 39479,41098 40108,40708 40738,40288
41338,39869 41907,39449 42477,39029 43016,38610 43496,38220 43945,37860 44365,37531 44755,37231
45055,36961 45384,36691 45744,36421 46104,36182 46493,35942 46853,35732 47243,35522 47633,35342
48022,35162 48412,35012 48802,34863 49191,34713 49551,34593 49911,34443 50270,34323 50600,34203
50900,34083 50360,34173 49791,34263 49191,34353 48562,34443 47872,34533 47183,34623 46434,34683
45684,34743 44935,34833 44125,34893 43346,34953 42537,34983 41727,35042 40888,35102 40079,35132
39269,35162 38460,35222 37650,35252 36841,35282 36092,35312 35312,35312 34593,35342 33873,35372
33184,35372 32524,35372 31895,35402 31295,35402 30756,35402 30246,35402 29797,35402 29377,35372 "/>
  <polygon class="fil0" points="32464,48442 31745,48322 31056,48232 30336,48112 29617,47992
28867,47902 28088,47782 27219,47663 26319,47513 25330,47393 24281,47243 23112,47093 21823,46943
20444,46763 18915,46583 17266,46404 15438,46194 13729,45984 12350,45774 11301,45564 10552,45384
10042,45204 9802,45025 9742,44845 9862,44695 10132,44575 10522,44425 11031,44335 11571,44245
12170,44155 12770,44095 13340,44065 13879,44065 14359,44065 14838,44065 15318,44095 15768,44095
16277,44125 16817,44185 17386,44245 18016,44305 18735,44365 19545,44485 20444,44575 21433,44725
22572,44875 23831,45055 25240,45264 26829,45474 28418,45714 29887,45894 31205,46044 32345,46164
33304,46254 34053,46314 34623,46314 34983,46254 35072,46164 34953,46044 34563,45834 33903,45594
32944,45294 31685,44965 30126,44545 28238,44065 27219,43826 26199,43616 25180,43436 24161,43286
23172,43166 22213,43076 21223,42986 20294,42926 19365,42896 18436,42896 17566,42866 16697,42896
15858,42926 15048,42956 14239,43016 13489,43076 12770,43136 12081,43196 11421,43286 10821,43376
10252,43436 9712,43526 9203,43616 8753,43676 8363,43766 8004,43826 7704,43886 7434,43945 7254,44005
7104,44035 7014,44065 6985,44065 6355,44755 5995,45324 5905,45834 6055,46224 6415,46553 6955,46823
```

```
7674,47003 8543,47153 9503,47273 10582,47333 11751,47393 12920,47423 14149,47453 15348,47483
16547,47543 17686,47603 18705,47693 19605,47752 20384,47842 21073,47902 21703,47992 22302,48052
22932,48142 23561,48232 24251,48352 25030,48472 25900,48592 26949,48712 28148,48862 29527,49041
31146,49221 33004,49431 34803,49611 36242,49791 37321,49911 38100,50031 38610,50121 38879,50181
38939,50241 38819,50270 38550,50300 38190,50300 37770,50300 37321,50300 36841,50300 36421,50270
36062,50270 35822,50270 35582,50270 35282,50300 34923,50300 34473,50330 33963,50360 33424,50390
32824,50450 32195,50480 31505,50510 30816,50570 30126,50600 29407,50630 28687,50660 27968,50660
27249,50690 26559,50690 25840,50690 25090,50720 24311,50720 23502,50750 22632,50810 21793,50840
20924,50900 20054,50960 19185,51020 18316,51080 17476,51140 16637,51230 15858,51290 15108,51380
14389,51440 13729,51530 13130,51619 12590,51679 12081,51769 11631,51859 11211,51949 10851,52039
10522,52159 10192,52309 9892,52459 9622,52639 9383,52848 9113,53088 8873,53358 8633,53628 8393,53988
8124,54347 7944,54737 7914,55097 8004,55426 8214,55726 8513,55996 8873,56236 9263,56446 9682,56626
10102,56775 10492,56895 10821,56985 11061,57045 11241,57045 11301,57045 11181,56985 10941,56895
10282,56685 9712,56446 9293,56146 9083,55846 9083,55456 9353,55037 9982,54527 10941,53928
11541,53628 12140,53388 12800,53148 13489,52968 14209,52789 15018,52639 15858,52549 16787,52429
17806,52369 18885,52309 20084,52249 21403,52219 22812,52189 24341,52159 25990,52129 27788,52099
29557,52069 31086,52009 32405,51949 33574,51859 34563,51799 35432,51679 36152,51589 36811,51470
37381,51350 37920,51230 38400,51110 38909,50990 39389,50870 39929,50750 40528,50660 41188,50540
41757,50420 42057,50330 42117,50181 41967,50061 41607,49941 41098,49791 40438,49641 39659,49491
38819,49371 37890,49221 36931,49071 35942,48922 35012,48802 34083,48682 33214,48562 "/>
    </g>
  </g>
</svg>
```

Now it's time to get that SVG file included behind some HTML. There are actually a few ways to display SVG in our HTML.

- We could actually paste the SVG code from Listing B-5 right into our page or we could append it to our DOM using JavaScript.

- The img tag supports SVG files directly, so we could just use something like `<img src="sailboat.svg"/>`.

- We could also set the background-image property of the element we want it to show up behind.

In this case, there's no reason not to use the img tag or set the background-image property. It's easier and serves our case. We would need to append the SVG code into our DOM (either manually or using JavaScript) if we were going to be manipulating, styling, or animating that SVG. In this case we're not, so we'll keep it simple. Listing B-6 sets the sailboat graphic behind the main div element by putting them both into a grid. You can see the result in Figure B-7.

Listing B-6. Adding a sailboat watermark behind a paragraph of text

```
<!-- HTML snippet -->
<div class="grid">
    <img id="sailboat" src="sailboat.svg"/>
    <div id="main">
        Ut commodo consequat leo...
    </div>
</div>

/* CSS snippet */
.lstb06 #sailboat {
    opacity:0.05;
}
```

```
.lstb06 .grid {
    display:-ms-grid;
}

.lstb06 #main {
    border:solid 1px gray;
    font-size:large;
    width:500px;
    height:500px;
    padding:10px;
}
```

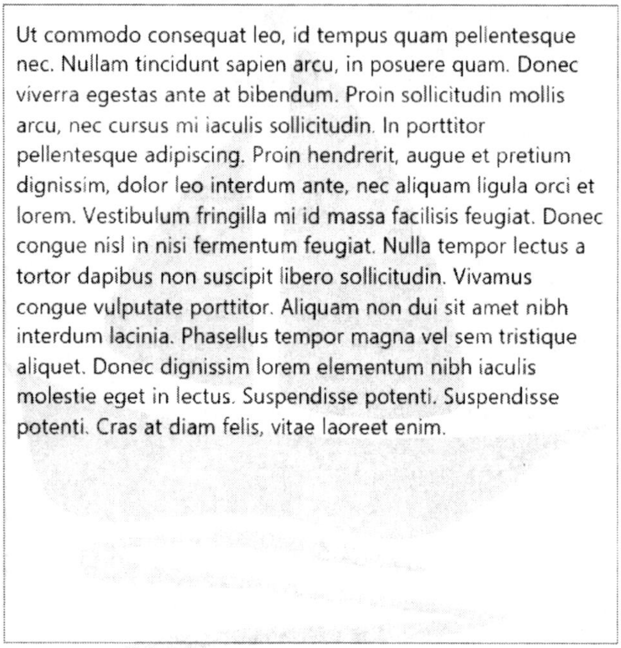

Ut commodo consequat leo, id tempus quam pellentesque nec. Nullam tincidunt sapien arcu, in posuere quam. Donec viverra egestas ante at bibendum. Proin sollicitudin mollis arcu, nec cursus mi iaculis sollicitudin. In porttitor pellentesque adipiscing. Proin hendrerit, augue et pretium dignissim, dolor leo interdum ante, nec aliquam ligula orci et lorem. Vestibulum fringilla mi id massa facilisis feugiat. Donec congue nisl in nisi fermentum feugiat. Nulla tempor lectus a tortor dapibus non suscipit libero sollicitudin. Vivamus congue vulputate porttitor. Aliquam non dui sit amet nibh interdum lacinia. Phasellus tempor magna vel sem tristique aliquet. Donec dignissim lorem elementum nibh iaculis molestie eget in lectus. Suspendisse potenti. Suspendisse potenti. Cras at diam felis, vitae laoreet enim.

Figure B-7. *A mostly transparent black sailboat appears very dim behind the paragraph text*

Fancy SVG Tiles on the Hub

Many Windows 8 apps use the built-in ListView control to show a grid of items. Typical Windows 8 grid items are rectangular and look like tiles. You're not stuck to that look, though the minimalism and efficiency it implements is a powerful design feature that should be considered.

Let's imagine you're creating a painting app and one section of your grid shows all of the users painting documents and you want those items to be represented in a shape that looks roughly like a rectangle except made from a few paint strokes. In this case, we still want to have tiles—except a bit fancier. You could, in this case, render out a bitmap and underlay it behind each item, but you would lose the advantages of SVG that I've mentioned. So let's use SVG and let's create the graphic ourselves.

I jumped over to CorelDRAW and quickly found a brush that allowed me to create the graphic in Figure B-8.

Figure B-8. *A graphic generated using CorelDRAW that we want to use for our hub tiles*

CorelDRAW can save that graphic out as SVG. I won't list that code because it's rather lengthy—still only about 125kb uncompressed though.

Our next step is to get that graphic behind the tiles of a ListView. Listing B-7 should do the trick.

Listing B-7. A ListView with CSS that places the paint strokes graphic behind each item

```
<!-- HTML snippet -->
<section aria-label="Main content" role="main">
    <div id="listview" data-win-control="WinJS.UI.ListView"></div>
</section>

<!--Templates-->
<div id="itemtemplate" data-win-control="WinJS.Binding.Template">
    <h2 data-win-bind="innerText:name"></h2>
</div>

/* CSS snippet */
.lstb07 #listview .win-item {
    display:-ms-grid;
    -ms-grid-columns:1fr;
    -ms-grid-rows:1fr;
    width:250px;
    height:174px;
    background: url(paint.svg) no-repeat;
    background-size:250px auto;
}

    .lstb07 #listview .win-item h2 {
        -ms-grid-column-align:center;
        -ms-grid-row-align:center;
        color:white;
        font-family:'Segoe WP';
        font-size:40px;
        font-weight:bold;
        position:relative;
        top:-10px;
    }
```

```
// JavaScript snippet
var list = new WinJS.Binding.List(
    [{ name: "Doc1" }, { name: "Doc2" }, { name: "Doc3" }]
);
var listview = element.querySelector("#listview").winControl;
listview.itemDataSource = list.dataSource;
listview.itemTemplate = element.querySelector("#itemtemplate");
listview.onloadingstatechanged = function (e) { debugger; };
```

And the result of all of that code is a ListView like the one you see in Figure B-9 complete with custom item shapes and overlaid text.

Figure B-9. *The resulting paint stroke items give the items some character*

A Timeline Graphic Built Using SVG

The previous two applications used the easy way of including SVG—that is using the img tag and the background-image CSS property and simply referencing an SVG file. Now let's take a little bit more difficult approach that gives us finer control over our vector image.

Imagine that we want to create a simple timeline graphic that contains a gray bar representing some length of time and then white dots for each time point. To accomplish this, we will create the SVG image, and then look at it to see how it is composed.

I started out again in CorelDRAW. This time I created a very simple, gray timeline with white dots marking points in time. Again, this particular graphic is simple enough that I certainly could have composed it by writing the SVG manually in Notepad, but in real life you would likely be working with a more complex graphic. The simple timeline graphic that I created can be seen in Figure B-10.

Figure B-10. *The timeline that we want to build dynamically with JavaScript*

I then generated the SVG, tweaked it a bit, and then looked at it using Notepad (Listing B-8).

Listing B-8. The SVG code generated by CorelDRAW for the timeline graphic in Figure B-10.

```
<svg xmlns="http://www.w3.org/2000/svg" width="1000px" height="200px" >
 <defs>
  <style type="text/css">
   <![CDATA[
    .str0 {stroke:black;stroke-width:2}
    .fil0 {fill:gray}
    .fil1 {fill:white}
   ]]>
  </style>
 </defs>
 <g>
  <rect class="fil0" x="30" y="90" width="940" height="20"/>
  <circle class="fil1 str0" cx="30" cy="100" r="10"/>
  <circle class="fil1 str0" cx="70" cy="100" r="10"/>
  <circle class="fil1 str0" cx="400" cy="100" r="10"/>
  <circle class="fil1 str0" cx="970" cy="100" r="10"/>
 </g>
</svg>
```

The elements themselves are inside the g element. The styles for those elements are in an embedded style sheet. We're going to use what this document tells us about how to create that timeline graphic and create it ourselves using JavaScript. That will give us the flexibility to place the points programmatically. We'll also pull the CSS styles out, put them in our document's style sheet, and give them more meaningful class names. It's nice to have all of our styles together in one spot. Just like with HTML, we want the SVG to be a *definition* of the graphics structure and let the style sheet deal with colors and such. Listing B-9 and Figure B-11 show how to dynamically create this timeline.

Listing B-9. The HTML, CSS, and JavaScript for building the timeline

```
<!-- HTML snippet -->
<div id="container"></div>

/* CSS snippet */
.lstb09 .circle {
    stroke:black;
    stroke-width:2;
    fill:white;
}

.lstb09 .line {
    fill:gray;
}
```

```
// JavaScript snippet
var points = [0,1,3,7,10];
var container = element.querySelector("#container");

//transform the points and generate SVG
var result;
points.forEach(function (p) {
    result += format("     <circle class='circle' cx='{0}' cy='100' r='10'/>", (p * 94) + 30);
});

//add resulting SVG to the DOM
container.innerHTML = format(
    "<svg xmlns='http://www.w3.org/2000/svg' width='1000px' height='200px' >" +
    "  <g>" +
    "    <rect class='line' x='30' y='90' width='940' height='20'/>" +
    "    {0}" +
    "  </g>" +
    "</svg>", result);
```

Figure B-11. *The resulting timeline is just what we were looking for and now the values can be changed easily*

It would be a good idea to turn this into a WinJS custom control so you can create them anywhere you want in your code with using <div data-win-control="MyApp.Controls.Timeline"></div>.

By the way, if you want to dig more into using JavaScript to generate and manipulate SVG graphics, there's a great post at http://www.farinspace.com/top-svg-javascript-libraries-worth-looking-at/ that will introduce you to eleven JavaScript libraries that will help you on this venture.

You've been introduced to the exciting SVG space and seen how it can enhance your Windows 8 app. We looked at a number (though certainly not all) of CSS style properties that affect SVG elements, and we walked through three robust applications of SVG within Windows 8 apps.

I hope you learned a bit reading this, but more importantly I hope you're inspired to go try it out and research the areas you don't know so you can master weaving SVG into your apps and styling it using CSS.

Index

CPSIA information can be obtained at www.ICGtesting.com
Printed in the USA
LVOW11s2200230114

370795LV00004B/94/P